"In *From Trauma to Transformation*, Muriel Prince Warren explores the long-term impact of the 9/11 attacks on the collective American psyche. Warren reveals the tragic state of unhealed minds while offering encouraging examples of transformation. Her brilliant use of hypnosis to quiet the amygdala, (the part of the brain that triggers the 'fight or flight' response), restores her patients' trust in their own minds. Warren suggests that only through controlling the amygdala, the little trouble-maker in the brain, will peace be restored to a traumatized mind. This book is a life-saving contribution to the field of trauma."
Christine A. Lawson, PhD
Author of *Understanding the Borderline Mother*

"A useful book that anyone currently involved with trauma therapy should read. Of particular help are the extensive treatment plans. Too often psychotherapy seems to be done 'on the hoof' and this author certainly attempts to correct that sort of malpractice."
Norman Claringbull
Lecturer in Counselling

"Written with professional wisdom and sensitivity, this groundbreaking volume offers a fresh and practical view of the connection between hypnosis and healing. Dr. Warren provides a thoughtful blueprint for the assessment, diagnosis, and successful treatment of those suffering from the impact of traumatic events. Her understanding of trauma and its treatment infuses her work with useful clinical information and valuable insights. This book is essential reading for all therapists who deal with trauma."
Pamela Roth
Senior Editor, Behavioral Science Book Service

From Trauma to Transformation

Muriel Prince Warren, DSW, ACSW

Foreword by Daniel Araoz, EdD, ABPP, ABPH

With contributions by

Rivka Bertisch Meir, PhD, MPH
Martin Tesher, MD, CCFP, ABFP
Bill O'Hanlon, MS
Rita Ghiraldini, DC
Michael Innerfield, MD

Crown House Publishing Limited
www.crownhouse.co.uk

Published by

Crown House Publishing Ltd
Crown Buildings, Bancyfelin, Carmarthen, Wales, SA33 5ND, UK
www.crownhouse.co.uk

and

Crown House Publishing Company LLC
4 Berkeley Street, 1st Floor, Norwalk, CT 06850, USA
www.CHPUS.com

British Library of Cataloguing-in-Publication Data
A catalogue entry for this book is available from the British Library.

10-digit ISBN 1904424902
13-digit ISBN 978-190442490-1

LCCN 2005929170

Printed and bound in the United States

To the Warren Trauma Institute:
Together We Can Achieve the Extraordinary.

Special thanks to:

Daniel Araoz
Harris Berger
David Bowman
Karen Bowman
Attillo Capponi
Anna Cicalo
Joanne Jozefowski
Rita Ghiraldini
Neal Levy
Bill O'Hanlon
Stefanie O'Hanlon
Michael Innerfield
Shawna Kristensen
Rivka Bertisch Meir
Michael Meir
Capt. Louis Siriotis
Kristina Siriotis
Mark Tracten
Joel Warren

And a very special thanks to Howard Matus for all his hard work in making this book possible.

When one door of happiness closes,
another opens; but often we look so long
at the closed door that we do not see the
one which has opened for us.

— Helen Keller

CONTENTS

LIST OF TABLES AND FIGURES

Tables

Figures

ACKNOWLEDGMENTS

I wish to thank the many people who have encouraged and supported me during this project. Special thanks go to my husband, Howard Matus, for his research and editorial skills, and to Dr. Daniel Araoz for writing the Foreword to this book. I would also like to acknowledge Norma Pomerantz for her meticulous editorial work and to Roberta Riviere for helping us put together the Warren Trauma Conference.

Since 9/11, all of our lives have changed. It is said that you can never walk through the same river twice. On May 15 and 16, 2004, I presented a conference on Trauma: Treatment and Transformation in New York City. Based on what emerged at the conference, I formed the Warren Trauma Institute in Orangeburg, New York. Within two short weeks, the center spread worldwide with the help of some very special people. They include Dr. Daniel Araoz, Dr. Attilio Capponi, Mark Tracten, Rev. Dr. James Law, Dr. Martin Tesher, Dr. Eleanor Laser, Dr. Harris Berger, Dr. Michael Innerfield, Anna Cicalo, Dr. Joanne Jozefowski, Pamela Roth, Carol Hadjinak, Karyn Korneich, Neal Levy, Carol Chetrick and Joel Warren. There is no way this book could have emerged from *Trauma: Treatment and Transformation* nor the Warren Institute grow worldwide the speed it did without their help and support.

To join the Warren Institute you can contact me at:

Dr. Muriel Prince Warren
Prel Plaza S. #15
60 Dutch Hill Road
Orangeburg, NY 10962
845-365-0801
Email: MPW0801@aol.com
Website: www.drmurielprincewarren.com

Some proceeds from this book will be donated to the Warren Institute.

FOREWORD

It is rare that anyone goes to a lecture to hear the lecturer being introduced. In books, the foreword is that introduction. Get it out of the way quickly because what comes after is a real treat. Abe Lincoln is supposed to have stated, "Most folks are about as happy as they choose to be." Dr. Warren gives us a comprehensive treatise on trauma in its many manifestations, focusing lovingly on the tragedy suffered by our country on 9/11.

One of the main points she emphasizes throughout the book is that we – yes, all of us – can learn to choose the thoughts that will free us from the trauma we have suffered. The effects of a horrible tragedy like that suffered by our country in 2001 do not have to victimize us forever. With care and compassion, especially for those who, in helping, suffer "secondary stress disorders," she proposes many methods to free us from the remnants of trauma after the painful event that affected our memories, feelings, and behaviors, often for a long time after the tragedy.

This is a book of liberation – "transformation" – in Warren's positive language. She uses the Phoenix metaphor to encourage us – clinicians and patients alike – to look at trauma in a less negative way. Trauma comes from a horrible experience we have suffered, but we can "transform" ourselves for the better because of it. To prove her point, Warren brings up many heroic examples of people who went through the excruciating suffering of 9/11 at close range, either physically or emotionally.

This book offers a unique benefit. Warren's innovative charts of behavioral goals for trauma therapy with children, adolescents, adults and families, are similar to the ones she gave us in 1999 in her *Behavior Management Guide*. Besides these practical aids for the clinician, Warren has spent much time in designing treatment plans, like the one for acute stress disorder (ASD). I consider these charts a creative contribution that will benefit all of us who deal with people in a clinical setting.

The ultimate goal of Warren's efforts is the person's reintegration, as she explains in the lucid section on hypnosis. She "depowers" trauma and empowers the individual who has gone through the trauma in order for him or her to reconnect with life. She leads the reader to a new space of optimism and happiness. It is as if she is saying that nothing, not even the most horrible experience of destruction and death, has the power to diminish us unless we consent to it.

Trauma: Treatment and Transformation is a very useful tome for clinicians in this country where we are living with "chronic stress," as Warren says, and where every psychotherapist will encounter patients suffering from traumatic events. But it is equally beneficial for people in general. Dr. Warren's style is uncomplicated, clear, and to the point. Unlike others who want to sound scientific, she writes to be understood; she offers practical, useful, techniques and methods to enjoy life after trauma. She gives enough help for both the emergency situations that cause unbearable stress and for a lifestyle without stress – with emphasis on mindfulness – in spite of any and all the negative surprises that life gives us.

We are lucky that the English language provides us with the solution to STRESS in the very word, summarizing what this great book teaches: S–T–R is a reminder to STOP, THINK, and RELAX in emergency stress situations; E–S–S encourages us to ESTABLISH SELF SECURITY, which is a matter of attitude and inner strength, the ultimate goal of mindfulness as taught by Dr. Warren.

Now that you've read the foreword, don't forget Lincoln's statement, and rush to assimilate the contents of the book in order to find out how to be happy in spite of life's tragedies.

Daniel Araoz, EdD, ABPP, ABPH
Professor, C. W. Post Campus
Long Island University, New York

INTRODUCTION

America may never be the same. Before 9/11, wars had always been fought on foreign soil, never here at home. But all of that changed with the collapse of the World Trade Center on September 11, 2001. We are at war against terrorism by fanatics within our borders as well as throughout the world. It is virtually impossible to predict and prevent every possible terrorist attack, even in our own backyard. As a result, we must learn to live under the constant threat of disaster.

That threat can give rise to emotions ranging from mild anxiety to sheer terror. Most people (Bracken, 2002) manage to "push it aside to get ready for the hustle and bustle of our everyday lives", (pp. 1–2). However, some people just can't shed the anxiety and must live out their lives with a constant feeling of dread. Their lives are not shaped by a taken-for-granted order, but are endlessly threatened by the quicksand of meaninglessness.

No one escapes a disaster without some degree of impairment that flows like a wave over the family, work group, and the community. In its wake, it leaves the seeds of severe and debilitating physical and psychological disorders. In reaction to the emotional shock wave that spread from Ground Zero, many people slipped into altered states of consciousness. Hospital emergency rooms were jammed with frightened people suffering from a variety of somatic reactions. My physician tells me that later, after the first signs of the biochemical attack, patients were begging him for antibiotics in case of anthrax exposure. A male patient I treated for depression and suicidal ideations is still, to this day, hoarding medication to combat anthrax.

One of the most difficult problems of disaster is dealing with the death of a loved one. Jozefowski (1999), outlines the stages of coping with death in her book, *The Phoenix Phenomenon*. "The death of a loved one," she explains, "forever changes the normal flow and rhythm of life, dividing it into before and after" (p. 15). In this sense, 9/11 has changed the normal flow of life in the world.

America is now on high alert. President Bush warned that we must quickly return to normalcy or become our own worst enemies. He tells us to be on high alert, but to remain calm. How is that possible? Incongruent messages such as these double-bind people, create innumerable psychological and physical problems, and generally drive the American public crazy. Kalb (2003, pp. 42–53) explains that living with fear will affect both the mind and the body.

As of this writing, one wonders how our troops will return from Iraq and what pathological consequences their psyches will suffer. There will definitely be a tremendous need for therapists who are trained to deal with trauma and its residues.

This book deals with trauma, its psychological and biological effects on mind and body, the psychology of terrorism, and treatment plans that deal with the resulting problems and transform them into growth.

1
CHANGE AND THE PROCESS OF HEALING

CHANGE AND ANXIETY

Change is being forced on us, and the human psyche's protective response is to fight to avoid the anxiety that always accompanies change. Paraphrasing Kierkegaard, Becker (1974) points out that:

> Man [is] lulled by the daily routines of his society, content with the satisfactions that it [life] offers him. In today's world, the car, the shopping center, the two-week summer vacation. Man is protected by the secure and limited alternatives his society offers him, and if he does not look up from his path, he can live out his life in a certain dull security (p. 74).

For Kierkegaard, there were three kinds of people: "Normal" man (or woman), who lives a life of quiet desperation to avoid or deny death anxiety; "Schizophrenic" man, who is crazy; and "Creative" man, who lives in a garden of anxiety. Becker explains, "As long as man is an ambiguous creature, he can never banish anxiety. What he can do instead is to use anxiety as an internal spring for growth into new dimensions of thought and trust" (p. 92).

The years since the 2001 terrorist attacks have presented us with new challenges. Man can no longer be lulled into a life of quiet desperation while terrorists confront us daily. We must learn to live with death anxiety. In this way, catastrophe can be used as a garden for growth.

Recently, I asked myself how I have changed since 9/11. I found myself working exhaustingly long hours trying to help my patients work through their individual traumatic reactions to the terrorism. I felt like

I was really doing something to help others, and found the effort heal-ing, not only for my patients, but also for myself. Many weeks later I also found that I had neglected certain parts of my practice that, in compar-ison, I considered less important under the circumstances. These include chart notes, a task required to meet the standards of the National Committee of Quality Assurance (NCQA).

I was trained as a psychoanalyst in the 1970s. In those days, thera-pists were taught not to keep chart notes because they would color the next session. A good psychoanalyst was advised to keep everything that was important in his or her head or else find another profession. When the NCQA was formed, chart notes became a must.

Trauma in any form (terrorism, the Twin Towers attack, auto acci-dents, sexual or emotional abuse, etc.) changes us biologically forever. It evokes a response that is both psychological and biological. If the response remains maladaptive and stuck, it can turn into dis-ease. As Peter Levine (1997) warns, "Psychology now becomes biology" (p. 99). It can feel like a mild anxiety attack or it can debilitate us. If a person's energies remain trapped in the trauma, it will become chronic, and over time the energy to heal and restore a person's equilibrium will dissipate. Drugs can be helpful for short periods of time, but basically we need to find new, creative ways to deal with our anxieties.

TRAUMA AND IMMOBILITY

Today, our survival depends on our ability to face our problems artfully rather than use our prehistoric defense resources: fight, flight, or freeze. Symptoms form in a spiraling response to the trauma. The human defense mechanism summons a response from the prehistoric part of our brain. The last option is freezing where the brain constricts the energy that would be discharged by either of the other options, fight (rage) or flight (helplessness). At this point psychology can turn freeze (immobility) into biology and people begin to go numb or lapse into altered states of being, (i.e., acute stress symptoms, post-traumatic stress disorder (PTSD), or depersonalization). The immobility is not eas-ily resolved because what the brain gets used to it repeats over and over. A good example is the body's response to cold. When you go swimming in a cold ocean or lake, the water feels freezing at first but then slowly becomes comfortable as your body adjusts to the temperature. The brain works in much the same way.

Trauma victims are trapped in their own fear and cling to the frozen part of themselves. That old defense saves them. If they feel any activa-tion toward thawing the numbness, they also feel the potential for vio-lence again. They remain in a vicious cycle of immobility, terror, or rage. These reactions are not confined to physical disasters. One patient who was sexually abused as a child became numb. Her father was a war veteran who medicated himself with alcohol to escape the horrors he experienced during World War II. When he was drunk he abused her. Although my patient is not an alcoholic like her father, she is terrified to get involved with a healthy man because (a) it is unfamiliar, and (b) she fears she will again feel the hurt she felt as a child. Thus, she remains inhibited by her fears. Meanwhile, the immobility often feels to her like a living death. Unconsciously, it becomes safer to remain in a cocoon guarded by her defenses than to face life.

The immobility of the freeze response often feels like death, and human beings will do just about anything to deny death. One of the ways to move through the immobility response is to gradually experience life in a safe environment (i.e., a therapist's office). If the freeze response is not treated, it becomes stronger, and with each freezing and refreezing the symptoms proliferate and become cumulative.

Some of the possible maladaptive patterns are: parasomnias, dyssomnias, sexual problems, eating disorders, substance abuse, acute stress disorder (ASD), depression, post-traumatic stress disorder (PTSD), generalized anxiety disorder (GAD), depersonalization, behavior problems, and attention deficit/hyperactivity disorder (ADHD).

The physical reactions to trauma include rapid heart beat, perspiration, sensitivity to light and/or sound, muscle tension, chronic fatigue, hyperactivity, reduced immune function, breathing and digestive problems, and blood pressure and blood vessel constriction. Mental reactions include racing thoughts, increased paranoia and worry, obsessions, compulsions, mood swings, numbness, hypervigilance, guilt, and dissociation. These reactions are often combined. Dissociation is the psyche's way of protecting itself from the attack. Mild dissociation produces a general spaciness, while intense dissociation can generate multiple personality disorder (MPD), distortions in time and/or perception, and out-of-body experiences (see Table 1).

Another patient explains that he is "here, but not here." He lives in constant fear that he will faint, leave his body, and never return. This patient was emotionally abused as a child by his mother, and subsequently sent to live with his grandmother, who was extremely superstitious. The grandmother taught the child to always exit a room by the same door that he entered or else some catastrophe would certainly occur. She also taught him that stepping on a sidewalk crack would "break his mother's back." To this day, my patient always exits a room through the door by which he entered and carefully avoids stepping on sidewalk cracks, despite the fact that his mother died many years ago. Although he has only screen memories of the abuse, the dissociation interrupts the hyperarousal state and prevents him from effectively reacting to his symptoms. For instance, he blames himself for the World Trade Center disaster. The patient actually feels it might not have

Table 1: Response to Trauma

Response*	Action	Leads to	Result
FIGHT	Attempted retaliation; Energy is discharged	Anger Rage Frustration Aggression Determination to "get even"	Anxiety disorders Eating disorders Substance abuse Sleep disorders Impulse control disorders Behavioral problems Relational problems
FLIGHT	Escape; Self-preservation	Fear Guilt Shame Imploded anger Lowered self-esteem	Acute stress disorder Depression Sleep disorders Relational problems
FREEZE	None; Inability to act; Energy is bound up	Immobility Guilt Terror Rage Helplessness Shame Death-like feelings	Post-traumatic stress disorder Obsessive-compulsive disorder Amnesia Forgetfulness Dissociative disorders Depression leading to neurosis Relational problems

*In response to trauma, the limbic part of the brain kicks into one of three responses: fight, flight, or freeze. In our culture, men are commonly taught to fight (e.g., the military, police, firefighters, etc.), while women are expected to freeze, or stoically endure stressful situations. Although there are signs that this may be changing, the pattern dates back to the time when men went out to hunt food, while women stayed home to raise children and clean the house.

happened if he had said all of his prayers that morning. Consciously, he realizes that he is not really responsible for the destruction. Unconsciously, he suffers from unrelenting guilt. He cannot stop worrying, nor can he find a safe place for himself. He also experiences night terrors and sleeps with all the lights and the TV on. To make matters even worse, this patient is afraid to travel far from home. He found menial employment within a mile of his house and is resigned to the fact that he will never lead a normal, healthy, or productive life.

Many patients experience feelings of rage and self-doubt generated by the initial trauma, and lose faith in the possibility of having a meaningful relationship with anyone. They isolate themselves from the rest of the world, and their lives are dominated by conscious and unconscious memories of the trauma.

Lord Protector Mask

This Tibetan Buddhist Mask appears angry. The figure represents our own ability to overcome evil, ignorance and suffering. It reminds us that from unsettling encounters can come great empowerment. We all need some empowerment!

Figure 1: Lord Protector Mask

TRAUMA IN CHILDHOOD

Perpetuation Across Generations and How to Overcome Its Effects

by Rivka Bertisch Meir, PhD, MPH

"Trauma" in everyday language means a highly stressful event. It refers to extreme stress that overwhelms a person's ability to function effectively. It is important to keep in mind that stress reactions are both psychological as well as physiological. Trauma overwhelms the individual's ability to cope, and leaves that person fearing death, annihilation, mutilation, or psychosis. The individual feels emotionally, cognitively, and physically overwhelmed.

Traumatic incidents include powerful one-time occurrences such as accidents, natural disasters, crimes, surgeries, deaths, and other violent events. Traumatic events also include responses to chronic or repetitive experiences such as child abuse, neglect, combat, urban violence, confinement in concentration camps, battering relationships, and enduring deprivation.

An individual's subjective experience determines whether or not an event is perceived to be traumatic. Survivors of repetitive trauma in childhood are likely to instinctively continue to use the same self-protective coping strategies that they employed to shield themselves from psychic harm at the time of the traumatic experience. Hypervigilance, dissociation, avoidance, and numbing are examples of coping strategies that may have been effective at some time, but later interfere with the person's ability to live the life she/he wants. Symptoms and/or repetitive patterns of behavior represent the person's attempt to cope the best way he or she can with overwhelming feelings.

Neurological research suggests that childhood trauma negatively affects development by interrupting biological and hormonal processes, which has long-term effects on physical, psychological processes, and behavior as well.

For some time, psychologists have been aware that children who experience trauma, violence, and abuse are more likely to commit acts of violence and abuse than other children.

This chapter will examine how violent behavior is determined by memories of past traumatic experiences and how belief systems perpetuate violence from one generation to the next. Children who experience trauma or witness violence early in life are more likely to act out this aggression with their peers and in society as they become teenagers, and with their families as they grow into adulthood and enter marriage (Halford, Sanders, and Behrens, 2000; Kalmuss, 1984). The dynamics of familial trauma and/or violence are about the assertion of power and control over other members of a family and peers through intimidating behavior patterns that are repeated over and over again.

Personal beliefs systems affect and perpetuate the transmission of violence. The author employs two primary methods to change beliefs: recall of recent trauma and regression to early childhood. In the first method, the patient recalls the most recent time that a conflict or illness has occurred; he/she then identifies which traumatic event occurred a few months earlier, and which limiting thoughts or fixed beliefs were constructed at that very moment. What was the issue that the client couldn't resolve in another manner, or could not communicate in another way? The second method is regression to early childhood. The regression allows the therapist to examine behavior patterns, or "Life Patterns." A Life Pattern is like a script that constantly repeats itself, causing one to obtain the same result in certain situations and making a person incapable of overcoming a situation despite the desire to do so.

Fixed Beliefs and Life Pattern Theory

When individuals experience trauma and suffering, they make decisions that may accompany them throughout life and determine their future behavior. These decisions are called "fixed beliefs," and they constitute the basis of behavior. Individuals act and make decisions based upon their beliefs, thereby dictating the quality of their relationships with themselves and others.

The inability to change behavior patterns based upon fixed beliefs generates separation, resentment, guilt feelings, feelings of victimization, criticism, and a desire for revenge. These feelings, if maintained for a long time, may develop into chronic and terminal illnesses.

Many conflicts occur because of "fixed beliefs" that are caused by conflicts experienced during childhood. Through regression we discover that this belief was already present very early in life. In other words, the childhood conflict just served as a reminder or trigger that people dredged up from previous experience so as to resolve it in this lifetime. Psychological and physiological impairments can be viewed as the result of imbalances from wounds left unhealed. Some proponents of this theory use the term "human bio-computer" to describe how memories are retained and can be accessed at a later time, similar to the way in which a computer retrieves a stored file (Lilly, 2004). The technique described here enables the patient to "retrieve old files" (fixed beliefs) and replace or rewrite them with beliefs that can produce good health and success in one's relationships and career. For this reason, we compare regression therapy to uprooting a plant, rather than simply cutting the surface of the grass as occurs with many other techniques.

Many serious illnesses could be partially or totally reversed using this technique. Nonetheless, in some cases in which a diagnosis is made and patients are regressed to the past, some individuals choose not to change their beliefs and prefer to maintain their maladaptive behavior. Some people refuse to admit that they were mistaken or made erroneous assumptions that have affected their lives and the lives of those around them. The therapist must respect such cases.

Definition of Fixed Beliefs and Life Patterns

A fixed belief is a repetitive or automatic thought that controls one's behavior (Bertisch, 1982, 1987). Fixed beliefs are present in every human being and are established very early in life, usually by the age of six. Children are good observers but poor interpreters of events, and based upon their observations they develop beliefs that may affect them for the rest of their lives. Such beliefs may make a person feel that he or she is superior to others and that he or she is in a contest with others and wants to "come out on top." Fixed beliefs create other unexpected and undesirable consequences. They incite a person to be critical of others, to become emotionally upset, and to become angry.

While fixed beliefs vary from individual to individual, they also take shape among entire groups such as families, communities, and nations. These collective fixed beliefs motivate conflict between religions, races, nations, sexes, indeed between any group and the nonmembers perceived by that group as "other."

A life pattern is a repetitive way of thinking and behaving that guides behavior. Life patterns operate throughout life and in all areas of life. They result from the relentlessly comparative structure of fixed beliefs that hinge on words like "more" and "less."

To be "more than" or "less than" someone else is to feel separate from that person. If you are "more than" others and separate from them, you are also in constant danger of becoming "less than" others and consequently, becoming destructively self-critical. These feelings of superiority or inferiority foster criticism of others and of oneself that is not at all constructive.

Negative life patterns that are repeated over and over again affect all areas of behavior, including health problems, problems in a couple's relationship, work problems, or problems with one's children.

These behavior patterns (life patterns) tend to be perpetuated and to become stronger because they are transmitted from one generation to the next generation as learned behaviors. Children tend to focus more on negative behavior and they tend to do it "better," or "stronger," than their parents.

A person with the fixed belief that violence is acceptable and that control over others is important is a person who is likely to have tendencies toward violence. A violent person will perceive his or her own family members as the group over which he or she feels they "must come out on top." Children who witness the trauma of violence at a young age come to believe that violence is "OK." Thus, they internalize this belief and incorporate it into their behavior patterns, both as adolescents and as adults.

In *Getting Well Again* (1978), Simonton, Mathews-Simonton, and Creighton describe the psychological process of illness. They have developed a theory of a five-step psychological process that precedes the onset of illnesses such as cancer:

1. Experiences in childhood result in decisions to be a certain kind of person.
2. A cluster of stressful life events rocks the individual.
3. These stresses create a problem with which the individual does not know how to deal.

4. The individual sees no way of changing the rules about how he or she must act, and so feels trapped and helpless to resolve the problem.
5. The individual puts distance between himself or herself and the problem, becoming static, unchanging, and rigid (pp. 72–5).

Simonton and his colleagues describe some of the conflicts faced by their patients in the period preceding their cancer diagnoses:

- *Experiences in childhood result in decisions to be a certain kind of person.* Children witness the behavior of their parents and make a decision early on how to behave or not to behave in a certain situation. Some of these decisions have a beneficial affect; others do not. Some children make the decision early on that they are responsible for how others feel. In adulthood, such feelings of accommodation are no longer appropriate.
- A *cluster of stressful life events rocks the individual.* Life stressors are often a precursor to illness and disease. Empirical evidence suggests a correlation between children who witness family violence and a higher incidence of illness, both as children and later as adults.
- *These stresses create a problem with which the individual does not know how to deal.* The inability to cope with the stresses placed on the individual creates a physiological and psychological state that may lead to illness or conflict.
- *The individual sees no way of changing the rules about how he or she must act and so feels trapped and helpless to resolve the problem.* The child who witnesses violence may perceive violence as the only means by which to solve problems, or as the way to solve certain types of problems. Violence becomes one of the ways in which a child who witnesses violence in the home must act. In feeling trapped and helpless regarding their own problems, children may internalize the violent behavior and act out in a violent manner as adults.

Consequences of Fixed Beliefs/Life Patterns

This section describes some of the negative consequences of fixed beliefs.

1. A fixed belief causes individuals to be critical, judgmental and unfairly evaluate those who seem to have less of the belief's quality. The criticism and judgment may be verbal or nonverbal, in the form of looks, gestures, etc. Mental criticism, as an attitude

expressed either openly or covertly, induces others to act in a certain way. This places limitations upon their behavior and prevents teamwork, synergy, and productivity.

2. A fixed belief creates a feeling of being "better than" others, a feeling of superiority to those who lack the quality.

3. A fixed belief creates a sense of separateness from others, aloofness, alienation, and loneliness.

4. A fixed belief distorts perception. Someone with the belief that he or she is, for example, more intelligent than others, is unable to see this quality in others, even when it is clearly present. His or her criteria are taken to be the only valid ones. Thus, the belief becomes a self-fulfilling prophecy. The belief becomes the glasses through which one sees and creates reality in all aspects of his or her life, including relationships with family, friends, and coworkers.

5. Fixed beliefs cause resistance, resentment, and revenge. These negative attitudes and behaviors make people react negatively. Sometimes they "give it back to you," either in very subtle ways or in very obvious ways. It turns out to be a clear example of the law of cause and effect: "What you sow so shall you reap."

6. A fixed belief drives the individual to have a chain of unconscious, negative thoughts about himself or herself and others, such as anger, frustration, guilt, or fear. These negative thoughts have consequences for an individual's health and his or her ability to cooperate with others.

7. A fixed belief produces health and physical symptoms of major and minor degree, including illnesses, digestive disorders, and headaches.

8. A fixed belief causes the individual to create many harsh rules for himself or herself and to set arbitrary standards for others that are expressed as "must," "should," and "ought" statements: "I must do this"; "I should be certain way"; or "Other people ought to act in certain way."

9. A fixed belief may actually prevent the individual from truly having the desired quality. The belief of being "more than" shuts one off from making an effort to attain the quality.

Once fixed beliefs are identified, they can be replaced or "rewritten" with other beliefs that produce health, harmony, cooperation, and financial success. "Rewriting" is the process whereby an individual becomes aware of fixed beliefs and is able to alter his or her behavior by changing these beliefs. Lipton (2001) has described this process: "As older children and adults, we can access the subconscious database of programmed beliefs and reactions, bringing them to consciousness for review and modification" (p. 179).

The Process

I have termed the method of changing these harmful beliefs "The Process." This method enables the patient to:

- Effectively modify and overcome problems and common concerns in life. This method is directed at the core of these problems – to the specific root of a conflict and not its ramifications.
- Improve personal relationships, self-esteem, well-being, and economic success.
- Demolish barriers among people, minimize conflicts and daily concerns, and improve communication and self-expression.

Using the Process will enable people to produce many of the vital changes they always expected and wished to have and to maintain, if they so decide, the experience of love, cooperation, and optimism.

This technique uses communication tools to engender a self-transformation, through improved self-knowledge. It provides a short cut to access the resources that each person has and to access the essence of each situation. This technique allows a real, effective, and genuine transformation.

One positive outcome of this technique is improved communication between oneself and others. The method helps to reevaluate oneself, to better evaluate others, to reposition one's self in relation to others, and to have a real vision of the environment. In this way one can experience being in "the shoes of other person" (i.e., total empathy with another human being).

This technique also enables the patient both to forgive himself for his mistaken assumptions and to forgive his parents for trauma that they inflicted during the patient's childhood. Once the patient understands fixed beliefs and how they affect behavior, he or she is able to see how situations and events have been misinterpreted and how the beliefs based on these faulty perceptions have affected behavior True forgiveness means understanding that it was wrong to place blame originally. Forgiveness is the key to happiness, releasing the individual from the prison of negative judgments. It is not surrender, but a conscious decision to cease to harbor resentment.

In conclusion, patterns of violence may be transmitted across generations and reappear in the next generation. The violent behavior of parents is transmitted to their children, where it may be replicated in situations such as marital conflict. The next generation has children, who grow up to repeat the pattern of violence that they saw as children. This theory holds that patterns of intimacy are transmitted across generations, largely through social learning from the nuclear family and the reactions of the extended family.

Other transgenerational issues that have been studied include the basis of depression, strictness/leniency in parenting, and eating patterns. Additional issues studies include divorce patterns, marital conflict, and child sexual abuse.

The Genesis of Fixed Beliefs

It is not the circumstances of our lives that configure us, but our beliefs about what those circumstances mean. In other words, our beliefs shape our structures of thinking and personality and mold the way we live our physical, emotional, mental, and economic reality.

Now we know that our thoughts create the external environment. So if we wish to change our relationship to the environment, all that we should have to do is to change our beliefs. However, before discussing how beliefs can be successfully changed in order to attract people instead of rejecting them, it will be helpful to analyze how and why we develop our beliefs.

The evolution of human consciousness has three phases. In each of these phases, the personality (integrated at the physical, emotional, and mental levels) develops its survival strategy.

Most beliefs are decided during the period of "individuation" (during adolescence). It is during that time that individuals need to differentiate themselves from their parents, by choosing beliefs and qualities that characterize and distinguish them from their parents and the family environment.

This process operates by deep observation and by deciding what qualities or characteristics to develop more and better than one's parents, in order to differentiate one's self from them.

These beliefs are basic and important in the teenage years because they guide, model, and differentiate the individual from his or her parents and others. But while these are key elements in adolescence, we often continue to apply them automatically in adult life, without even perceiving the negative consequences that they provoke in all areas of life.

In my book *Re-Creating Your Life: Self-Transformation Step-by-Step* (Bertisch Meir and Meir, 2004), I outlined the development of this natural evolution from mass consciousness to individual consciousness and then to group consciousness:

Mass Consciousness (Childhood and Preadolescence)

Before learning to be individuals, people find themselves in the mass consciousness, that is, in a state in which others make the decisions.

This state is characteristic of infants, small children, and preadolescents. If this state is carried over into adulthood, one may feel like a victim and feel that someone else is responsible for what happens to oneself: a spouse, or a boss, coworkers, children, parents, neighbors, etc. In this stage one is unable of seeing how he/she is responsible for his/her current situation. When that situation becomes intolerable, one makes a great effort to extricate oneself, appealing to beliefs such as: "I am better," "I know more" etc., that is, declaring one's independence.

In childhood and preadolescence, this belief is effective, since it permits us in a short time, to feel strong and handle the situation. But these beliefs become a barrier that distorts communication with others and relationships in adulthood.

Individual Consciousness (Adolescence)

This is the period that children begin to feel that nobody "understands them" and they may become aggressive out of fear of losing their identity. Any form of commitment or cooperation is viewed as a trap, and is interpreted as a return to "mass consciousness" or "dependency."

This is the period when many fixed beliefs are established. Even if a person adopts the role of "weak" or "worse than," he/she is making an attempt to stay in the individuation stage or to be in control of the situation.

If the individual does not control the situation, he/she thinks that he/she will return to the mass consciousness or dependency phase. This anxiety compels him/her to be in constant competition with and opposition to others, and is a major cause of pain and suffering.

Group Consciousness (Interdependent Consciousness and Synergy)

Many individuals remain stuck in one of the earlier stages of consciousness. However, the natural evolution is from mass consciousness to individual consciousness and then to group consciousness. Independent individuals are capable of interrelating with others at a level that appeals to all of their abilities and experiences, resulting in a relationship that is more than the sum of the individual parts.

The results obtained in this way, either in work, in relationships, in health, family, studies, etc., are the product of synergy. In order to operate with optimal capacity, at full power, people need to feel that their identity is kept within any relationship. One needs to recognize that a satisfactory and full interpersonal relationship emerges from active cooperation with other people.

The same concept can be applied to relationships with family members, friends, coworkers, and others in service to the community. This last postulate is important in that each person contributes his/her virtues, ideas, abilities, but always maintains his/her own individuality. In order to achieve cooperation, we need to identify the wrong fixed beliefs and replace or rewrite them with those that consistently preserve a good purpose, working in solidarity for the good of all.

Parallels to Other Contemporary Theories

The author postulates the existence of a universal, easily observed, and verifiable psychological structure that underlies much of human behavior. If indeed that structure exists and operates as predicted by Life Pattern Theory, we can expect that other researchers and therapists/counselors have also observed its effects. They would have seen the same patterns of behavior, even though they would, naturally, give them other names, attribute them to other causes, and deal with them in other ways.

I present below a list of common "clinical" observations selected from contemporary psychological theories. The challenge, then, is to account for such phenomena in terms of life patterns.

> Observed phenomena: Illogical thinking; distorted perception; superficial and deep communication; paradox; life "script" or life style; meta-communication; primary, secondary, tertiary beliefs; dichotomous thinking; criticism of others, self-criticism, and feelings of inferiority; projection, rationalization, and "other defense" mechanisms; feelings of alienation; adult behavior; child behavior; negative emotions such as anger; pushing people's "buttons," which automatically triggers upsets; insecurity; inability to be in the "here and now" ; conflict with others; "rules"; need "to be right."

- **Albert Ellis's** Rational-Emotive Theory (Ellis, 2001) holds that problems are caused by "dogmatic, irrational, unexamined beliefs." He says that because problems are unrealistic, they will not withstand objective scrutiny, and that when empirically checked and logically assailed they tend to evaporate. Bertisch Meir's findings are similar in this area.

  Ellis also blames much unhappiness on people's "rules," their "musts," "oughts," and "shoulds" that are applied to oneself and others. Life Pattern Theory agrees, and illustrates how rules are created primarily to "support" the fixed belief.

Ellis emphasizes that the irrational beliefs also produce "deifications and/or devilifications" of oneself or others. Life Pattern Theory observes the same, but attributes the self-deification to the pride of "I'm more x" and the self-devilification to the self-criticism caused by one's inability to continually maintain the belief.

- **Alfred Adler** theorized that a person's problems originate in faulty goals, values, and perceptions (Adler, 1927). The person acts "as if" certain things are true. Assisting a person, for Adler, meant reeducation, allowing him to see that the "as if" things he thought were true, were, in fact, not true. Adler also observed that a person developed a "life style" based on his thoughts, faulty or otherwise. Adlerians feel that people develop a "private logic" in order to stay consistent with their original mistaken assumptions.

The relationship between beliefs, Life Pattern Theory, and the above Adlerian observations are obvious.

- **Richard Bandler and John Grinder** are the originators of Neuro Linguistic Programming (NLP). In *The Structure of Magic* (1990), they wrote that many problems could be traced to their source by analyzing a person's language usage. Problems exist as deep structures. People talk in "surface structures" that are the outer manifestations of the deep structures. Deep structures are the fullest linguistic representations of the patient's experience. The deep structures form the patient's mistaken model of the world. The therapist's task is to help the patient clarify what his or her model is. To accomplish that, the deep structure needs to be uncovered. Fixed Beliefs/Life Pattern Theory is in complete accord. Indeed, it easily furnishes real clinical and real life examples to illustrate the concept of deep and surface structures.

- **Eric Berne's** theory of Transactional Analysis (Berne, 1986) posits that each person views himself or herself and others as being okay or not okay. We observe the same phenomenon, but again believe that we add a more fine-grained explanation: A person views himself or herself as sometimes okay (when he or she is being x) and sometimes not okay (when he or she is not being x). Other people are also classified as okay or not okay, depending on their amount of x.

In summary, we can easily diagram the sequence in which a fixed belief is a consequence of a trauma or negative experience that affects the structure of personality and future behavior, often with undesirable results. To change beliefs and life patterns through the specific psy-chotherapy/counseling techniques called "processing" means to work in the nucleus of a situation and to restructure its core rather than the periphery, as other classical techniques tend to do. We are facing a new paradigm concerning personality structure and innovative psycho-therapy/counseling methods.

Whenever we change our beliefs, we can learn to choose our thoughts. We can choose positive, proactive thoughts. This has a trans-formative effect upon the individual, his or her relationships, and his or her environment. This is the best way to start transforming ourselves from victims of trauma and/or past negative events and beliefs to become powerful and proactive people who contribute their best to their families, careers, and society at large. Individuals can choose happiness, success, and positive outcomes from every experience.

References

Adler, A. (1927). *The practice and theory of individual psychology. New York: Harcourt, Brace.*

Bandler, R. and Grinder, J. (1990). *The structure of magic.* Palo Alto, CA: Science & Behavior Books.

Berne, E. (1986). *Transactional analysis in psychotherapy.* New York: Ballantine Books.

Bertisch, R. (1982). *A model for conflict resolution techniques: Fixed belief/life pattern counseling.* Unpublished master's thesis, University of Hawaii, Honolulu.

Bertisch, R. (1987). *Life pattern theory and practice.* Doctoral disserta-tion, University for Humanistic Studies, San Diego, CA.

Bertisch Danziger, R. and Danziger, S. (1984). *Mind map of life patterns: A map on beliefs, life patterns and behavior.* Honolulu, HI: Self-Mastery Systems International.

Bertisch Danziger, R. and Danziger, S. (1987). *You are your own best counselor.* Honolulu, HI: Self-Mastery Systems International.

Bertisch, R., and Kliksberg, N. (1990a). "Psychic surgeon of the Philippines, truth or fraud? The case of Emilio Laporga in Argentina." *Argentine Journal of ASPR (American Society of Psychical Research),* 84(2), 185–6.

Bertisch, R., and Kliksberg, N. (1990b). "Psychic surgeon of the Philippines, fraude or real?". *Argentine Journal of Paranormal Psychology,* 1(2), 35–40.

Bertisch, R., and Mordkowski, F. (1992). *Multiphasetic and interdisci-plinary advance approach to detain, prevent and revert the ischemic cardiopathy.* Argentinean Society of Cardiology. Argentina, 87(7), 7–10.

Bertisch, R., and Mordkowski, F. (1993). *Autotransformación y longevidad*. Buenos Aires, Argentina: Synergistics International.

Bertisch Meir, R., and Meir, M. (2004). *Re-creating your life*. Philadelphia: Xlibris.

Bertisch Meir, R. (in press). *Stop beliefs that stop your life*. Bloomington, IL: AuthorHouse.

Bertisch Meir, R. (2004). Del miedo al éxito. In H. Iglesias (ed.) *Exitistas o exitosos*. Buenos Aires, Argentina: Cefomar editora, 137–46.

Bertisch Meir, R. (2005). *El poder de sus pensamientos*. Bloomington, IL: AuthorHouse.

Ellis, A. (2001). *Overcoming destructive beliefs, feelings, and behaviors: New directions for rational emotive behavior therapy*. Amherst, NY: Prometheus Books.

Halford, W. K., Sanders, M. R., and Behrens, B. C. (2000). "Repeating the errors of our parents? Family-of-origin spouse violence and observed conflict management in engaged couples." *Family Process*, 39, 219–37.

Kalmuss, D. (1984). "The intergenerational transmission of marital aggression." *Journal of Marriage and Family*, 46, 11–19.

Lilly, J. C. (2004) *Programming the human biocomputer*. Berkeley, CA: Ronin Publishing.

Lipton, B. H. (2001). "Nature, nurture and human development." *Journal of Prenatal and Perinatal Psychology and Health*, 16(2), 167–180.

Piaget, J. (1972). *The child's conception of the world*. Lanham, MD: Rowman and Littlefield.

Pribram, K. (1971). *Languages of the brain*. Englewood Cliffs, NJ: Prentice-Hall.

Simonton, O. C., Mathews-Simonton, S., and Creighton, J. L. (1978). *Getting well again: A step-by-step, self-help guide to overcoming cancer for patients an their families*. New York: Bantam Books.

THE MIND OF A TERRORIST

It is important that we make an effort to learn how the mind of a terrorist works. Even more important, the U.S. media must understand how they feed terrorism for their own gains. For most of these insights I am indebted to Dr. Salman Akhtar (1999). He tells us that the word "terrorism" dates back to 1795, when it was coined to denote acts of intimidation. The term was usually applied to a group. Yesterday's terrorist can become today's hero. Terrorist organizations are usually led by a charismatic leader. His followers idealize him and the group while devaluating the rest of society. The terrorist group is different from cults or gangs, which can break out into acts of self-destruction.

The majority of terrorists are men who have been traumatized as children and suffered chronic physical and emotional abuse. Their psyches were violated, and the essential feeling of safety needed for developing a healthy psyche was not available to them. The violation of their psychological boundaries led to a childhood marked by hate, intense anxiety, lack of trust, and a loathing for passivity. In order to control their fears, they must "kill" their personal view of themselves as victims and turn their passivity into active sadism. They buttress self-esteem by devaluing others. The resulting "malignant narcissism renders mute the voice of reason and morality" (Akhtar, 1999, p. 350). This makes it possible to "justify" outright cruelty. Their paranoid mentality is covered over by a patina of rationalization.

A terrorist organization consists of a leader followed by sexually inhibited young men who have been similarly traumatized, usually closet narcissists who have no cohesive identity (James Masterson, personal communication, 1996). Closet narcissists do not become exhibitionists, but derive their power from joining with a full-blown narcissist. The leader offers a new family. Through fiery oratory and exaggerated glories, he appeals to the infantile hungers of the group. He reminds the group members of their individual traumas through exaggerated accounts of injustices against the group by outsiders. In this way, the followers shift their anger and aggression toward their enemy and feel enormously bound to their new "father." It is as if this "destructive Pied Piper" has a trance effect on them. Their shame and guilt are diminished, while their narcissism comes into full bloom. They lose any sense of right and wrong, and their values come from group approval. "The oppressed of yesterday become the oppressors of today. Such violent medleys provide the discharge of repressed sexual impulses as well and prepare the psychological floor for an invisible dance with death" (Akhtar, 1999, p. 252).

The secondary role of the group is furthered by the praise of agencies supporting its causes as well as overt and covert financial aid. The terrorists' narcissism is paradoxically fueled by the shock and horror of their victims. "The dynamic is akin to the satisfaction a sexual exhibitionist draws from his onlooker's startled response. The notoriety achieved through the public media serves a similar function" (Akhtar, 1999, p. 352).

The terrorist organization is based on the victimization of the followers and therefore cannot afford to succeed. If they succeed, they will no longer be victims and their identity will collapse. As a result, the terrorist leader unconsciously aims for the impossible.

Hezbollah suicide bombers are promised the love of hoors (celestial maidens) in heaven. Akhtar (1999, p. 353) claims that is similar to the insistence of psychiatric patients that all of their self-induced suffering is acceptable because "someday their childhood traumas will be completely reversed."

In conclusion, terrorism has multiple determinants that range from childhood trauma to social and economic deprivations and abuses. Lessening the pain of a terrorist would help defuse his malignant sadomasochistic needs. As therapists, we cannot even begin to devise a plan to treat them. Nevertheless, our politicians and the national media must develop the restraints to defuse the narcissistic sadism of the terrorists rather than fuel their pathological needs.

THROUGH THE EYES OF A BYSTANDER

This is the story of the personal experience of an off-duty firefighter who found himself suddenly immersed in the traumatic events of 9/11:

> Tom is a 32-year-old volunteer fireman who was attending a training class in downtown New York City when the disaster took place. He lives and works in upstate New York. That morning he was assigned to take a class on dealing with fires in tall buildings. Most of the structures in Tom's hometown are small, but a new six-story office building was under construction and the fire department wanted to be ready. Tom's wife was home, and his four children were in school.
>
> He was walking to class with a buddy, Kevin, only a couple of blocks from the Twin Towers when the first plane hit. "Everybody was running away from the building toward the waterfront. I figured some sort of tragic accident had occurred and that maybe I could help. We were headed in the opposite direction of the crowd when I stopped to get my bearings. Kevin was nowhere to be seen. It was so confusing, like I was watching myself watching a movie. I knew I was in my body, I just couldn't feel it," Tom said.
>
> When the second plane hit, Tom realized that New York City was under some kind of attack. Without a commander or his squad for backup; he wasn't sure what to do. "I could see the flames and smoke billowing from the buildings. As I looked up, I could see people jumping out of the buildings. I frantically tried my cell phone and then the radio, but nothing was working. Then I just went numb," the firefighter explained. He slipped into an altered state of consciousness. Tom didn't understand what was going on around him and he didn't have a clue as to what he could do. Trained as a firefighter, he instinctively began running toward the scene of the incident to see if he could be of help. Then the towers crumbled, and Tom knew he was out of his league. He

crumbled too. He was overcome with grief and fear and started to sob. He felt ashamed of himself.

Tom ran into some other firefighters, but he was in street clothes, and they were too busy to stop and talk with a civilian. At that moment he felt small and insignificant. His whole perspective about life had changed forever. When a stranger told Tom the Pentagon had also been attacked, an icy sense of doom swept over him. He suddenly realized that in all the excitement he hadn't even once thought of his wife and kids.

That's not unusual for firefighters: Firefighters and police officers are trained as professionals first and family men or women second. This is a major reason for familial disputes among this population as well as divorce and alcohol and drug abuse.

They are also afraid to ask for help for fear their guns or equipment will be confiscated and they will be given desk jobs and be regarded by their buddies as "sissies." That is one of the reasons debriefing failed to work during and after 9/11. These are men and women of action, not talk. It is called the "silent conspiracy."

This has made it impossible to recruit a knowledgeable firefighter or police officer to speak at a trauma conference or to join the Warren Trauma Center. A firefighter is a firefighter first. It is a rule that becomes part of their personalities.

Tom kept dialing his home number on the cell phone without success, and finally realized that there was no way to communicate with the firehouse or his family. As the scene got worse, it became obvious that New York City had been shut down and the site of the tragedy had been isolated. It was total chaos at and near Ground Zero. "People were running and crying. I just wasn't sure how to help them or, for that matter, how to help myself. In all the confusion, I heard an airplane overhead, and was sure more bombings were imminent. I began to run aimlessly, following other silent runners whose eyes seemed fixed in blank, frightened stares. It was absolute chaos," he said.

Tom knew that without his specialized equipment and the rest of his team, there was little, if anything, he could do. He had to get home to make sure his family was safe and to catch up with his squad. He headed for the Path trains, hoping they were still running. He was covered with gray soot and dirt. All around him, people were running and crying. Feeling ashamed and embarrassed, he got on the train with other terrified men and women and made his way across the Hudson River. Once he got across the bridge, his cell phone was working, and Tom hurriedly called the firehouse, only to find that while he was on his way home, his squad was en route to New York and Ground Zero. His wife was home watching the scenario unfold on television, and was convinced now that Tom was dead. The children were safe in a lockdown at school.

The schools in Tom's hometown had shut down all communication with the outside world. Teachers were ordered not to talk about the disaster for fear of mass hysteria. Nevertheless, some children found out what was happening, and the word spread through the student population like a flu epidemic. The ineffectual stonewall technique only exacerbated their fears.

Meanwhile, Tom hitchhiked the rest of the way home. Once there, instead of the welcome he anticipated, Tom found anger and disappointment. Instead of being thankful that her husband was alive, Tom's wife became angry that once again she was the last to know whether or not he was alive and safe. He decided to drown his emotions in a bottle of scotch, and finally collapsed from mental exhaustion. He awoke the next morning to find his wife and children traumatized by the events and angry at his alcoholic binge.

Tom was well aware that heart disease is the leading cause of death among firefighters because of the stressful lives they lead. He started to somatize and feel heart palpitations. When he checked in at the firehouse he discovered that some of his buddies had died in the collapse of the second tower. The rest of the squad was still in New York City helping out at Ground Zero. He immediately headed for the hole in the ground where the Twin Towers had stood to search for some of his fallen comrades who were reported missing. Almost in a hypnotic trance, he kept searching for body parts. Although not formally on duty, Tom was sent for debriefing at the South Street Seaport. He was a man of action, not talk, and the debriefing only made his problems worse.

In response to the smoke and dust, he developed a cough that combined with the continuing heart palpitations, convinced him he was having a heart attack. He kept reliving the events of 9/11. His physiology had turned into biology, and the next stop was his doctor's office. After a thorough exam, the physician referred Tom for psychotherapy, an idea he refused to accept. "You can't talk away what happened. After all, talking could not and would not take away the memories of 9/11 or the gnawing guilt I feel for not doing more to save my buddies and other victims," Tom told himself.

Instead of treatment, Tom returned to his squad and spent every waking minute with them searching for their missing buddies and self-medicating with alcohol when not on duty. It seemed to work for Tom. At last, he was doing something, but it didn't work for his family. His wife eventually decided to file for divorce and, because of his drinking, sought to restrict his contact with the children except under formal supervision. Tom sank into a world of despair and confusion. He had lost himself and now his family. All he had left was the squad. Many of his buddies were killed, and Tom felt ashamed and guilty that he didn't do anything to help them. He had no understanding of why his wife and children left him or why he continued to have flashbacks of the disaster. The quest for his fallen comrades continued until the search was formally called off and firefighters were banned from the disaster site. That last night, Tom and his squad slept with their fallen comrades amid the dust and debris in the gaping hole that had once been the Twin Towers.

Postscript

On September 27, 2002, about fifty-four weeks after 9/11, it was reported that a firefighter from Squad 288 made a makeshift shrine to the firefighters who died on 9/11 and, sitting before it, put a shotgun in his mouth and blew his brains out. Tom finally found his own peace rather than seeking therapy and perhaps working out his problems. But did he really find peace or unleash a whole new set of problems? What about his family? What legacy did he leave them? Anger, drinking, and suicide are not the answer.

As therapists, we all know children learn from identification, imitation, and introspection. Introspection is subliminal and the most dangerous because it is simply unconscious and you act on it without your thinking mind. What kind of legacy has Tom left for his children? A life of drink and high risk for suicide (like their father).

Most of us do not realize that our unconscious minds are developed by age 12 to 15, providing a general map of how we will lead our adult lives. This fireman has actually put his family in danger of not being able to cope with future problems, except by drinking, and if that doesn't work, to shoot themselves. How much peace does that provide? Consciously, I'm sure he would not want that solution for his family. But unconsciously he could not find another way.

TWO TYPES OF TRAUMA

There are two types of trauma: Type 1 Trauma, or Individual Trauma, (Erickson, 1976, p. 38) is a "blow to the psyche that breaks through one's defenses so suddenly and with such brutal force that one cannot react effectively." Type 2, or Collective Trauma, "is a blow to the basic tissues of social life that destroys the bonds that hold people together and impairs the prevailing sense of community."

Dr. Charles Figley of the Institute of Traumatology estimates that 30% of all women have been beaten or raped by their spouses or other males. Every nine seconds a woman is beaten in America. It is unknown just how many children are abused because many female victims repress the memories, and the event may not become conscious until the victim reaches adulthood. Male victims are usually too embarrassed to report an abusive event and feel they should be able to handle subsequent reactions by themselves. When such events occur repeatedly, they become more traumatizing and overrun our personal resources. Trauma by Proxy involves seeing the event on television, reading about it in the newspapers, or hearing about it from a friend.

The National Institute of Mental Health (NIMH) has still been unable to complete statistics on depression for people in the United States that would reflect the impact of 9/11. Meanwhile, recent clinical trials of six popular antidepressants failed to show a "clinically significant" difference between the drugs and the placebo. The drugs include: Prozac, Paxil, Zoloft, Effexor, Serzonne, and Celeza. Startling was the unusually high number of study dropouts because of adverse drug side effects.

It is estimated that 30% of Vietnam veterans are suffering from post-traumatic stress disorder (PTSD) and are homeless as a result of it. Prior to 9/11, it was estimated that 10–15% of these veterans suffered from anxiety disorders and that about 75% of their medical complaints that go undiagnosed are usually psychosomatic.

Although this book presents comprehensive programs for dealing with both Type 1 and Type 2 trauma, it deals mainly with Type 2 Traumatic Event Stress. The individual behavioral symptoms in Type 1 and Type 2 stress appear to be similar except that in Type 2 there is a greater tendency toward fear and group helplessness, combined with fear that the world itself will collapse. The emotional symptoms include overwhelming fears or anxieties, feeling lost, guilt, grief, excessive death anxiety, feeling detached from others, a restricted range of feelings, a sense of a limited future, and displays of irritability or outbursts of anger. Behavioral symptoms may include withdrawal from or clinging to others, sleep disturbances, unusual behaviors, changes in eating patterns, communication problems (silences, pressurized speech), changes in work habits, flashbacks, experiencing the event as a dream or recollection, and intense reactions to cues reminiscent of the event. Included in the cognitive impairments are poor concentration, shorter attention span, memory problems, impaired ability to focus, difficulties making decisions, slower problem solving, trouble with calculations, memory loss with respect to certain aspects of the event, hypersensitive startle reaction, and lack of interest in usual activities. Physically, the victim may experience muscle tremors, chest pains, gastrointestinal distress, difficulty breathing, headaches, or elevated blood pressure.

The behavioral symptoms related to physical or sexual abuse include physical signs of abuse, impaired ability to think, problems with control and self-mastery, post-traumatic stress disorder, acting out sexually or aggressively, depression and/or anxiety, and a plethora of other psychiatric symptoms such as low self-esteem, "damaged goods" syndrome, suicidal ideations and/or attempts, guilt, repressed anger, blurred role boundaries, pseudomaturity in children, failure to accomplish developmental tasks, poor social skills, social withdrawal, nightmares, acute stress disorder, and underlying death anxiety.

CHILDREN'S RESPONSES TO DEATH AND TRAUMA

Harper (2002 pp. 18–19) traces the shifting attitudes toward death of children as they gradually mature to adulthood. From infancy through early childhood children have no concept of death, but can experience a great sense of loss and grief that sets the stage for later realizations. From ages three to five children think of death as a kind of reversible sleep, but deny death as a normal and final process. Although at ages six through nine children accept death as final, they still believe it won't happen to them. It isn't until pre-adolescence, ages 10 through 12, that children view death as final and inevitable. The may hide their fear of death by joking about it. By adolescence they have acquired concepts of time, space, quantity, and causality, and are ready to add death to the list. The denial of death may explain some of their risk-taking behavior. Defiance replaces the jokes about death that marked the previous phase. In fact, adolescents are actually seeking the meaning of life. Although we finally accept it as inevitable, our views of death continue to be modified throughout adulthood.

"When we talk about death anxiety, we are embarking on a journey into the mysterious regions of the mind where people have shelved these thoughts" (Warren 1991, p. 28). However, in today's environment, the issue has raised its ugly head, and we must face it square on. Recommended treatments for dealing with the issue of death and death anxiety have been largely ignored in philosophical, religious, or medical points of view.

Children's reactions to fear often appear exaggerated and strange to adults. Common childhood reactions may include nightmares, fear of sleeping alone, and above all, fear of the dark. They may become "clingy" or revert to early childhood behavior like thumb sucking to soothe themselves. Other children develop somatic complaints (i.e., headaches, stomachaches). Children from birth to age two, before they develop language skills, may become irritable, cry, or want to be held or cuddled.

Pre-kindergarten or kindergarten children may feel helpless or powerless. They do not understand permanent loss and believe that consequences can always be reversed. Abandonment is a major fear. Children in the seven to eleven age range may understand the permanence of loss from trauma. Nevertheless, they may react by having difficulty concentrating, and step back into earlier behaviors. They may feel guilt, anger, or a sense of personal failure. Children ages 12 to 18 generally have a great need to prove themselves and appear knowledgeable to others. If they survive the trauma, they may even feel immortal, a reaction that may lead to other reckless behavior. Sometimes overwhelmed by such intense reactions, teens may be unable to discuss them with others.

When I was about seven years old, I realized that we all had to die some day, and I got up the courage to ask my father about death. "Stop that nonsense," he replied. "Everybody has to die sooner or later. Just put it out of your mind." I was scared and didn't know what to do. After thinking about the problem for some time, I decided to make a deal with myself. I put the question off for 10 years. When I was 17, I put it off for another 10 years. That was how my own private denial of death arose, but I cannot put it off any longer. Life in 2005 is different. We can't make deals like that. We must find a better way to deal with the ever-present threat of death in a world overrun by worry.

Kabat-Zinn (1990, p. 3) talks about "an art to facing difficulties in ways that lead to effective solutions and inner peace and harmony. When we are able to mobilize our inner resources to face our problems artfully," he says, "we can use the pressure of the problem to propel us through it" to a solution. That's much like a sailor who skillfully positions his sails to make optimum use of the wind's energy to get the boat where he wants to go.

Whether we ignore our problems or focus on them exclusively, they are certain to multiply. The things we worry about seldom actually happen. The things we don't know enough to worry about might well happen after all. Therefore, living in the here and now, while focusing on solutions to everyday life, will help people to lead a more meaningful existence.

The Atom Bomb Story

A patient once told me about living under the constant fear of the atom bomb when she was growing up during World War II. People were building bomb shelters. School children were taught to hide under their desks (not that that would have protected them from the destruction or the subsequent radiation). Fear was in the air. She remembers awakening every morning, afraid that this was the day she would die. Finally, at age 18, she realized that her entire childhood was ruined by fear, anxiety, headaches, and related gastrointestinal problems. She learned to remind herself every morning that her worry about the bomb that never came had wasted her childhood. Now, every time she catches herself worrying, she reminds herself of the Atom Bomb story.

"Full catastrophe living" (Kabat-Zinn, 1990) means living fully in the here and now. It does not mean one should not plan for the future or forget the lessons of the past. It means you are aware of the future and the past, but you don't live there. He adds:

> In our era, the full catastrophe is much in evidence on all fronts. A brief reading of any morning newspaper will drive home the impression of an unending stream of misery in the world, much of it inflicted by one human being on another. If you listen with an attentive ear to what you hear on radio or [see on] television news programs, you will find yourself assaulted daily by a steady barrage of terrible and heart-breaking images of human violence and misery . . . . Even if we don't read or listen, or watch the news, we are never far from the full catastrophe of living (p. 6).

That was written 15 years ago. When we now listen to the news, violence is rampant, and we are all in the midst of one critical traumatic incident after another. In the early phases of the war against terrorism, the media tended to misfire. Skepticism and colored reports (Wall Street Journal, December 2001) only scared the American people and did not put us in good light with many countries around the world. Newscasters often attempt to reel you in and rile you up so you keep listening.

AFTER THE CRASH

Most mental health clinicians have been trained to work with individuals, since collective trauma in the past was not the major concern it is today. People are now finding it difficult, if not impossible, to heal when communities like New York City are torn and we are routinely bombarded with new threats. During and immediately after a disaster, people are usually able to pull together and function, albeit with diminished effectiveness. This is known as the Heroic Phase or the Honeymoon Phase of disaster characterized by widespread altruism. As time goes on and fatigue sets in, illusions become disillusions, and stress begins to appear as people lose their focus and develop symptoms.

Fear is contagious, and when it takes over, all reason flies out the window. We know better than to yell "fire!" in a crowded theatre. When people are frightened, they panic and it spreads like a wave quickly through the crowd. Everyone rushes for the exit even though it is obviously blocked. In the stampede some are trampled and die.

ESCAPING THE DOUBLE-BIND

The public has been caught in a double-bind by official advice from our national leadership. We have been told that we must return to our normal way of life. At the same time, we are also admonished to be on constant alert, putting us in a "damned if you do and damned if you don't" position, the traditional double-bind. It was recognized as far back as 1956 by Gregory Bateson and his colleagues (Bateson et al., 1956) that the pathological double-bind produces a wide range of disturbing affect: helplessness, fear, exasperation, and rage, among others (Bateson et al., p. 251). Therefore, it is important that we find a new way to alert the public without "double-binding" them. The almost-constant news coverage of probable outbreaks of terrorist biochemical warfare is out of sync with reality. In 2002, the American Psychological Association estimated that 40,000 Americans die annually in automobile accidents. In comparison, the statistical odds of contracting anthrax are minimal.

Changing how one perceives what is happening can control the fear. Focusing on outcomes rather than possibilities can help. For example, how many people are actually going to contract a fatal disease from opening their mail? The odds must be similar to those that have made the state lottery a resounding financial bonanza.

A technique I find useful with my patients comes from living a life that is mindful (staying in the here and now rather than what might be in the future), which is well explained by Jon Kabat-Zinn (1990):

> This leads directly to new ways of seeing and being in your life because the present moment, whenever it is recognized and honored, reveals a very special, indeed magical power: it is the only time that any of us ever has. The present is the only time that we have to know anything. It is the only time we have to perceive, to learn, to act, to change, to heal. That is why we value moment-to-moment so highly. While we may have to teach ourselves how to do it through practicing, the effort itself is its own end. It makes our experiences more vivid and our lives more real (p. 29).

Research indicates that the way in which people cope with crisis will determine how much control they will have in this new world. Those who go on with their work, pleasure, etc., seem to have an internal locus of control and will develop further. People with little locus of control will feel they are at the mercy of environmental (e.g., natural, political, economic) forces around them.

I have been particularly concerned about one of my patients because of her suicidal ideations, anxiety, and depression. After the first anthrax attack, she arrived in my office fully loaded with enough Cipro and Doxycycline, prescribed by her medical doctor, to get her through the next millennium. While previously she felt some tenuous control over her life, now she felt a complete loss of control over her work and play. She requested her physician to provide the medication in case she opened an anthrax-contaminated letter or there was a germ warfare attack on the train trip to work.

Life is full of ups and downs, but when the downtimes get longer or appear never to end, what happens to mental health in America? There are a variety of major mental disorders in the United States. These include anxiety disorders such as panic disorders, obsessive-compulsive disorder, post-traumatic stress disorder, generalized anxiety disorder, and various phobias; depressive disorders such as dysthymic disorder, bipolar disorders, and schizophrenia; eating disorders; and attention deficit/hyperactivity disorder. People with these disorders have a fragile locus of control that will be exacerbated by the constant barrage of news warning of biochemical warfare and further terror on the home front.

Since 9/11, we have experienced day after day of warnings and alerts. Yet, for some reason there have been no published statistics by the American Psychological Association or the National Institute of Mental Health about the effect of the World Trade Center crisis on mental health in the United States or the world. This only leads me to believe we are in a state of denial. More and more people are turning to drugs, alcohol, and other substances to cope with the stress. We are truly living in a state of National Trauma Syndrome. Dr. Andrew Weil warns us to limit the amount of time we spend watching TV news and stay in the here and now in order to survive.

Contrary to common belief, people do not seek mental health treatment immediately after a disaster, and shock syndrome and pathological grief symptoms are not rampant. Years after the World Trade Center disaster, the American Red Cross asked people to reach out for help since financial and other resources were available but largely unused. It is only recently that people finally are beginning to ask for help. Yet, as far as the police and firefighters are concerned, there remains a silent conspiracy. They are still afraid to talk about their fears, even to their brothers and sisters (personal conversation 2004). They are afraid they will be thought of as "crazy" and put on desk patrol or, worse yet, lose their guns or status as firefighters or police officers. It was suggested that people declined the Red Cross services because they felt others needed it more.

Second Disaster

Actually, the problems people face immediately after a disaster are concrete in nature: locating their loved ones scattered by the incident, food, clothing, and shelter. They are usually faced with an impersonal bureaucratic system that moves slowly and is hampered by endless red tape. It is no surprise that many victims cannot collect their benefits in a timely manner.

One of my patients had been fighting with Social Security Administration for more than a year about her disability benefits. She was injured at work and needed approval for an operation. Before a decision was handed down by the Social Security Administration, her disability checks arrived sporadically or not at all, and she simply ran out of money. In constant pain, she still traveled from doctor to doctor, seeking approval for back surgery. To make matters worse, she had diabetes, a heart condition, and Addison disease, and had no family to turn to for help.

When the Twin Towers crashed on September 11, her medical records were buried forever in the rubble, along with her hope of back surgery in the near future. Money and food became critical concerns for her. Next, she received an eviction notice for nonpayment of rent. She turned to her attorney when she had no money and when she contacted the agencies established to help victims of the disaster, her circumstances did not fit the usual profile, and her pleas went unanswered. She became scared, angry, and helpless.

This, and incidents like it, have been recognized as the "Second Disaster" in which victims are made to feel even worse, or more helpless, with nowhere to turn due to bureaucratic red tape (Farberow and Frederick, 1978; Hesse, 2002). Years after the World Trade Center destruction, my patient is still fighting daily with long telephone menus that lead nowhere. She cannot stand for hours on slow-moving lines with other victims patiently seeking help with their problems. The frustration is almost overwhelming. The maintenance of ongoing treatment with a patient in these crisis circumstances is challenging at best. My priority was to intervene as quickly and efficiently as possible, an approach made possible by using the telephone.

Franklin Delano Roosevelt, in his first inaugural address, reassured the American people that, "There is nothing to fear but fear itself." In contrast, our government continues to frighten us by warning that the terrorists are developing weapons of nuclear, biological, and chemical warfare, and will not hesitate to use them on us unless we strike first. How much more scary can it get?

In actuality, security is just an illusion. It has never existed, and we have never known what to expect from the terrorists from one moment to the next. Important things in life are seldom planned, and sooner or later we are confronted with pain. The challenge is to face it and live our lives as richly as we can. A truly traumatic event invites us to reevaluate our lives.

In trauma, a person's breathing is greatly affected, the body tightens, and maladaptive character logical patterns occur. Most people dissociate when traumatized.

During the Oklahoma bombing and on 9/11, people were walking around stunned. The terrorist gets new thrills as the public is systematically terrorized. What does that do for our national psyche? As we go forward we must come to the understanding that all we have is the here and now.

Trauma may be the root cause of war. Every day we witness mindless killings carried out in the name of peace. Trauma begets trauma. People are afraid to travel or to spend money. It is difficult to be effective when one feels helpless, and it is virtually impossible to trust in rules or be guided by empathy when one feels his/her life is threatened.

We need to find solutions rather than constantly revisiting the problem and reinfecting ourselves with fear. The answer is to develop stability and connective relationships that lead to peaceful solutions. The meaning of trauma not only becomes integrated into the social history of our times,) but also in the private recording devices of the individual spirit in an effort to make sense of the chaos (Williams-Keeler, 1998).

An anonymous Holocaust survivor observed that each generation must create its own humanity. We are products of history and must change with it. There is nothing as resilient as the human spirit.

The range of human response to terror is varied. Some people look at it as a way to find meaning in their lives. Others withdraw or become embittered. Frankl (1990) at a conference in Anaheim, California, told of how he and others in World War II made it out of the Nazi death camps by finding new meaning in their lives. Finding something that can get you through the day and night can give you hope and possibilities for the future. Staying frozen in the trauma keeps one in a negative trance. In order to move forward, you must find new solutions or connections in your life.

This is a time to be innovative. Creative minds have always known how to survive. We now live in a time when we must learn to transcend our predicament of living with the fear of terrorism and discover an adequate guiding truth to help our children and ourselves when the government puts us on alert without any viable solutions for our anxieties.

As psychotherapists, we must dedicate ourselves in these trying times to finding creative solutions by following our conscious commands to carry out our professions in the best way we can. If we really want to end terrorism in the world, we will have to start in our own backyard by recognizing the bullying and terrorism that exist in our schools, families, neighborhoods, and the workplace. These are our own citizens. The terrorists are mirrors of our own culture, and we must take responsibility for our part in the problem.

Many schools have developed excellent contingency plans to deal with a 9/11-type disaster. These include special emergency committees of school psychologists, social workers, and guidance counselors together with the principal. In most cases, the teacher has been overlooked. Yet it is the teacher who is on the front line in the classroom. All school personnel, including teachers, should be familiar with the age-appropriate reactions of children to traumatic stress.

J. S. Volpe, Director of Professional Development of the American Academy of Experts in Traumatic Stress, explains, "A response that identifies and responds to a crisis in a unified and collaborative manner can alter the aftermath of the crisis. A preconceived and organized intervention is better than reacting in a haphazard way."

People react differently to trauma. Some people can move on, while others seem to never get over it. Some see it as a wake-up call, while others become embittered and withdraw from the world. There is no right or wrong way to deal with it. In this book, I have tried to provide some suggestions to guide you in searching for and finding a personal meaning in life and a connection with the possibilities of the future. That does not mean living in a future fantasy because we must develop adaptations for living in these times. Find something to get you through the day. Remind yourself that the more mindful you are, the less likely you are to frighten yourself or dilute your personal power. People who are traumatized often get frozen in time. You can't change the past, but you can change the way you are currently living. Often people do not realize that they have the power to change what they focus on. Cognitions can be changed, but we cannot change the past or effectively peer into the future.

Panic is to fear as a match is to fire. Bin Laden's followers attacked our country, but we can't let them control our minds or allow them to shut down our lives. One way to help yourself is to mentally downgrade outcomes that frighten you while remaining prepared for any possibility. Bodily confront your fear by monitoring the conversations in your head. When you feel fear, acknowledge it, see it, but don't become frozen in it. Fear is one thing, but letting it control you mind and your life is something else. Life is either an adventure you are willing to take, or it is nothingness. When things go bump in the night, both as individuals and as a nation we need to remind ourselves that we come well equipped with resources we can rely on.

2
DEALING WITH TRAUMA
IN AN AGE OF CHRONIC STRESS

THE NATIONAL TRAUMA SYNDROME

Chronic stress emerges as a result of living in ongoing stressful situations that are not short lived. Life in our post-9/11 world poses stressful situations in which the classic reactions of fight, flight, or freeze are continually suppressed. Under persistent stress, all parts of the human body (brain, heart, lungs, muscles, blood vessels) are over or under activated and produce psychological and physical damage over time. The effects include increased vulnerability to stroke, cancer, infections, and immune and gastrointestinal disorders. Unfortunately, stress is an unavoidable consequence of life, and we need to learn how to effectively deal with it.

Secondary or vicarious traumatization (Hesse 2002, p. 295) "desperately needs to move to the forefront of American consciousness" since "hundreds of rescue workers and mental health providers who have worked with trauma victims have undoubtedly been victims . . . themselves." Figley (1995) warns that secondary traumatization can emerge suddenly with little or no warning, causing helplessness and confusion. He has described four distinct "waves of assistance" for victims in the aftermath of disaster (see Table 2).

USE OF THE TELEPHONE

Aronson (2000) explains that sometimes the work of the therapist seems more practical than psychological, such as locating a food hotline to save the patient from starvation. It's impossible to think about anything else

Table 2: Four Waves of Assistance

I.   COPING AND STABILIZATION
     Basic Needs (Maslow)
     Safety and Security

II. STRESS MANAGEMENT
     Arousal Reduction
     Facilitation of Coping with Life

III. GRIEF AND TRAUMA RESOLUTION
     Debriefing
     Arousal Containment

IV. LOSS ACCOMMODATION
     Stabilization of Emotions and Behaviors

     Six Loss Accommodation Functions
     Recognize the Loss
     React to the Separation
     Re-experience the Loss
     Relinquish Old Attachments
     Readjust to the New World without Forgetting the Old
     Reinvest in the New World

From *Compassion Fatigue: The Stress of Caring Too Much* (1994) (DVD transcript)
Charles Figley, ed., Panama City, FL: Visionary Productions. Used with permission.

when you're broke and hungry. Aronson quotes Sue Elkind, a specialist in patients with serious impasses. Elkind's priority is to "intervene as quickly and efficiently as possible, an approach facilitated through work by phone." Noting the adaptability of human beings, she explains, "When visual cues are unavailable, auditory sensitivity is sharpened" (Aronson, 2000, p. xxv).

The telephone has quietly slipped into clinical practice and many practitioners have adopted its use under special circumstances, Dr. Aronson explains. "Since it is rarely discussed in public or written about, the phone is not recognized as the important tool that it is" (Aronson, 2000, p. xxi). The phone is the quickest way to stay connected with your patients in times of crisis. In a disaster, therapists must do what is needed, including adapting their services to meet the unique requirements of their patients.

Farberow and Frederick (1978) point out that the traditional office space is of little use in a disaster, and that most victims will not approach a mental health worker for counseling in such times of stress.

The immediate aim is to rebuild, educate, and connect people to the support systems available as quickly as possible. Sometimes, talking on the telephone helps patients feel connected and increases their ability to become adaptive and creative out of necessity.

DEMOBILIZATION, DEFUSING, AND DEBRIEFING

Demobilization, defusing, and debriefing are the three major techniques for dealing with the victims of a critical event like the 9/11 disaster.

Demobilization

Demobilization refers to the process in which victims are removed from the scene of the critical event, supplied with necessary staples (food, clothing, shelter), provided information about stress and trauma, and taught effective coping techniques.

Defusing

Defusing was used during 9/11 but proved to be a technique that created more havoc than usefulness. I have included it in this chapter as a piece of memorabilia, not as a suggested technique. However, some people still find it useful.

The technique of defusing, which is conducted within 12 hours of a crisis, is less detailed than debriefing. It consists mainly of group discussions aimed at reducing the acute stress. Defusing is more flexible than debriefing and is designed to restore normal functioning. It can be repeated as often as required. The format for defusing includes three phases:

1. *Introduction*. Explain goals while setting ground rules and expectations.
2. *Exploration*. Review the facts of the crisis and discuss personal reactions to the event.
3. *Information*. Teach stress management and practical coping skills; normalize symptoms.

In every critical event, there are more victims than you might expect. Everyone experiences physical or psychological impairment to some degree. Those impairments spread across the landscape of family, work, and community relations, setting the stage for a range of disorders, both physical and psychological, and exacerbating those disorders already in existence. It has been suggested that at least 90% of adults who witnessed the 9/11 disaster at Ground Zero or on television will experience a resulting trauma. In actuality, I believe the figure is higher than we realize.

Although the statistics are still unclear, it was shown that the rate of heart problems in the United States just 30 days after 9/11 had more than doubled from 3.5% to 8.0% of the population. More New York City firefighters than ever are now smoking, reversing a pre-9/11 trend. More than a third of our children and teens report being worried compared with 21% before the World Trade Center tragedy.

One of my patients, Mr. A., a police officer, was at Ground Zero when the Twin Towers collapsed. He returned home that night feeling guilty that he had not done more to help. He was instructed to return to Ground Zero for debriefing, but found himself having an acute stress attack with difficulty breathing. He was afraid of losing his job or being ridiculed by his fellow policemen for not going to the meeting. Fear of losing face is not a recognized *DSM-IV* category, but very much a reality, especially in a military-like environment. This only added another layer of fear and guilt to a man who was already stressed out by the original event. Stone (2001) reminds us:

> Unlike some occupations, a [police] officer has difficulty leaving his responsibilities at work. The expression "once a cop, always a cop" is based on truth. The unwritten code of behavior that officers live by becomes a part of them as surely as the personality they begin developing from infancy (p. 99).

Mr. A's commanding officer immediately ordered a psychiatric evaluation for him and removed him from duty. His guns were sequestered pending a full valuation. Eventually, he was placed on temporary leave and suffered even more stress from the humiliation and shame of the suspension and having his guns taken away.

Different personality types (Millon, 1995) process information in their own distinctive ways. The initial response of cognitive personalities is action oriented. They want to solve the problem, and intervention attempts may be regarded as intrusive. In contrast, affect-oriented personalities need a cathartic experience such as the opportunity to ventilate, and generally do well with the debriefing, except when the worker inappropriately attempts to solve the problem. They need the space to ventilate before looking for solutions. Depressive people feel guilt more acutely during a trauma and are likely to become immobile, while obsessive people want to run from their feelings and are more likely to be triggered into action.

Debriefing

Note again, this technique should be used with caution and only at the patient's request. If an individual wants to be left alone, respect the individual's right. I like to use the analogy of the lobster; when a lobster loses his or her shell, it hibernates until it gets a new shell.)
The goals of debriefing are:

1. *Stabilization* and mitigation of an individual's acute stress symptoms.
2. *Restoration* of a more "steady state" of psychological functioning (i.e., psychological homeostasis).
3. *Reduction* of the level of manifest functional impairment; i.e., assist persons in returning to an adaptive level of functioning (Everly and Mitchell, 1999).

Debriefings are usually held between two and ten days after the event and are designed to provide a sense of closure to the traumatic event I personally believe this is impossible, and that the aim of debriefing should be to bring people together and help them grieve and see that this is a normal state of affairs. Bringing closure to a traumatic event can't be accomplished overnight. It requires extensive work and a great deal more time than a simple debriefing. In mass critical disasters, debriefings can be effective three to four weeks after the event. Critical Incident Stress Debriefing (CISD) refers to a seven-stage model of crisis intervention (Everly and Mitchell, 1999) designed for use with homogeneous groups who have experienced a traumatic event (see Tables 3 and 4). It is most effective when done with a trained crisis therapist alongside a police officer or firefighter (one of their own). CISD has been found to be less effective when conducted with only a therapist. The patient needs one of his or her own who has experienced the crisis to lead the group with the therapist; otherwise, he or she feels intruded on.
There are some unresolved problems associated with debriefing. The sessions are usually carried out by intervention teams that may or may not include a mental health professional. However, the team members are usually trained in traumatology. There are multiple phases of psychological and emotional responses to trauma that must be recognized. For instance, if the victim is in shock or denial, those defenses need to be respected. Probing or asking inappropriate questions before the victim is ready to deal with them can cause further harm.
The purpose of this book is to suggest how to help our patients through critical incidents in and out of the treatment room. It includes treatment plans to help patients who have been traumatized deal with life after disaster. It is not a training manual on debriefing or defusing techniques. To learn more about debriefing and defusing, I recommend

Table 3: The CISD Process

PHASE	CISD OBJECTIVES	LEADER'S PROMPTS	DOMAIN
Introduction	To introduce intervention team members, explain the process, and set expectations and ground rules.	"My name is... Our purpose for being here is... The 'ground rules' are as follows...."	Cognitive
Fact	To allow participants to describe the traumatic event from his/her own perspective (ask each participant, but make it clear that one can choose to be silent).	"Tell me who you are, what your role in the incident was, and just what you saw and/or heard take place."	Cognitive
Thought	To allow participants to describe their cognitive reactions to the event and to begin to transition to the affective domain. (Once again, ask each participant to volunteer his/her perspective.)	"Now, I'd like you to tell us what your first thoughts were in response to the crisis."	Cognitive to Affective
Reaction	To identify the most traumatic aspect of the crisis for participants who wish to speak and to allow for cathartic ventilation, simply ask the probing question to group collectively.	"What was the worst part of the incident for you personally?"	Affective

(continued)

Table 3: The CISD Process (continued)

PHASE	CISD OBJECTIVES	LEADER'S PROMPTS	DOMAIN
Symptom	To identify any symptoms of distress or psychological discord that the group of participants wishes to share and to potentiate the initial transition from the affective domain back to the cognitive domain.	"What physical or psychological symptoms have you noticed, if any, as a result of the incident?"	Affective to Cognitive
Teaching	To facilitate a return to the cognitive domain by normalizing and demedicalizing the crisis reactions of the participants and to teach the basic personal stress management/coping techniques that can be used to reduce current distress.	"We've heard numerous symptoms that are being experienced. Let me explain their nature and give you some suggestions on how to reduce their negative impact."	Cognitive
Re-entry	To provide closure to the CISD process, remembering that the goal of CISD is to provide psychological closure to the crisis.	"Let me try to summarize what we have covered during this process together."	Cognitive

From *Critical Incident Stress Management* (1999) (2nd ed.) by George Everly, Jr. and Jeffrey T. Mitchell. Ellicott City, MD: Chevron. Used with permission.

reading *Critical Incident Stress Management (CISM): A New Era and Standard of Care in Crisis Intervention*, edited by George S. Everly and Jeffrey T. Mitchell (1999), and *Critical Incident Stress Debriefing: An Operations Manual for the Prevention of Traumatic Stress Among Emergency Service and Disaster Workers,* also by Jeffrey T. Mitchell and George S. Everly (1996).

At the time of writing, I do not believe this technique has proven to be effective. The men and women of the New York City Fire and Police Departments are people of action. They do not want to sit around and talk about what is happening. During 9/11, all they wanted to do was look for their comrades. CISD led to the "silent conspiracy." These men and women of action were afraid to talk and were also afraid that if they talked they would be considered sissies by their colleagues and, even worse, have their guns or jobs taken away and assigned to desk jobs. Today, they are still refusing to talk or to seek private counseling.

TRANSFORMATION

We are still living in an unusually stressful environment and need to prepare ourselves to deal with the insecurity of our times. The war on terrorism that began on 9/11 really dates back to the Crusades when it started in the name of justice or to undo or prevent violence in the name of God. Osama Bin Laden believes he is going to heaven by destroying evil Americans. We believe the only way to bring peace to this world is to bring him to justice. All of the warfare (Levine, 1997, pp. 225–6) is "a direct result of the unresolved trauma that is being acted out and repeated in an unsuccessful attempt to re-establish a sense of empowerment." Once traumatized, it is almost certain that we will repeat or reenact parts of our traumatic experiences. To paraphrase James Gilligan, Levine adds, "The attempt to achieve and maintain justice or to undo and prevent injustice, is … universal" (p. 178).

Akhtar (1999) points out that as children, the major players in a terrorist organization "suffered chronic physical abuse and profound emotional humiliation."

> The "safety feeling," which is necessary for healthy psychic growth, was thus violated. They grew up mistrusting others, loathing passivity, and dreading the recurrence of violation of their psychophysical boundaries. At the base, this intense anxiety over future loss is driven by the semiconscious inner knowledge that passivity ensures victimization. To eliminate this fear, such individuals feel the need to "kill off" their view of themselves as victims. One way to accomplish this is to turn passivity into activity, masochism into sadism, and victimhood into victimizing

others, which is manifest by hatred and violent tendencies toward others. Secondarily, the shock and horror of the victims paradoxically fuels the narcissism of the terrorist. This dynamic is akin to the sexual satisfaction an exhibitionist draws from his onlookers' startled response. The notoriety received by the terrorists in the public media serves a similar mirror function (p. 351).

Levine (1997, p. 179) tells us that the only way out of this vicious circle is through "renegotiation of the trauma," in which "the repetitive cycle of violent reenactment is transformed into a healing event." Transformation is shifting the emotional systems of trauma victims from fear to safety. It's as if a black cloud were removed, bringing us to a broader perception, a fluidity and receptivity without judgment.

Trauma can rob us of our lives, or it can be used as a tool to help us to grow. The process of healing starts from within. When we are overwhelmed by trauma, it is important to remember that there is no reality except our own perception of the trauma. War is a necessary reenactment of the past. One war begets another war, which begets another war, and so on.

The same is true of individual stress disorder. Trauma has a universal fascination for humans. How many people watched the Twin Towers fall over and over again on television, creating hyperarousal with them and re-infecting themselves with each subsequent newscast? Arousal increases aggression, and terrified Americans wanted revenge.

Trauma will need great leaders to defuse the sadomasochistic tendencies of terrorism and negotiate peaceful solutions. It will also require skilled therapists to help individual patients safely go through their perceptions, and teach them the art of conscious living.

The internal world of the psyche is much more negotiable than most people realize. The brain's rapid response system (Cowley, 2003, p. 46) sends the body into a state of high alert. The amygdala found in the lower anterior lobes of the brain, "produces corticotrophin, a substance which signals the pituitary and adrenal glands to flood the bloodstream with epinephrine (adrenaline) and Cortisol, shutting down the non-emergency systems." This eventually gives way to chronic anxiety, which affects the immune, memory, and gastrointestinal systems. Once acute anxiety become chronic anxiety, the brain remains on constant high alert.

The common denominator among all the stressors in today's society is the feeling of helplessness and fear, which triggers the autonomic nervous system (primarily the pituitary and adrenal glands) to produce stress hormones. Long-term effects can include impaired memory, weakened immune system, high blood pressure, and gastrointestinal problems. Short-term fear involves specific phobias, and long-term effects include a generalized anxiety in which the brain can no longer distinguish between disasters and minor bumps in the road.

POSTSCRIPT TO 9/11

Although conceptually logical, debriefing proved to be a disaster during and after 9/11. Helpers (i.e., police, firefighters, men and women of action, and even therapists) did not want to stop working. I couldn't imagine canceling patient appointments to get debriefed or to sit around with other therapists talking about my feelings when I could be helping someone else.

When Mayor Guiliani ordered everyone out of the "hole," as Ground Zero was called, the firefighters and police officers continued looking for the remains of their buddies, and even slept in the hole until the mayor called it quits. He ordered the police to remove the firefighters, which touched off a small war. The honeymoon was over for the police and firemen who had been working side by side since the beginning of the crisis.

At the debriefing at the South Street Seaport, therapists sat around. No one would talk to them. Weeks later, the American Red Cross was advertising for people to come in for counseling. They had plenty of money available to cover the costs.

What we learned is that during a disaster, debriefing may be a viable strategy for some people; it just won't work with police and firefighters. Even today, many survivors are still not ready to talk about it. They are afraid to even talk to their buddies about it, so they suffer in silence with anxieties and flashbacks.

Dr. Beverly J. Anderson, Clinical Director of the Metropolitan Police Employee Assistance Program in Washington, D.C., and president of the American Academy of Police Psychology (Volpe, 1998), explains that the real reason police don't talk about trauma is that they are "trained on the job to suppress their emotions. ... If they begin talking about it at home ... they may become overwhelmed with emotion, and they don't know what to do with those feelings. ... Many officers are uncomfortable with their own emotions" (p. 6).

There are some unresolved problems associated with debriefing. The sessions are usually carried out by intervention teams that may or may not include a mental health professional. However, the team members are usually trained in traumatology. There are multiple phases of psychological and emotional responses to trauma that must be recognized. For instance, if the victim is in shock or denial, those defenses need to be respected. Probing or asking inappropriate questions before the victim is ready to deal with them can cause further harm.

The protocol for immediate intervention includes normalizing and validating feelings. After that, a choice of future debriefing times is offered to the officer who will attend six mandatory sessions on department time. They are co-led by officers who have been through a critical incident. This system appears to be effective.

One policeman had the courage to come to me for help. He was immediately removed from active duty, his guns were turned in, and his position on the list for sergeant was frozen. What did that do for his psyche? What did it tell his buddies? Do you think they were going to seek help, too? He came to me as a last resort since I am in private practice and not part of the system. We used the Trauma Release Technique (TRT) (for further information on this technique, refer to Chapter 6) to cure his flashbacks. We purposely did not use his insurance. His wife was also a therapist and knew that his records would be confidential. We both agreed that since I believed he was fit for duty and should be reinstated, I would contact the police department psychologist. With his written permission, I wrote to her. After several exchanges of letters, the patient was reinstated and given his gun. Six months later, he was promoted to sergeant.

Experiencing flashbacks after witnessing a disaster such as 9/11 is a normal reaction, and requesting therapy to help deal with the flashbacks should not be a punishment. The Warren Trauma Center was established in May 2004 to deal with such issues, and we hope to provide confidential services without the red tape for all who request it in addition to providing education, training, and research.

DEVELOPMENTAL MODELS OF GROWTH

There are many different ways of dealing with our fears, but first let us look at Abraham Maslow's "Hierarchy of Needs" (1954) and compare it with Jozefowski's (1999) "Model of Grieving."

Maslow developed a schema for the healthy personality in which certain needs take precedence over others. For example, if you are hungry and thirsty, you will try to find water, since you can survive without food for a longer period of time. He developed this "hierarchy of needs" in which healthy people develop. The first three needs that a healthy, functioning person must meet he termed "deficit needs." These include physiological, safety-security, and belonging. The final two needs are self-esteem and self-actualization; a state, Maslow claimed, that could be reached by approximately 2% of the population (see Table 4).

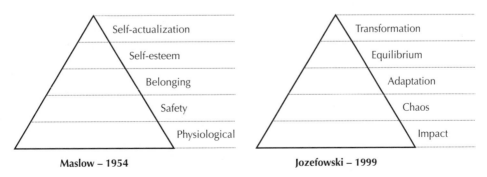

Maslow – 1954   Jozefowski – 1999

Figure 2: Models of Growth

Table 4: Maslow's Hierarchy of Needs

	Example	Anecdocte
1. Physiological Needs		
Oxygen, water, protein, salt, sugar, calcium, vitamins. Be active, get rest, eliminate wastes, avoid pain.	When the Twin Towers crumbled, basic needs went unmet. Obviously, this increased the stress levels.	In response to President Bush's admonition that we go on with our normal lives, it became normal to behave abnormally. People started hoarding food and bottled water and stocked up on antibiotics out of fear of continuing terrorism, thus increasing stress.
2. Safety & Security		
Safe circumstances, stability, protection, structure, order, and limits. Without these, we develop fears and anxieties.	Safe neighborhood, job security, nest egg, some insurance coverage. Failure to have any of these will increase stress.	After 9/11, people felt a loss of safety, not only the loss of the buildings and the massive loss of life, but a loss of innocence. America no longer felt like a safe haven and people went into fight, flight, or freeze modes. *U.S. News & World Report* (November 12, 2001) reported that the new "normal" for Americans was an altered state of consciousness on high alert.

(continued)

Table 4: Maslow's Hierarchy of Needs (continued)

	Example	Anecdocte
3. Belonging		
The need for family, friends, and community. Without them, we feel lonely and develop social anxiety, which increases our stress level.	During crises, people run to family and friends for comfort and support.	In an effort to keep children from becoming frightened that family or loved ones were involved in the 9/11 disaster, school administrations isolated their facilities and completely shut down incoming and outgoing communications. This proved to be a miserable mistake, since some students overheard teachers discussing it, while others had access to computers and radios. The super security only created more havoc and stress. The secrecy contributed to the chaos among the children and exacerbated their separation anxiety. Unable to fight or flee, they froze, increasing their stress hormones. The Warren Trauma Team expects to develop a program of education that will teach educators and administrators better techniques for dealing with traumatic events.
4. Self-Esteem		
Need for respect by self and others, status, reputation, appreciation, dignity. Low self-esteem leads to a sense of inferiority.	During economic failure and job loss people lose self-esteem and need to integrate skills and qualities while maintaining balance in life.	A patient of mine threatened to jump out of a window unless he found a job comparable to the one he held at the World Trade Center.

(continued)

Table 4: Maslow's Hierarchy of Needs (continued)

	Example	Anecdocte
5. Self-Actualization Maslow suggested that only 2% of our population could ever reach this level. Self-actualization is the desire to fulfill your dream, to be all that you can be. In today's world, very few of us are able to reach our highest goals. Under stressful conditions, we regress to lower levels of expectation. When bombs start falling, we look for safety. These needs do not involve homeostasis, the principle that controls our personal thermostats. When it gets too hot, the thermostat switches off. When it gets too cold, it switches on again. The body searches for equilibrium. If you jump into a cold lake, the body reacts to the shock and eventually adapts. The mind works the same way.	People who were able to self-actualize were those who were comfortable being alone, relatively independent, and relied on their own experience and judgment. They were not susceptible to social pressure and had a quality of acceptance of themselves and others. They tended to have more peak experiences than others and regarded life's problems as opportunities.	People who reach this level face their fear and move beyond it. They do not get stuck in the fight, flight, or freeze syndrome. Today there is a new concept of evolution through intellectual and psychological adaptation. Christopher Reeve is a good example. People with low self-esteem and an external focus of control will be at the mercy of natural, economic, and political forces, and will have difficulty functioning mentally and physically. People with an internal locus of control, like Mr. Reeve, obviously function as well as they can under a great deal of stress and are able to self-actualize under the most difficult of circumstances. Although at the end, Mr. Reeve only had his breathe or his voice to keep him going, he did not give up until the day he died.

Joanne Jozefowski (1999) developed an updated model, termed The Phoenix Model, for overcoming grief, which is equally appropriate for anxiety and depression arising from a traumatic event or major loss (see Table 5). The first phase involves "feeling the impact," followed by "going through the chaos of the trauma," and arriving at a sense of "equilibrium." The final two phases are "adaptation" and "transformation."

The initial "Impact" phase includes shock, denial, holding on, and a feeling of emotional Novocain, which numbs the body against unbearable pain. The second phase is "Chaos," which is marked by a complete lack of safety and security. There is no order or structure to the world around you. After losing a loved one, one of my patients found her thoughts running out of control. She felt a sense of impending doom and could not find a comfortable place for herself. She described her mind as reacting like a runaway train. The third phase is "Adaptation." This is the time to take new risks, assume new roles, and find something to believe in, people to connect with, or groups you can belong to. It culminates in new levels of self-esteem and self-confidence, which mark the "Equilibrium" phase. In the final "Transformation" phase, the anxiety, depression, and post-traumatic stress disorder resulting from the traumatic event are transformed by self-actualization. The victim starts to fulfill his/her full potential and find new meaning and purpose in life.

Table 5: Jozefowski's Phoenix Model

	Example	Anecdote
1. Impact	Shock, denial, holding on; feeling an emotional Novocain, which numbs mind and psyche from unbearable pain. Need for physiological stability and safety. Protection from fear and anxiety.	When someone close to us dies, our first reaction is denial, which helps us feel safe and stable. We freeze.	A colleague of mine died while I was at a conference in London. Another colleague was stunned and in obvious denial or altered state of consciousness. "He can't be dead," my colleague blurted, waving a piece of paper he took from his pocket. "I just received a letter from him before I left New York."
2. Chaos	Lack of safety, security, attachment, and belonging. No structure or order.	Emotional numbing wearing off. "Crazy times," feeling anxious, fear, guilt, anger, depression, and alienation. Amygdala becomes activated.	After losing a loved one, a patient of mine felt her thoughts were out of control. She started to obsess about her health, her family's well being. She felt a sense of impending doom and could not find a safe place for herself.
3. Adaptation	Belonging, risk-taking, new roles.	Being in the world without the deceased loved one, or living in today's world, during crisis.	People began spending more money on fixing up their homes rather than traveling. They worked to be close to friends and family to avoid stress.

(continued)

Table 5: Jozefowski's Phoenix Model (continued)

	Example	Anecdote
4. Equilibrium		
Finding self-esteem and self-confidence.	Integrate new skills and qualities. Maintain balance in new life. Develop some sort of spirituality, something to believe in.	Helen Keller tells us that although the world is full of suffering, it is also full of overcoming it.
5. Transformation		
Self-actualization.	Fulfilling unique self-potential. Discovering purpose and meaning in your life. Finding new mountains to climb...	Renowned hypnotist Milton Erickson visited a very depressed woman in Phoenix who refused to leave her house. The house was completely dark with the exception of one room, which had light coming in through the window. Next to the window was a table of thriving African violets. The woman perked up a bit as she spoke with pride of her magnificent violets. Realizing that the woman was quite religious, Erickson suggested that people in the church might enjoy seeing the flowers. Without further discussion, he left the house. Months later, he heard that the woman was doing much better. For some reason, she began to grow more violets. First, she set some violets near the window then opened the curtain for more light. She kept repeating this scenario with every window until the entire house was filled with violets. Many people at church ended up with the beautiful flowers.

From *The Phoenix Phenonemon: Rising from the Ashes of Grief*, (1999) by Joanne T. Jozefowski. Northvale, NJ: Jason Aronson. Used with permission.

TALKING TO THE AMYGDALA: EXPANDING THE SCIENCE OF HYPNOSIS

David Barlow of the Boston Center for Anxiety and Related Disorders claimed in a *Newsweek* magazine article (Cowley, 2003) that it is actually possible to talk with the amygdala, a key component of the brain that deals with emotions like fear. Since this idea was consistent with the basic tenets of hypnosis, it intrigued me.

Although talking to the amygdala is an abstract concept, in hypnosis I believe that when a person is in a hypnotic trance, the amygdala is relaxed and therefore not giving signals to the pituitary or adrenal glands to go into a fight, flight, or freeze response and flood the body with stress hormones. This gives the immune system a chance to build up and allows the body to begin to heal itself. That is why I believe hypnosis heals people. It is that simple: under hypnosis, the amygdala shuts down the rapid alert system, the stress hormones become nonactive, and the body's inherent wisdom system goes to work all by itself. All the hypnotherapist need do is to help the patient to relax the amygdala and the brain actually signals the body to relax, and thus the relaxed body begins to heal itself.

Hypnosis is a way to access the untapped power of the mind and alter brain functions. In this state of intense relaxation and concentration, the mind is able to focus on positive suggestions that can be carried out at a future time. These subliminal messages are surprisingly powerful.

Michael I. Posner, professor emeritus of neuroscience at the University of Oregon (*New York Times*, November 22, 2005, pp. F1–F4), proved through brain scans that hypnotic suggestion can change the mechanism of perception. In the same article, Dr. David Spiegel explains that when we imagine something different, it becomes something different. This isn't magic. Under hypnosis, when you are relaxed, the amygdala is automatically shut down. When you imagine a peaceful scene, your immune system starts to build up and your body has time to heal itself.

"The mind is like an onion. The outer layer, or conscious mind, deals with intelligence, reality, and logic. The inner mind is concerned with emotion, imagination, and memory, as well as the autonomic nervous system, which automatically controls our internal organs (i.e., how we breathe, send oxygen to our blood cells, or walk without using the conscious mind.) The internal mind is on autopilot, reacting to the dictates of the pleasure principle. It seeks pleasure and avoids pain" (Warren, 2003, pp. 175–6).

It is these characteristics that make hypnosis a highly effective therapeutic tool in dealing with a wide spectrum of mental and physical disorders. In fact, hypnosis has been used to reduce trauma in many chronic illnesses (i.e., irritable bowel syndrome (IBS), bulimia, cancer, high blood pressure, and Parkinson's disease) (Frank and Mooney, 2002). The *Wall Street Journal* (Friedman, 2003) has documented how hypnosis has entered the medical mainstream and trance states are being used when treating fractures, cancer, and burns, and to speed recovery time.

Dr. David Spiegel, Stanford University researcher, speaking at the 54th Annual Conference of the Society for Clinical and Experimental Hypnosis in November, 2003, in Chicago, reminded us that although we don't fully understand how it works, there is significant evidence that hypnosis can be effective in helping people reach into their own unconscious resources to solve problems normally beyond their ability. Not only does it work, but also it often succeeds where modern medicine has failed.

That evidence continues to pile up. Hypnosis is now being used in dentistry, childbirth, and to treat fertility, allergies, eating disorders, headaches, and to improve academic and sports performance. Eleanor Laser, PhD, a hypnotherapist, assists physicians like Elvira Lang, MD by performing hypnosis and analgesia during operations at the Harvard and Iowa University Medical Schools. Hypnosis is not sleep, but an altered state of consciousness in which a person accesses that part of his or her mind that is capable of adjusting the problem without the conscious, thinking mind directing it.

In addition to being a psychotherapist, author, researcher, and educator in private practice in Rockland County, New York, I am also an experienced hypnotherapist. So I decided to put David Barlow's statement to the test. Patients don't have to know where the amygdala is located and what it does. The unconscious mind knows. The unconscious mind knows how to work without the conscious mind directing it. That's one thing I have learned from years of conducting hypnotherapy. You can rely on the patient's unconscious mind to come up with the answers, while the therapist contributes positive suggestions.

First, I researched the amygdala and was surprised to find that tremendous progress has been made in just the past few years in our understanding of the brain and how it works. I was also amazed that no one has put it all together in one place. So I decided to conduct my own experiment.

The Amygdala

The amygdala is located on either side of the middle of the brain known as the limbic system. There are two of them, each 1.5 centimeters – the size of a walnut. The amygdala is critical for certain kinds of negative emotions, particularly fear, but it can also provide an important link to creativity and increased intelligence Richard J. Davidson, Director of the Laboratory for Affective Neuroscience and the W. M. Keck Laboratory for Functional Brain Imaging and Behavior at the University of Wisconsin in Madison, has studied this area of the brain and mind-body interaction since 1999. He explains that many parts of the brain work together to produce complex behaviors such as emotions (Gyatso, T. and Goleman, D., 2003). It was found that the amygdala plays a key role in the circuitry that activates emotion, while the prefrontal cortex does much of the regulation. Evidence suggests that regions of the left frontal cortex play an important role in positive emotions, while the right frontal lobe plays that role in certain negative emotions.

Another key part of the brain is the hippocampus, a long structure directly behind the amygdala that has been linked to memory. The hippocampus is essential for the appreciation of the context of events. Some emotional disorders such as post-traumatic stress disorder and depression involve abnormalities in the hippocampus. In both these disorders, it was found that the hippocampus actually shrinks.

The amygdala, the hippocampus, and the frontal lobes (Gyatso and Goleman, 2003, p. 193) are all extensively connected with the body, and, in particular, with the immune system; with the endocrine system, which regulates hormones; and with the autonomic nervous system that regulates heart rate, blood pressure, and other functions.

The brain provides a complex system of feedback circuits involved in the reaction to stress and trauma. This process starts with the actual or perceived threat of death or injury that activates the higher reasoning centers in the cortex (Sapolsky, 1993). The cortex, in turn, sends a message to the amygdala, which is the principal mediator of the stress response. The amygdala then releases corticotrophin-releasing hormone (CRH) to stimulate the brain stem to activate the sympathetic nervous system by way of the spinal cord. This triggers the adrenal glands, located atop the kidneys, to release epinephrine and glucocorticoids. These two hormones act on the muscles, heart, and lungs to prepare the body for the fight, flight, or freeze response. When the stress becomes chronic, glucocorticoids induce the locus coeruleus to release norepinephrine that makes the amygdala produces even more CRH and other stress hormones as the reaction escalates.

Dr. Hillary P. Blumberg and a team of researchers at Yale University ("Scanning a Brain..." New York Times, December 30, 2003) have found that the amygdala and hippocampus are much smaller in teenagers and adults with bipolar disorder. That finding may provide doctors with a new tool for early diagnosis and treatment of the disorder. Teenagers and adults with bipolar disorder are at high risk for suicide.

Recovery function is the time it takes for a person to come back to a quiet baseline condition of the brain after being provoked by an emotion, as in a traumatic event. Certain people have a prolonged response and others return to the baseline very quickly. It has been shown that people with quick recovery function have less activation in the amygdala. The amygdala and hippocampus in their brains are larger and of a more normal size than those of anxious people. These people show more activation in the left prefrontal cortex. They report that their everyday experience is filled with feelings of vigor, optimism, and enthusiasm (Gyatso and Goleman, 2003, p. 197).

Other Research

Other research projects have centered on the memory, which has been linked to adrenaline, the hormone secreted by the adrenal glands in response to anxiety, stress, and fear. Dr. Jim McGaugh at the University of California at Irvine demonstrated that rats injected with adrenaline just after learning a task had enhanced retention (Friedman, 2003). Dr. Larry Cahill, also at Irvine, showed that blocking the effects of adrenaline could prevent emotional arousal from enhancing memory. That implies that any emotionally charged situation that causes adrenaline release will produce stronger memories.

Dr. David Barlow of Boston University's Center for Anxiety and Related Disorders, claims that we can actually *talk* to the amygdala and reduce stress in our minds and bodies. As a hypnotherapist, I know that the unconscious mind is best addressed by hypnotic language in a trance state.

I was further encouraged by numerous scientific studies in recent years showing that the hypnotized mind can exert a real and powerful effect on the body. Hypnosis is increasingly being used today to help women give birth without drugs, for muting dental pain, treating phobias and severe anxieties, helping people lose weight, stop smoking, or even improve their performance in athletics or academic tests (Waldholz, 2003). The stage was set for my first trial.

Three Cases

My first example involves a patient who feared an upcoming operation and the possibility of his blindness or death. He explained that he was a professional golfer and had been diagnosed with osteosarcoma. His physician had just found a tumor the size of a golf ball behind his left eye. He had been warned that he had a slim chance of retaining his eyesight after the tumor was removed. Furthermore, there was a real possibility that he would not make it through the operation. We had five consecutive sessions during the week before his operation. The patient told me that he was a multimillionaire at age 40. All he wanted was to play golf, and his wife would not let him. He was deeply depressed and without a *"causa sui"* (a reason for living) (Becker, 1974, p. 119), and often dreamed of dying. Dr. Norman Shealy, a Harvard-trained neurosurgeon and researcher, and many others, have concluded that the immune system becomes compromised by depression, stress, anger, and guilt, leading to many diseases, including cancer.

In each hypnosis session, I relaxed the patient's amygdala, shutting down the fear and enhancing the outcome. I did not explain to the patient that I was talking to his amygdala, but under hypnosis in a trance state, the amygdala shuts down the stress hormones, giving the patient an opportunity to rebuild his immune system. I am not a golfer. But I suggested that when the surgeon drilled into his skull, he would hit a hole in one and the tumor would pop out. On the day of the operation, the patient showed no fear of the procedure. When the surgeon made the initial incision just behind the eye, the tumor simply rolled out of his head without further intervention. The patient arrived at my office the following day with his eyesight intact and nothing but a band aid covering the incision. The tumor was sent to Johns Hopkins and the Mayo Clinic for analysis. To this day, the surgeon and his colleagues don't understand what happened. They think they made an error in diagnosis. The tumor was just not as serious as they originally thought. This patient decided to become a golf coach, thereby reducing his depression and finding a *"causa sui."* His immune system was now functioning well.

About six months later, he began having difficulty with his prostrate. Because of their constant fighting, his wife turned to smoking pot, which made her more amorous. His amygdala was activated by her sexual demands and the fear that he would not be able to perform. The prostate is a male sexual gland that surrounds the neck of the bladder and the beginning of the urethra. The gland secretes a thin, opalescent fluid that forms part of the semen.

"An activated amygdala doesn't wait around for instructions from the conscious mind," explains Claudia Kalb (Kalb, 2003, p. 46). Once it perceives a threat it can trigger a body wide emergency response within milliseconds. Jolted by impulses in the amygdala, the nearby hypothalamus produces a hormone called Corticotrophin Releasing Factor, or CRF, which signals the pituitary and adrenal glands to flood the bloodstream with epinephrine, adrenaline, norepinephrine, and cortisol. These stress hormones then shut down non-emergency services such as digestion and immunity, and direct the body's resources to fighting or fleeing. The heart responds, the lungs pump, and the muscles get an energizing blast of glucose. The stress hormones also act on the brain, creating a heightened awareness and supercharging the circuitry involved in memory formation.

In autoimmune diseases, the immune system is confused and attacks the body. Hypnotherapy can help stimulate healthy immune system functioning where only foreign invaders or mutant cells are attacked. A general understanding of how autoimmune diseases operate is helpful to patient and therapist alike. Sometimes pictures of the disease process and immune system help to facilitate the internal changes necessary for healing or remission.

This patient underwent tests that indicated a PSA of 2.4 µg/L. We began hypnosis focused on his prostrate. In a quiet, relaxed state, I asked him to locate the pipe that controlled his prostate gland, reminding him that the back of his mind knew better than I just how to put it in working order. His PSA level has now been reduced to 1.66 µg/L (see Figure 3). (The normal range is 0.0 to 4.0.)

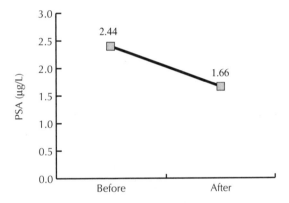

Figure 3: Prostrate Therapy

Perhaps even more dramatic is the case of a 75-year-old man with kidney failure who was facing the prospect of dialysis. This patient had been through three heart attacks and showed an allergic reaction to the contrast or dye used in angioplasty. His kidney function, as measured by the level of creatinine in his blood, had declined to about 20–25% of normal. Using the same technique of inducing trance and reducing all stress hormones, I asked the patient to visualize himself in a healing garden, and using all of his senses, imagine through the powers of his own pure subconscious mind – which knows better than I do – sending healing energy to the parts of his body that need it most. In a sense, I was using his own intuition to empower him. After three sessions of hypnosis focusing on improvement of his kidneys, blood tests showed his creatinine level was reduced from 3.0 to 2.0, equivalent to approximately 50% of normal and a 100% improvement (see Figure 4). Although his kidneys are not perfect, dialysis is no longer necessary. We are now working on his carotid artery, which shows a partial blockage.

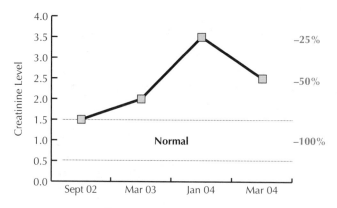

Figure 4: Kidney Failure

Serious medical malfunctions are not the only areas susceptible to the power of hypnosis. This case involved a 16-year-old girl who was failing math with a 53 average despite attempts to tutor her. After three months of hypnosis once a week, her average climbed steadily to an amazing 85. Through hypnosis, I was able to shut down the stress hormones that can impair memory and taught her how to anchor those feelings of calmness. Eventually, she was able to perform her own self-hypnosis prior to scheduled tests at school. I helped her to realize that her brain was like a computer, only better. In fact, it was the prototype for all manmade computers. We went over the fact that in the first five years, she learned more than at any other time in her life. She learned a language, to tell one person from another, to distinguish different objects, to begin mastery of her ABCs, how to color, brush her teeth, and many other things. All of this was data she was able to program into her brain before she was five years old. Now that she was 16, those tasks slipped in to her subconscious mind. Just like breathing or sending oxygen to her blood cells, she didn't have to think with her conscious mind about how to do it.

The same principle holds true for math, science, and anatomy. Only now, it is much easier. Data we store in our computer brain can be retrieved just the way we retrieve the method for tying our shoelaces. First, the patient is given a simple way to anchor the feeling of calmness, perhaps by simply placing his pointer finger and thumb together, putting her into a state of self-hypnosis so the stress hormones do not interfere with her memory bank. Then she is told to tackle the easiest questions first, giving the patient a feeling of success. Success breeds success. Reducing stress hormones and strengthening the ego combined with desensitization helps patients with school and test taking.

I can't claim that every case is an absolute success, but I can say that more and more and with the perseverance of my patients, I have been getting better and better results.

As Stephen Kahn and Erika Fromm have told us, therapists go through change every day. The profound transformation in my work came about with the hypothetical understanding of how hypnotherapy works. Until then, I was confident it worked, but I didn't understand how. That understanding has reassured me and made it possible for me, in turn, to reassure my patients. As continuing research unlocks the secrets of the brain, hypnosis will emerge, breaking the barrier between art and science.

There are other cases, some more critical than others, but they all end the same way. In all cases, even the patients find it difficult to accept that hypnosis was effective in eliminating the problem. They sometimes would prefer to think that the original diagnosis and the laboratory tests had been wrong. Since it often appears so simple, hypnosis may not get the credit it deserves. The main thing is that the problem that brought the patient to me has been solved.

Method

Let me clarify what I mean when I say "talking to the amygdala." Obviously, I do not mean to imply that the amygdala is capable of speech. What I am saying is that the amygdala acts *as if* it is receptive to messages from the unconscious mind, whether it is the patient's or the therapist's. Only the light of scientific research can prove or disprove this hypothesis. If it is true, we can regard the amygdala as the gateway to the unconscious and hypnosis will have a powerful, new technique.

When I hypnotize a patient, the amygdala normally shuts itself off. The body and mind are at rest. There is no fight, flight, or freeze response, and all stress hormones are shut down. The patient is constantly reassured that he/she is in control, and that the patient's unconscious mind will intuitively know where to direct the healing power. The critical point is that the patient's brain knows how to solve the problem even if the patient doesn't consciously know that he knows.

The procedure is no different in principle from any hypnosis session, and consists of six discrete steps:

(1) **Set-up**, in which the subject is reassured of his/her control and offered the choices of staring at a spot on the ceiling, opening or closing their eyes, etc.

I often tell them that I don't want them to go into a trance too fast or too slow. It is all up to the patient. This reinforces their sense of control.

(2) **Induction**, direct or indirect using parallel process narratives to reinforce the realization of the power of the brain, in which the patient enters the trance state and goes to a deeper and deeper level. An

example of parallel process narrative might be Erickson's famous story in which a horse wandered into his family's yard when Erickson was a young man. The animal had no identifying marks (Rosen, 1982) but Erickson offered to return the horse to its owners.

Rosen explains:

> In order to accomplish this, he simply mounted the horse, led it to the road, and let the horse decide which way he wanted to go. He intervened only when the horse left the road to graze or wander in to a field. When the horse finally arrived at the yard of a neighbor several miles down the road, the neighbor asked Erickson, "How did you know that that horse came from here and was our horse?" Erickson said, "I didn't know – but the horse knew. All I did was keep him on the road" (pp. 46–7).

The analogy is obvious. Like the horse who knew his way home without intervention, the unconscious mind knows instinctively how to solve the problem.

(3) **Talking to the amygdala (warning: this is an abstract concept and should not be taken literally),** in which the therapist uses metaphors and ego strengthening suggestions to facilitate healing intuitively. I sometimes suggest that patients can marvel at the metamorphis that took place overnight, like trees that are barren in winter and flourish in spring. I tell them that they know their pure subconscious – which is active day and night – can repair, rejuvenate, and regenerate, creating new energy and letting one's own intuition to send to the part of the body that need it most. You may be amazed or surprised where it sends it first but your unconscious mind will know what is best for you, better than I do. My voice will disappear while the back of your mind – your pure subconscious – does the work for you now. When you are ready to continue, you can let me know by wiggling your finger. This is known as 'ideo-motor' signaling. Even though the patient may not have consciously heard what I said, his or her unconscious mind heard me suggest or call on the patient's unconscious mind to solve the problem.

(4) **Post-hypnotic suggestion,** in which the patient is reassured that he/she will awake feeling physically well and refreshed with no ill effects from the trance. I often give them a post-hypnotic trigger, in the form of words or simple actions that serve as anchors to help them stay calm so the healing can continue. An example might be the words "easy control." Another anchor would be to put their pointer finger and thumb together anytime during the day they feel the need to calm down.

And (5) **Return,** in which the patient is brought gradually to full alertness. Then we discuss their experience and how it felt.

Summary

In order to reach transformation in today's world, we will need a new concept of evolution that includes intellectual and psychological adaptation. Barlow (2002) suggests that we will need to find new ways to communicate with the amygdala, the part of the brain that alerts our stress hormones. Jon Kabat-Zinn (1990) calls it "full catastrophe living" and, in keeping with that theme, this book contains treatment plans, behavioral techniques, and hypnotherapy suggestions to illuminate the path to transformation.

3
MAJOR DISORDERS RELATED TO TRAUMA

On September 11, 2001, I sat in my office amazed at the range of the various responses of my patients. Since I was trained as a psychoanalyst, I watched closely to see what would unfold as each patient entered the treatment room. Some were in denial and acted as if nothing was happening. Others were in acute distress and could only focus on their own anxiety or guilt. Some talked about moving to the Amazon, while others wanted to visit Ground Zero for a better look at the destruction. I used the telephone and e-mail to contact those who were too upset to make it to my office. I felt it was important for us to stay connected. In the process, I found the best way for me to deal with my own anxieties was to keep on working. I even volunteered to work on weekends with children who lost loved ones in the disaster. By the end of the week, I was beginning to feel stress and realized that it could easily develop into compassion fatigue (see Figures 5 and 6).

COMPASSION FATIGUE

I was instructing my patients to stay informed by watching television or reading newspapers, but to avoid the addictive television replay of the towers falling over and over again. However, I was hearing the same stories over and over again, and absorbing the trauma secondhand through the eyes of my patients. This, too, was addictive.

I knew there was little I could do at Ground Zero, and that my focus was on helping my patients get through these terrible days. I was exhausted, but couldn't stop. At the end of the day, I went home only to have difficulty falling asleep or staying asleep. All I wanted to do was to return to the office and work with my patients. I was helping them to help me. I also found it impossible to address the comparatively

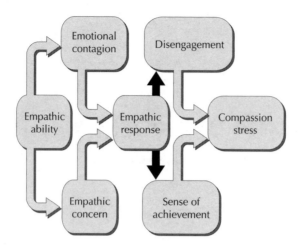

Figure 5: A Model of Compassion Stress

From *Compassion Fatigue: The Stress of Caring Too Much* (transcript) (1994). Charles Figley, ed., Panama City, FL: Visionary Productions, used with permission.

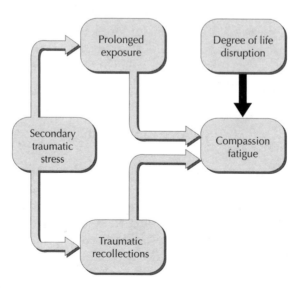

Figure 6: A Model of Compassion Fatigue

From *Compassion Fatigue: The Stress of Caring Too Much* (transcript) (1994). Charles Figley, ed., Panama City, FL: Visionary Productions, used with permission.

meaningless bureaucratic paperwork (e.g., chart notes, outpatient treatment reports, billing, etc.).

It is difficult for clinicians to admit, even to themselves or other caregivers, that they may need the help of another professional. After all, if they cannot help themselves, how can they help their patients? Denial is a universal first line of defense against trauma. A clinician in denial cannot permit himself or herself to be upset or to ask for help.

Compassion fatigue is usually derived from the strong desire of clinicians or trauma workers to help people who are suffering. At the heart of the concept are empathy and exposure. Whether we like it or not, working with traumatized people changes the caregiver for better or worse. This phenomenon is known as "secondary victimization" or "secondary trauma stress," which is the normal result of continued empathic response over time with trauma survivors. Victims may see or experience a single critical incident, but therapists absorb the trauma over and over again through the eyes and ears of their multiple patients.

Compassion fatigue can be a signpost on the road to burnout – a disillusion with one's practice – resulting in depression and low energy. In contrast to burnout, in compassion fatigue the clinician feels deep sorrow for the traumatized victims, accompanied by a desire to alleviate their pain. Since we never can be powerful enough or smart enough to answer all of our patients' needs, we develop a feeling of anguish in our own souls.

Compassion fatigue is a state of tension from prolonged exposure to suffering that becomes contagious. The caregiver may experience acute stress disorder, depression, or post-traumatic stress disorder by reexperiencing the event, or avoidance (flight), or numbing (freeze) as a response to reminders of the event. If the victim is a firefighter or police officer, treatment is compounded by his or her difficulty in talking about his or her feelings. They are action-oriented people and many regard talking about feelings as a waste of time.

At the time of writing, we found out that debriefing did not work because of the "conspiracy of silence" among firefighters and police officers. Talking with a counselor or therapist meant risking the confiscation of your weapon and the prospect of a desk job. All they wanted to do was go back into the hole where the Twin Towers once stood and search for the remains of their brothers and sisters. Now, first responders are being told that if faced with another similar tragedy to "run the other way." It goes against their basic instincts and everything they have been taught. They are caught in a real double-bind and have nowhere to turn, not even to their comrades, for fear of being ridiculed. Many find solace in alcohol or other addictive substances.

It is absolutely insane to believe that any man or woman of action (i.e., police officers, firefighters, other first responders, even therapists) would turn their backs on their work and sit in a group to discuss his or her fears and problems during a disaster. I would not cancel an appointment to be debriefed, defused, or demobilized. I can only imagine how these men and women felt going to the South Street Seaport during 9/11. The real imperative was back in the hole where their buddies gave their lives to help others.

One way professionals can help themselves is to take the time to monitor themselves, and, in a sense, do their own self-debriefing. Since empathy is a major resource for therapists and trauma workers, they are particularly vulnerable to compassion fatigue. Those who regard themselves as saviors are even more vulnerable, especially if they have experienced some kind of trauma. It has been shown that between 25% and 30% of all people who experience trauma develop post-traumatic stress disorder or other major psychiatric disorders.

BEHAVIORAL SYMPTOMS

COMPASSION FATIGUE

Let us look at the symptoms of compassion fatigue:

- Anxiety
- Preoccupation with the trauma or the traumatized victim
- Numbness or freezing response
- Flashbacks (persistent arousal)
- Absorbs emotional suffering of others
- Aches and pains (headaches, backaches, etc.)
- Changes in sleeping and eating patterns
- Sweating or heart palpitations
- Compromised immune system (increased susceptibility to illness)
- Sleep problems, nightmares, night terrors
- Easily startled
- Feelings of helplessness/hopelessness
- Shock and/or denial
- Hypervigilance
- Poor concentration
- "Chicken Little Syndrome," feeling of doom
- Restricted range of feelings

OBJECTIVES OF TREATMENT

COMPASSION FATIGUE

- Educate clinician/worker about compassion fatigue
- If appropriate, use debriefing process to talk about the experience
- Encourage sharing experience with other involved clinicians/workers
- Reduce addictive exposure to news media coverage of traumatic event
- Identify triggers of compassion fatigue
- Identify clinician/worker's own personal trauma
- Reduce anxiety related to the disorder
- Reduce other symptoms (restlessness, sleep disturbance, eating disorders, poor concentration, hypervigilance)
- Identify patient's personal and social resources (support systems)
- Develop strategies to stay in the here and now
- Reshape irrational beliefs
- Ease work schedule
- Develop boundaries between work and private life
- Develop ways to prioritize and partialize work schedule
- Encourage compliance with educational programs and referrals
- Reduce need for perfection
- If appropriate, recommend further professional supervision
- If appropriate, help clinician avoid unhealthy substances (alcohol, over-the-counter drugs) and overindulgence in food
- Encourage replenishing activities (time off, relaxation, vacation, etc.)

TREATMENT PLAN

COMPASSION FATIGUE

PROFESSIONAL CAREGIVER'S SHORT-TERM GOALS	THERAPIST'S INTERVENTION
Join with therapist in collaborative treatment.	Establish a collaborative or therapeutic alliance to build trust and enhance outcome.
Identify symptoms.	Explore symptoms, mindful that professional caregivers may be highly sensitive about having such symptoms and feel they should know best how to handle their own problems.
Understand the distinction between compassion fatigue and burnout.	If professional caregiver is uninformed, outline the differences between compassion fatigue and burnout.
Become aware of the risk factors for burnout.	Identify the risk factors for burnout (role ambiguity; unrealistically high self- or job expectations; perfectionism; discrepancy in job functions; boundary problems; loss by death, divorce, or personal trauma; substance abuse; lack of social supports).
Recognize the risk factors for compassion fatigue.	Review risk factors for compassion fatigue (prolonged exposure to suffering; emotional contagion; traumatic recollections that trigger reactions; empathy for the suffering; a need to rescue others; feeling a sense of achievement when one does. Prolonged exposure can lead to disengagement (numbing oneself to the misery), and compassion stress).

PROFESSIONAL CAREGIVER'S SHORT-TERM GOALS	THERAPIST'S INTERVENTION
Realize which preventive measures are most appropriate to reduce the compassion fatigue.	Identify the appropriate preventive measures needed: Set boundaries, modify work schedule, identify triggers that might cause vicarious trauma, find ways to self-soothe, discover personal meaning in the trauma, or seek further supervision if appropriate.
Pay more attention to your personal life and find ways to replenish yourself.	Since much of theory is based on empathy, help patient recognize that "the best empathizers seem to have a tendency toward depression" (Greenson, 1967, p. 383). Encourage increased focus on personal life.
Relate in detail the trigger event and your reactive feelings toward it.	Investigate with professional caregiver the traumatic event, your feelings, and reactions.
Describe flashbacks and dreams of the event.	Explore flashbacks and analyze dreams to reduce their impact on the patient.
Undergo evaluation for sleep disorder.	Evaluate patient for sleep disorder. If positive, treat the disorder (see appropriate treatment plan).
Discuss dynamics of anxiety.	Explain that anxiety is not dangerous, not permanent, and can be a potential "garden for growth."
Reexperience the traumatic event using relaxation technique or hypnosis.	Use hypnosis as a guide to relive the traumatic event.
Examine reactions to discover distortions and exaggerations.	Identify anomalies in reaction to the trauma.

PROFESSIONAL CAREGIVER'S SHORT-TERM GOALS	THERAPIST'S INTERVENTION
Using evidence-based reality, replace exaggerated reactions.	Attempt to reframe negative reactions with reality.
Learn diaphragmatic breathing to aid relaxation and calm self.	Teach clinician to use diaphragmatic breathing in relaxation.
Understand the "fight," "flight," or "freeze" reactions to trauma and their implications.	Discuss the fight, flight, or freeze reactions. Explain that energy is released in "fight" and "flight," and blocked in "freeze," leaving us to re-experience the trauma again and again as post-traumatic stress disorder (PTSD).
Become aware of "secondary trauma" and develop plans to reduce this hazard.	Teach the professional caregiver the hazards of working with trauma victims and the need to protect themselves from "secondary trauma." Encourage a counterbalance between work and outside activities.
Share experiences with other colleagues involved with trauma.	Encourage professional caregiver to share experiences with other caregivers involved in the critical incident and get ideas of how they are handling stressors. Get support from significant others.
Understand how your background impacts your choice of profession and your practice.	Encourage professional caregiver to explore his/her motivation in selecting this career to get a better understanding of his/her own psychology and acknowledge his/her own satisfactions and gratifications. Many therapists find their way into this profession because of their own emotional wounds.

PROFESSIONAL CAREGIVER'S SHORT-TERM GOALS	THERAPIST'S INTERVENTION
Enhance understanding of compassion fatigue and stress management.	Suggest professional caregiver read *Compassion Fatigue* and *Critical Incident Stress Management*.
Become aware of your unconscious reasons for becoming a professional caregiver and their implications.	Suggest professional caregiver read *A Curious Calling*.
Develop a plan of action to address compassion fatigue.	Develop a SMART plan: Small, Measurable, Achievable, Realistic, Timelined goals (see Change, Behavioral Techniques, Chapter 6).
Learn more about the human capacity for growth from grief and how personal transformation can save lives.	If professional caregiver is also dealing with issues of death, refer to *The Phoenix Phenomenon: Rising From the Ashes of Grief* (see Resources, Chapter 8). Other suggested readings, as appropriate, include: *Full Catastrophe Living: Using the Wisdom of Your Body and Mind to Face Stress, Pain, and Illness*; and *Waking the Tiger: Healing Trauma* (see Resources, Chapter 8).
Attend self-help groups with other colleagues, or get further professional supervision.	If appropriate, refer patient to professional group or further supervision.
Explore with therapist the issues of separation and dependency. Discuss treatment termination plan.	Resolve issues of separation and dependency and terminate treatment.

CRITICAL INCIDENT STRESS DISORDER

Critical incident stress management (CISM), in itself, is not psychotherapy, but a system of interventions in a group setting designed to prevent or mitigate adverse psychological reactions. It was developed in 1999 by G. S. Everly and J. T. Mitchell. If crises or disasters become epidemic, we will need immediate, effective strategies to deal with our patients. Individual, family, and group interventions will be needed at any time and any place with the goal of reducing fear and returning to normal functioning as much as possible. This plan has been adapted for individual treatment, which may require the therapist to adapt his or her usual protocol.

In critical incident stress disorder (CISD), the patient has witnessed or experienced an actual or threatened event that placed him or her or another person in danger of death or serious injury, and has reacted with feelings of intense horror, fear, or helplessness. No one who experiences a disaster in person, or sees it on television, is untouched by it. People who did not experience the event can be affected by a secondary disaster by watching the trauma unfold over and over on television. Even the therapist who treats trauma victims may be exposed to secondary victimization in the form of compassion fatigue. After a disaster, most people will pull together, but their effectiveness will be diminished. Many will not see the need for mental health services and may reject assistance of all types. This is a special time, and therapists need to put aside their usual methods to use a more practical, active outreach approach that is appropriate for each phase of the disaster.

Patients may react to disaster in a wide range of ways. They need to be reminded that their reactions are normal. In the beginning, people will need more practical advice than psychological help. There are four waves of assistance:

1. **Coping and stabilization**, with a focus on basic needs and safety
2. **Stress management**, including arousal reduction strategies and coping with current and future life circumstances
3. **Resolution of grief and trauma**
4. **Accommodation, adaptation, transformation, and reconnection**

Warning: This plan should only be used if requested or agreed to by the patient and not if ordered by an agency. After 9/11 it proved to be a critical mistake and patients refused to cooperate. They want to be doing their jobs rather than undergoing therapy.

BEHAVIORAL SYMPTOMS – ADULTS

CRITICAL INCIDENT STRESS DISORDER

Emotional
- Overwhelming fear or anxiety
- Feeling lost or overwhelmed
- Depression
- Guilt, grief
- Excessive death anxiety
- Feels detached from others
- Range of feelings is restricted
- Has increased sense of limited future
- Irritable, displays outbursts of anger

Behavioral
- Withdrawal from others
- Sleep disturbances
- Unusual behaviors
- Changes in eating patterns
- Excessive silence or problems in communication
- Changes in work habits
- Persistently reexperiences traumatic event as a dream or recollection
- Has flashbacks of the event
- Displays intense distress at cues reminiscent of the event
- Avoids people, places, activities, and thoughts associated with the event

Cognitive
- Poor concentration
- Memory problems, poor attention span
- Difficulty making decisions
- Slowed problem solving
- Difficulties with calculations
- Unable to remember an important aspect of the event
- Interest in usual activities is diminished
- Is easily startled

Physical
- Muscle tremors
- Chest pains
- Gastrointestinal distress
- Difficulty breathing
- Headaches
- Elevated blood pressure

BEHAVIORAL SYMPTOMS – CHILDREN AND ADOLESCENTS

CRITICAL INCIDENT STRESS DISORDER

In addition to some of the above symptoms, children may also exhibit the following:

- Regression to earlier developmental stages
- Hyperactivity
- Persistent controlling behavior
- Easily startled
- Nightmares, night terrors
- Bedwetting
- Clinging behavior
- Acts out in school
- Difficulty in concentration
- Headaches, stomachaches, or other physical ailments somatic in nature

OBJECTIVES OF TREATMENT
IN CHILDREN AND ADOLESCENTS

CRITICAL INCIDENT STRESS DISORDER

Select one or more:

- Identify if basic needs are being met (i.e., safety, food, shelter, etc.)
- If necessary, refer to Federal Emergency Management Agency (FEMA)
- Explain "secondary disaster" to reduce unnecessary anger and frustration and to avoid further trauma and helplessness in already traumatized patients. You don't have to be at the disaster site. Trauma affects everyone, even those who just watch it repeatedly on television news. They are the secondary victims.
- Educate parents or caregivers about the cognitive, emotional, behavioral, and physical symptoms associated with being involved in a critical incident.
- If patient has lost a loved one, use the bereavement plan or post-traumatic stress disorder plan in addition to this one.
- Help patient and family regain internal and external control.
- Reduce cognitive, behavioral, emotional, and physical stress symptoms.
- Diminish symptoms of anxiety or survivor guilt. Survivor guilt includes the unshakable feeling that you should have been killed instead of a loved one or partner. It is a common reaction.
- Help mourners through the grieving process.
- Teach strategies to reduce stressors to critical events.
- Identify stress reactions of significant others.
- Resolve feelings of despair and hopelessness.
- Help each patient tell his/her story and identify how they are dealing with trauma.
- Eliminate sleep disturbances and nightmares.
- Demonstrate appropriate communication skills: active listening, questioning, mirroring, paraphrasing.
- Restore appetite, stop weight loss.
- Teach the Phoenix Model of dealing with bereavement and crisis (i.e. Impact, Chaos, Adaptation, Equilibrium, and Transformation or Self-Actualization).
- Encourage compliance with educational programs and referrals.
- Develop personal plans to ensure safety and empowerment.
- Reframe irrational beliefs.
- Promote socialization, reconnection, reduce alienation.
- If appropriate, encourage family to develop spiritual side for grounding.
- Develop discharge plan for coping with everyday life.

TREATMENT PLAN

CRITICAL INCIDENT STRESS DISORDER

SHORT-TERM BEHAVIORAL GOALS: ADULTS	THERAPIST'S INTERVENTIONS
Explain needs to therapist.	Determine if basic needs are being met (food, clothing, shelter, safety, etc.).
Reduce anger and helplessness. Prepare to deal with difficulties you will encounter in attempting to get help.	Educate patient about "second disaster" and seeking help from a bureaucratic system to avoid further erosion of self-esteem.
Follow-up with referral.	Refer to Federal Emergency Management Agency (FEMA).
Feel supported and connected while undergoing first stages of dealing with trauma.	If patient cannot get to office, offer telephone sessions to stay connected and help with debriefing. Reach out in any appropriate manner (e.g., go to disaster site, telephone session, e-mail).
Collaborate with therapist to reduce stressors immediately associated with the event.	Establish therapeutic alliance with patient as soon as possible to help deal with overwhelming stressors of traumatic event(s).
Relate in detail the traumatic event and your reactive feelings to it.	Investigate with patient the impact of the traumatic event and how it is affecting him/her.
Patient is treated for bereavement as well as critical incident stress management.	If anyone in the family has died, revise diagnosis and see bereavement plan to use with critical incident stress management.
Describe flashbacks and their intensity.	Explore for flashbacks and assess intensity.

SHORT-TERM BEHAVIORAL GOALS: ADULTS	THERAPIST'S INTERVENTIONS
Understand the different types of trauma.	Help patient understand the different types of trauma: Type 1, individual; and Type 2, collective.
Become aware of ways to reduce stress during critical incidents or disasters.	Educate patient about ways to reduce stressors to the critical event.
If patient requests therapy, reduce stigma of therapy and secure absolute confidentiality, otherwise therapy cannot be effective.	If patient is firefighter or police officer, determine first if he/she wants help. If not, do not intervene. Always "meet the patient where he/she is." These are men and women of action. Allow them to come to you. Forcing therapy on anyone cannot work. Do nothing unless asked.
Realize it is normal to feel abnormal in times like this.	Help patient to understand and accept his/her feelings as normal.
Help identify hidden toll of critical event.	Explore for symptoms associated with disaster and identify the hidden toll of the critical event on the patient (sleep disorders, flashbacks, post-traumatic stress disorder, etc.; see appropriate plan).
Identify your response to disaster.	Investigate response to disaster: fight (anger), flight (helplessness), or freeze (immobility), which constricts energy and makes victim feel helpless with imploded anger, depression, acute stress disorder, and post-traumatic stress disorder (see appropriate treatment plan).

SHORT-TERM BEHAVIORAL GOALS: ADULTS

Learn how to reduce stressors to the critical event.

THERAPIST'S INTERVENTIONS

1. Help patient to structure time; keep busy.

2. Help patient to stop labeling himself/herself as crazy. It's normal to feel abnormal under stress.

3. Urge patient to talk to others.

4. Help patient understand that attempting to numb pain with drugs, alcohol, or excessive food will just complicate problems.

5. Get patient to reach out and connect with others.

6. Encourage him/her to show feelings.

7. Tell patient to help coworkers and let them help him/her.

8. Ask patient to write his/her feelings in a journal, especially during sleepless hours.

9. Urge patient to do things that feel good.

10. Help patient to realize that hoarding out of fear will cause more trouble for everyone.

11. Tell patient not to make any major life decisions at this time.

12. Instruct him/her not to fight flashbacks. Talk about them. Realize they will become less painful over time. (See Trauma Release Technique, Chapter 6).

13. Do things that help you feel you have some control over your life.

SHORT-TERM BEHAVIORAL GOALS: ADULTS

THERAPIST'S INTERVENTIONS

14. Listen carefully to traumatized persons.

15. Do not deny reality, but reduce the time listening to radio and watching TV to avoid reinfecting yourself.

Learn to identify symptoms of stress reaction: emotional, behavioral, cognitive, or physical.	Help patient to identify the stress reactions he/she is having to the traumatic event(s).
Help yourself and your family move through a transitional period toward greater development.	Educate patient about the five phases of the Phoenix Model: Impact, Chaos, Adaptation, Equilibrium, and Transformation.
Identify the Phoenix developmental stage you are in.	Help patient identify where he/she is in the Phoenix Model and what to expect.
Understand your need to maintain stability, establish security measures, and begin to belong or reach out to others.	During the Impact Stage, help patient understand the needs for food, shelter, sleep, safety, security, and preliminary belonging. Guide him/her in designing a support system.
Recognize the need to maintain physiological stability while acknowledging and expressing grief and resisting isolation.	During the Chaos Stage there is still a need for food, shelter, sleep, safety, and security, but the major task is to maintain physiological stability and be able to talk about and acknowledge grief while staying connected and resisting isolation.
Understand that during times of crisis and fear there can also be growth.	The following Adaptation Stage is aimed at normalization. Remind patient "Although the world is full of suffering… it is also full of overcoming it." Create a realistic outline to live in today's world while encouraging the expression of feelings.

SHORT-TERM BEHAVIORAL GOALS: ADULTS	THERAPIST'S INTERVENTIONS
Learn strategies to deal with anxiety.	Teach patient the dynamics of anxiety: not permanent, not dangerous; running away only increases it.
Develop proactive strategies to reduce helplessness and hopelessness.	Help patient gain equilibrium and develop proactive strategies for living in the new world.
Look for ways to create meaning from the tragedy.	Help patient through the Transformation Stage by creating meaning from the grief and loss of life.
Confront thoughts of unrealistic or exaggerated consequences.	Guide patient to confront distorted reactions that trigger situations.
Identify cognitive distortions.	Weigh the actions against evidence-based reality.
Learn to self-soothe rather than catastrophize.	Help patient to develop coping mechanisms that are soothing rather than frightening, such as staying in the here and now. Even though this may be very difficult during times of critical disaster, help him/her see that what they worry about often doesn't happen, and what they don't know to worry about may well happen.
Realize that many others are affected when traumatic events occur.	Explore for low self-esteem or survivor guilt and explain it as normal reaction to trauma.
Identify irrational beliefs.	Reframe irrational beliefs about death, fears, and anxieties.
Use guided imagery and relaxation technique to gain control over feelings.	Teach relaxation technique and guided imagery to master anxieties.

SHORT-TERM BEHAVIORAL GOALS: ADULTS	THERAPIST'S INTERVENTIONS
Learn diaphragmatic breathing as relaxation technique.	Teach belly breathing to assist in relaxation.
Undergo treatment for other disorders.	Explore for other psychopathology (depression, marital discord, sleep problems, etc.) and treat or refer for treatment (see appropriate treatment plan).
Comply with referrals for medical and psychiatric evaluations.	Provide referral for medical and psychiatric evaluations if appropriate.
Use Resources (Chapter 8) to enhance coping strategies.	If patient has the time and energy, recommend he/she read *I Can't Get Over It, Life After Trauma: A Workbook for Healing*, or *The Phoenix Phenomenon: Rising From the Ashes of Grief* (see Resources, Chapter 8).
Learn new skills.	Assign patient to read *Becoming Stress-Resistant* or *Building Self-Esteem* (see Resources, Chapter 8).
If you are on medication, report all negative reactions and failure to take meds.	If patient is on medication, emphasize need for regular schedule and need for feedback that may indicate required change in dosage.
Resolve separation and dependency issues and terminate treatment.	Address issues of separation and dependency. Terminate treatment.

TREATMENT PLAN

CRITICAL INCIDENT STRESS DISORDER

SHORT-TERM BEHAVIORAL GOALS: CHILD/ADOLESCENT	THERAPIST'S INTERVENTIONS
Identify how you are attempting to deal with the traumatic event.	Investigate the impact of the traumatic event and how the patient is affected by it.
Get help to deal with the crisis if you need it.	Determine if basic needs are being met (food, clothing, shelter, safety.) If necessary, refer to Federal Emergency Management Agency (FEMA).
Child: Engage in play therapy. **Adolescent:** Develop a therapeutic relationship to help you through the traumatic event or loss of loved one.	Engage patient in therapeutic relationship to help deal with the traumatic event.
Realize you can look to others for support.	Explore available support systems. Are there aunts, uncles, other relatives, and/or friends available to help patient adjust to the emotional shockwave? If parents or caregivers are unavailable, call in emergency resources (i.e., Social Services, Child Welfare, etc.)
Understand the stages of trauma and be reassured that you will get through the grieving process.	Educate patient about the stages of trauma: (1) Shock, denial, disbelief; (2) Anger: "Why did it happen?"; (3) Chaos, despair: "How can it ever get better?"; (4) Bargaining: "If I am a better person, things will improve." Help patient reorganize and create a new life to reduce the effects of trauma.

SHORT-TERM BEHAVIORAL GOALS: CHILD/ADOLESCENT	THERAPIST'S INTERVENTIONS
Learn to identify the symptoms you are experiencing and recognize them as a response to trauma.	Help child to identify his/her stress reactions: emotional, behavioral, cognitive, physical.
Undergo treatment for specific disorders as appropriate.	See appropriate treatment plans for indicated disorders (i.e., ASD, PTSD, bereavement, etc.).
Realize that human beings are not perfect and reduce stressors imposed on self.	Teach the patient that human beings are not perfect.
Determine the impact of the trauma on schoolwork.	Explore for academic problems related to the trauma and treat accordingly (refer to appropriate treatment plan).
Become aware of ways to reduce stressors to the critical event.	Educate patient about ways to reduce stressors to the critical event:

1. Structure time; keep busy.

2. Don't label yourself crazy. It's normal to feel crazy under stress.

3. Talk to others.

4. Understand that attempting to numb pain with drugs, alcohol, or excessive food just creates problems.

5. Reach out and connect with others.

6. Show feelings.

7. Help others, and let them help you.

8. Write your feelings in a journal, especially during sleepless hours.

SHORT-TERM BEHAVIORAL GOALS: CHILD/ADOLESCENT	THERAPIST'S INTERVENTIONS
	9. Do things that feel good.
	10. Do not begin hoarding out of fear. It will cause more trouble for everyone.
	11. Do not make any major life decisions.
	12. Do not fight flashbacks. Talk about them. Realize they will be less painful over time.
	13. Do things that help you feel you have some control over your life.
	14. Listen carefully to other traumatized persons.
	15. Do not deny reality, but reduce the time spent listening to radio or watching TV to avoid reinfecting yourself.
Learn how to manage the different stages of grief.	Teach patient to understand the five phases of the Phoenix Model: Impact, Chaos, Adaptation, Equilibrium, and Transformation.
Learn to identify the Phoenix development stage you are in.	Help patient identify where he/she is in the Phoenix Model and what to expect at this stage.
Recognize that you need to maintain stability and safety, and begin reaching out to others.	During the Impact phase, help patient understand the need for food, clothing, shelter, safety, sleep. Start a support system.
Recognize the need for psychological stability while being able to express grief.	During the Chaos Stage, basic needs continue, but the major task is to maintain physiological stability and be able to talk about and acknowledge grief while staying connected and resisting isolation.

SHORT-TERM BEHAVIORAL GOALS: CHILD/ADOLESCENT	THERAPIST'S INTERVENTIONS
Develop proactive strategies for living in the new world.	Help patient regain equilibrium after the trauma by developing proactive strategies for reducing helplessness and hopelessness.
Look for ways to find meaning in the tragedy.	Guide patient through the Transformation Stage by attempting to find meaning in the grief and loss of life.
Understand that during times of crisis and fear, there can also be growth.	The following Adaptation Stage is aimed at normalization. Remind the child of Helen Keller's words, "Although the world is full of suffering, it is also full of overcoming it." Develop a realistic outline to live in today's world while encouraging the expression of feelings.
Confront thoughts of unrealistic or exaggerated consequences.	Guide patient in confronting distorted reactions to trigger situations.
Identify cognitive distortions.	Weigh the actions against evidence-based reality.
Learn to self-soothe rather than catastrophize.	Help patient develop coping mechanisms that are soothing rather than frightening (i.e., staying in the here and now). Even though this may be difficult during times of critical disaster, help him/her realize that what we worry about often doesn't happen, while what we don't know enough to worry about may well happen.
Realize that others also feel bad when critical trauma incidents occur.	Explore for low self-esteem or survivor guilt, and explain it as a normal reaction to trauma.

SHORT-TERM BEHAVIORAL GOALS: CHILD/ADOLESCENT	THERAPIST'S INTERVENTIONS
Identify irrational beliefs.	Explore irrational beliefs about death.
Reframe beliefs about fears and anxieties.	Discuss the beliefs and develop rational alternatives.
Understand anxiety, and realize that avoidance does not help.	Teach patient the dynamics of anxiety: not dangerous, not permanent; confrontation can promote change; running away only increases anxiety.
Communicate your life story to therapist.	Have the child/adolescent relate the story of his/her life.
Express suppressed feelings about saying goodbye to a loved one.	If appropriate, play the *The Goodbye Game* to dispel myths and false ideas about death (see Therapeutic Games, Chapter 7).
Discuss personal coping mechanisms developed to handle stressful situations.	Investigate with patient possible patterns of social withdrawal or becoming overly active as a way of dealing with feelings about trauma.
Recognize and discuss how the family affects the problem.	Explore the family's impact on the problem. Are they supportive? Do they talk about the tragedy or pretend it never happened? Remind the patient that anxiety and uncertainty are normal parts of grief.
Learn positive self-talk.	Teach patient positive self-talk to interrupt negative patterns.
Learn new techniques for relaxing and dealing with anxieties.	Teach belly breathing to help the patient relax and reduce stress (see Behavioral Techniques, Chapter 6).
Agree to allow therapist to confer with school to help in development of a comprehensive psycho-educational treatment plan.	Interview child/adolescent to determine if he/she thinks the school should also be involved in helping.

SHORT-TERM BEHAVIORAL GOALS: CHILD/ADOLESCENT	THERAPIST'S INTERVENTIONS
Comply with referrals for medical and psychiatric evaluations.	Provide referrals for medical and psychiatric evaluations, if appropriate.
Develop new coping strategies.	Assign adolescent to read or parents to read to child, *I Can't Get Over It* or *Trust After Trauma* (see Resources, Chapter 8).
Identify ways you have changed.	Investigate ways in which the child has changed in attempt to create meaning for what he/she has gone through.
Shift focus of attention from problems to accomplishments.	Ask patient to describe accomplishments of past week.
Feel more confident as self-esteem improves.	Compliment patient to provide positive reinforcement whenever possible.
Learn that grieving is a natural process and learn skills to cope.	If adolescent has time and is willing, have him/her read *The Hyena Who Lost Her Laugh* (see Resources, Chapter 8). Parents can read the book to younger children.
Learn positive problem-solving techniques and how famous people have overcome obstacles.	Assign adolescent to read *Conquer Anxiety, Worry, and Nervous Fatigue: A Guide to Greater Peace* or *Facts to Relax By*. Have parents read to child, *Anybody Can Bake a Cake* or *Don't Despair on Thursdays!* (see Resources, Chapter 8).
Learn methods you can use to advocate for yourself.	Instruct patient in the technique of self-advocacy.
Understand that you can deal with these issues and bring treatment to a successful conclusion.	Develop treatment termination plan and resolve issues of separation anxiety and dependency. Let them know you will be available should they ever need further counseling.

TREATMENT PLAN

CRITICAL INCIDENT STRESS DISORDER

SHORT-TERM BEHAVIORAL GOALS: FAMILY

Improve communications among family members to reduce familial anxiety.

Identify unsatisfied needs and get help. Be aware of the problems with red tape, long lines, and other frustrations that are normal in times of trauma.

Identify outside sources that can lend temporary support during the grieving process.

Each family member shares his/her reaction to the loss.

Family members understand the normal stages of grieving and what to expect from each other.

Each family member shares his/her unique reaction to the critical incident.

THERAPIST'S INTERVENTIONS

Conduct family sessions to reduce alienation, improve communication skills, and enhance understanding of trauma in the entire family.

Explore how basic needs are being met, (i.e., food, clothing, shelter, safety, etc.) and, if necessary, refer family for Federal Emergency Management Agency (FEMA). Explain "secondary disaster" to avoid unnecessary stress.

Identify any other members of the extended family who can provide additional support.

Explore individual reactions to the trauma. See how each family member felt before and after the traumatic event.

If the rest of the family is unfamiliar with the stages of grief, explain them using the Kubler-Ross Model: Denial, Anger, Bargaining, Depression, and Acceptance (Kubler-Ross, 1997), or the Phoenix Model: Impact, Chaos, Adaptation, Equilibrium, and Transformation (Jozefowski, 1999).

Have each member explore his/her individual feelings and response to the critical incident to give their sorrow words that can be cathartic.

SHORT-TERM BEHAVIORAL GOALS: FAMILY	THERAPIST'S INTERVENTIONS
Identify each family member's methods of coping with the disaster.	Discuss individual methods of coping.
Identify irrational thoughts related to death.	Explore irrational methods of coping in all family members. Do they feel guilty for the death? Blame each other?
Each family member identifies his/her unfinished business with the deceased and psychodynamically works through relevant issues that are unresolved.	If any family members died in the critical incident, at the appropriate time use role-playing with an empty chair representing the deceased. Ask family members to express what they would like to relate to the dead person. Include any unfinished business they would like to complete.
Become aware of ways to reduce stressors to the critical event.	Educate family about ways to reduce stressors to the critical event:

1. Structure time; keep busy.

2. Don't label yourself crazy. It's normal to feel crazy under stress.

3. Talk to others.

4. Understand that attempting to numb pain with drugs, alcohol, or excessive food just creates problems.

5. Reach out and connect with others.

6. Show feelings.

7. Help others, and let them help you.

8. Write your feelings in a journal, especially during sleepless hours.

9. Do things that feel good.

SHORT-TERM BEHAVIORAL GOALS: FAMILY	THERAPIST'S INTERVENTIONS
Become aware of ways to reduce stressors to the critical event.	10. Explain that hoarding out of fear will cause more trouble for everyone.
	11. Refrain from making any major life decisions at this time.
	12. Do not fight flashbacks. Talk about them. Realize they will be less painful over time.
	13. Do things that help you feel you have some control over your life.
	14. Tell family that writing – even writing in a journal – is a way of expressing feelings and can help eliminate anxieties.
	15. Do not deny reality, but reduce the time spent listening to radio or watching TV to avoid reinfecting yourself.
Expose hidden blame in order to resolve it.	Explore for hidden blame among family members.
Family members disclose survivor's guilt.	Investigate for survivor's guilt, and educate family members that it is a normal part of the grieving process.
Family realizes they can find hope through growth and adaptation.	Educate family about the Adaptation phase and help them realize their old life has ended. Help them to let go and see that this process can be the birthplace of hope and transition.
Family members are empowered by realizing how they can take on new roles and grow.	Assist family to establish equilibrium by taking on new roles and on planning how they can live in times of crisis.
Stay in the here and now to reduce stress.	Realize that staying in the here and now will calm you down.

SHORT-TERM BEHAVIORAL GOALS: FAMILY	THERAPIST'S INTERVENTIONS
Recognize the uselessness of worry.	Reassure family members that worry is useless since what we worry about very rarely happens and the things we do not worry about often take place. Remind them of the Atom Bomb story (see Chapter 1).
Each family member strengthens himself/herself by developing new, productive roles.	Help each family member to build self-confidence through actual realistic achievements.
Each member individually develops a SMART plan to help them get through the crisis.	Develop a SMART action plan: Small, Measurable, Achievable, Realistic, Timelined Goals (see Change in Behavioral Techniques, Chapter 6).
Family members recognize they have the power to make important changes even if they seem small.	Help family members realize they have an opportunity to do some things differently.
Realize that major change is the result of small changes taken one at a time.	Help family members to identify and prioritize achievable goals.
Identify individual transformation.	Have each member identify ways they have transformed since the tragedy.
Discuss the books to enhance your understanding of grief.	If someone in the family has died in the tragic event, assign adolescent to read and parents to read to child, *The Phoenix Phenomenon* and *Living Beyond Loss: Death in the Family* (see Resources, Chapter 8).

SHORT-TERM BEHAVIORAL GOALS: FAMILY	THERAPIST'S INTERVENTIONS
Make use of available community resources.	Refer family to available community groups. Remind them of secondary victimization. Although community resources may be available, the waiting lines for assistance may be formidable.
Reduce negative communication.	Develop a system of positive reinforcement with family to help members interact better with each other and reduce scapegoating.
Work together to develop a treatment termination plan.	Discuss termination issues and develop a plan to terminate treatment.

ACUTE STRESS DISORDER

Acute stress disorder (ASD) is marked by anxiety, dissociation, and other symptoms within one month after an extreme traumatic event such as the World Trade Center collapse and other terrorist attacks. Symptoms may include a sense of numbing, detachment, lack of emotional responsiveness, reduced awareness of surroundings, derealization, depersonalization, or dissociative amnesia. The traumatic event is persistently reexperienced, and situations that may trigger a remembrance of the event are actively avoided. The disturbance lasts for at least two days, but usually does not endure for more than four weeks. During that time, the disorder may significantly interfere with the individual's normal functioning. If the symptoms of acute stress disorder persist, a revised diagnosis should be considered.

Post-traumatic stress disorder requires a history of more than one month. Before the World Trade Center attack, 52 million Americans were diagnosed with stress disorders. There is no doubt that the figure is even higher after 9/11.

When traumatic events such as a disaster occur, basic needs must be addressed immediately. Food, clothing, and shelter are primary concerns. Although extraordinary measures (i.e., use of the telephone or visiting the site) may be advisable, it is better if the patient can get to your office. In today's environment therapists should be knowledgeable about available resources (FEMA, online help, emergency 800 numbers, hotlines, Red Cross, etc.), which may or may not help, although patients should be warned about the "secondary disaster" and the need to deal with long lines and bureaucratic red tape.

Once the patient's basic needs have been assured, it is time to attempt to build a therapeutic alliance to enhance the outcome of treatment. The critical elements that make an event traumatic (van der Kolk, McFarlane, and Weisaeth, 1996) are the victims' subjective assessments of how threatened and helpless they feel. At this point it is important to explore the patient's experience of the event and determine how victimized and helpless he/she might have felt. Caroline Myss (www.Myss.com) reminds us that illness can develop as a consequence of patterns and attitudes that we do not realize can be dangerous until they have already become biologically toxic.

Today, almost everyone – police officers, firefighters, and civilians in government – is warning us of imminent terrorist attacks and acute stress disorder is ubiquitous. We have become more accustomed to red alerts. Children are acting out worse than ever before. War toys are everywhere. Video games that seem to get more and more violent with every new version, are tolerated or ignored by adults and met with glee by their children. Is this where children learn that violence is okay? I am afraid to be alone with two of the children in treatment with me for fear they will punch me, or worse. I require one parent in the room with them at all times. Cursing is normal in their speech patterns, and I have forbidden it in my office. Their parents see nothing wrong. They claim their children's behavior was learned from their friends or TV. The problem has gotten considerably worse since 9/11. Where are we headed?

BEHAVIORAL SYMPTOMS

ACUTE STRESS DISORDER

- Intense feelings of anxiety that can be unpredictable
- Numbing or lack of emotion
- Feels dazed or disconnected
- Derealization or depersonalization
- Inability to recall an important part of the traumatic event
- Difficulty coping with everyday stresses
- Recurring images, thoughts, dreams, or flashbacks of the event
- Strained relationships
- Distress at reminders of the event
- Excessive worry of further catastrophic events (i.e. terrorism, bio-chemical warfare, etc.)
- Avoids people, places, and things associated with the event
- Eating patterns disturbed
- Sleep problems, anxiety, irritability, lack of concentration, restlessness, exaggerated vigilance
- May suddenly burst into tears without apparent provocation
- May become isolated from usual friends and colleagues
- Other major impairment of daily activities

OBJECTIVES OF TREATMENT

ACUTE STRESS DISORDER

Select one or more:

- If event just occurred, assess real danger to patient and others
- Identify impact of event on the patient
- Determine if basic needs are being met (i.e., food, clothing, shelter, etc.)
- Refer to Federal Emergency Management Agency if necessary
- Explore cognitive and affective reactions that perpetuated acute stress disorder
- Investigate for support systems (familial, social, worker) patient can turn to for practical and emotional help
- Educate patient about the disorder
- Investigate coping pattern: fight, flight, or freeze
- Reduce anxiety related to the disorder
- Reduce other symptoms (restlessness, sleep problems, irritability, poor concentration, excessive vigilance)
- If patient is a child or adolescent, educate parents or caregiver about the cognitive, emotional, and behavioral symptoms of acute stress disorder
- If appropriate, see other family members and have each of them explain how they are experiencing the critical event
- In children, reduce regression, hyperactivity, controlling bedwetting behavior, somatic complaints, and acting out
- If patient has lost a loved one, use the bereavement plan.
- If 30 days after the event, use the post-traumatic stress disorder plan in addition to this one
- Help family gain internal and external control
- Help patient understand that it okay to stay informed, but addictive watching of television or reading news accounts of the tragedy can reinfect him/her.
- Diminish symptoms of anxiety or survival guilt
- Help mourners through the grieving process
- Teach strategies to reduce stressors to critical events
- Identify stress reactions of significant others
- Resolve feelings of despair and hopelessness
- Eliminate sleep disturbances and nightmares
- Encourage compliance with educational programs and/or referrals
- Reduce irrational beliefs
- Restore realization and personification
- Promote socialization

- Eliminate need for avoidance of people, places, or things reminiscent of the traumatic event
- Reduce alienation
- Help patient understand he/she can stay informed, but that addictive listening to radio or television, or addictive reading of newspapers or news magazines may increase anxieties and reinfect him/her
- Demonstrate appropriate communication skills (active listening, questioning, mirroring, paraphrasing, etc.)
- Attempt to restore appetite
- If patient has lost someone in the disaster, teach the Phoenix Model for dealing with bereavement and crisis (Impact, Chaos, Adaptation, Equilibrium, and Transformation/Self-Actualization)
- Encourage compliance with educational programs and referrals
- Attempt to develop personal rituals to ensure safety and empowerment
- Promote socialization and reconnection; reduce alienation
- If appropriate, encourage family to develop spiritual side for grounding
- Restore to optimum level of functioning
- Develop discharge plan for coping with everyday life

TREATMENT PLAN

ACUTE STRESS DISORDER

SHORT-TERM BEHAVIORAL GOALS: ADULTS	THERAPIST'S INTERVENTIONS
Get help with basic needs and understand protocol to follow to assure basic needs.	Explore whether basic needs are being met (food, clothing, shelter, safety, etc.) and refer to FEMA as necessary.
Collaborate with therapist in development of a treatment plan.	Join with patient in creating a treatment plan.
Relate personal view of the trauma and identify the amount of helplessness and victimization you feel.	Determine patient's view of the trauma and estimate level of helplessness and victimization.
Learn nature of acute stress disorder.	Teach patient the causes and features of acute stress disorder.
Remain connected; reduce fears and isolation.	If patient is in distress and cannot accommodate a normal office visit, resort to telephone sessions temporarily to maintain level of support.
Recognize "hidden toll" of the disaster.	Explore for symptoms associated with the disaster to identify the "hidden toll" of the incident on the patient, especially firefighters and police officers who may be reluctant to speak about their symptoms.
Eliminate stigma of feeling abnormal.	Help patient realize that it is normal to feel abnormal in times like these.
Identify your natural response to the critical event.	Explore patient's response to the critical incident (fight, flight, or freeze).

SHORT-TERM BEHAVIORAL GOALS: ADULTS	THERAPIST'S INTERVENTIONS
If you have children, recognize your responsibility as a role model.	Help patient understand he/she is a role model for his/her children. How the parents react to disaster will impact their children's reactions. Anxiety is contagious.
Stay in the "here and now" to reduce stress even in the most traumatic times.	Teach patient how to stay in the here and now and reduce catastrophizing.
Identify underlying dynamics.	Examine underlying dynamics that exacerbate anxieties.
Understand double-bind theory and reduce addictive listening to media coverage of the event, reducing individual and familial anxiety.	Explain double-bind theory ("Damned if you do, damned if you don't") and relate it to addictive news watching during the crisis: Repeated watching reinforces anxiety, while not watching creates the feeling you are uninformed. Solution: Confine coverage to one-half hour a day; avoid addictive watching.
Understand that it is normal to feel abnormal in stressful times.	Help patient understand there are times when it's normal to feel abnormal.
Identify where and how you feel anxiety.	Since trauma is both cognitive and physiological, most trauma victims are affected somatically. Determine how the patient is affected.
Identify sensorimotor reactions to traumatic event.	If patient is stabilized, explore sensorimotor reactions (i.e., sounds, smells, intrusive images, numbing, inability to regulate hyperarousal).
Identify life changes since traumatic event (in economics, home life, work, style, relationships, etc.)	Identify changes in patient's life as result of the trauma.

SHORT-TERM BEHAVIORAL GOALS: ADULTS	THERAPIST'S INTERVENTIONS
Attempt to build emotional tolerance for painful feelings.	Encourage patient to stay with feelings even if patient reports he/she cannot talk about highly charged emotional issues.
Realize that your feelings are appropriate and do not indicate a flaw in your character.	If patient feels foolish, shameful, or weak because of anxiety disorder, reinforce idea that feelings are feelings and there's no right or wrong to them.
Examine your reactions to trauma, and identify distortions and exaggerations.	Explore patient's reactions and point out distortions or exaggerations.
Replace exaggerated reactions with more positive reactions using evidence-based reality.	Reframe negative reactions with positive reality-based cognitions.
Learn to use diaphragmatic breathing to calm self.	Teach patient diaphragmatic breathing.
Practice coping skills in real-life situations to diminish and eliminate anxiety reactions.	Instruct patient to challenge persons, places, activities, and things related to the event to overcome stress and fear reactions.
If children are acting out, explore how much TV they watch and the games they play. Set new limits.	If children are watching violent or sexual shows on television, it is time to set limits. Sign up for a class in parenting.
Explore with therapist the issues of separation and dependency. Review treatment termination plan.	Prepare treatment termination plan, and address termination issues.
Attend self-help group meetings to reinforce coping skills.	Refer patient to self-help group dealing with acute stress disorder.

TREATMENT PLAN

ACUTE STRESS DISORDER

SHORT-TERM BEHAVIORAL GOALS: CHILD/ADOLESCENT	THERAPIST'S INTERVENTIONS
Assess basic needs. Identify available support systems.	Investigate whether patient's basic needs are being met. If not, meet with parents to help child/adolescent and family find help.
Learn about diagnosis and develop realistic expectations of self.	Educate patient about the diagnosis and discuss symptomatology so he/she can adjust self-expectations.
Child: Engage in play therapy. **Adolescent**: Enter non-threatening therapeutic interaction geared to appropriate development level.	Engage child in play therapy and adolescent in age-appropriate therapeutic relationship.
Describe the event that triggered the stress reaction.	Explore with patient how the traumatic event has affected him/her.
Understand it is normal to feel abnormal in times of crisis.	Help patient realize it is normal to sometimes feel abnormal under the circumstances.
Help identify your response to disaster.	Investigate response to disaster: *fight* (get angry and retaliate), *flight* (run away from feelings), or *freeze* (constricts energy and makes one feel helpless with imploded anger, depression, and/or post-traumatic stress disorder). (See appropriate treatment plan.)

SHORT-TERM BEHAVIORAL GOALS: CHILD/ADOLESCENT	THERAPIST'S INTERVENTIONS
Identify available support systems.	If parents are unavailable, investigate if aunts, uncles, grandparents are available to provide practical and emotional support.
Understand underlying dynamics that led to maladaptive behavior and stress.	Explore ways in which anxieties manifest themselves (need for perfection, worry about nuclear or biochemical war or catastrophic thinking), and clarify underlying dynamics.
Recognize that human beings are not perfect and reduce stressors imposed on yourself.	Help child/adolescent to ease up and realize that no human being is perfect.
Recognize underlying feelings of anger or depression and express appropriately.	Explore for underlying feelings of anger and/or depression (see appropriate treatment plan).
Identify response to stressors.	Explore for fight, flight, or freeze reactions so appropriate interventions can be employed in treatment.
Child: Use puppets. Observe how they behave. Begin to see new role models deal with anxieties.	Use puppets to shape child behavior and use role-playing to help adolescent learn new ways to deal with anxiety.
Adolescent: Observe new ways to deal with anxieties.	
Learn that it is okay to feel anxious and just face it head on. Learn the dynamics of anxiety.	Encourage patient when he/she faces anxiety. Learn that it isn't dangerous or permanent and can be reduced by confrontation.

SHORT-TERM BEHAVIORAL GOALS: CHILD/ADOLESCENT	THERAPIST'S INTERVENTIONS
Identify how you feel inside.	Teach patient to create a climate for healing. It is not difficult, but is like learning the customs of a foreign country. Shift from thought to basic sensations. "How are you feeling inside?"
Child: Realize others also feel bad and relate to puppets in overcoming the feeling. **Adolescent**: Investigate underlying feelings and cooperate with treatment.	Explore underlying feelings and treat (see appropriate treatment plan). In children, have puppets talk about their feelings and what to do about them.
Child: Imitate puppets and learn how to better deal with fear. **Adolescent**: Understand how you increase anxiety by distorting reality.	Instruct patient to keep a journal of thoughts to better understand his/her cognitive distortions. In children, use puppets to role model dealing with fear.
Identify irrational beliefs about stress, fears, and anxieties.	Explore irrational beliefs. In children, change irrational beliefs by having the puppets develop and discuss rational alternatives.
Learn how to reduce stressors to the critical event.	Teach rational alternatives: 1. Help child structure time in a better way; keep busy. 2. Teach patient to realize he/she is not crazy. It's normal to feel that way under stress. 3. Talk to others about your feelings. 4. Understand that attempting to numb the pain with drugs, alcohol, or food just complicates the problem.

SHORT-TERM BEHAVIORAL GOALS: CHILD/ADOLESCENT	THERAPIST'S INTERVENTIONS
	5. Reach out and connect with others.
	6. Don't suppress your feelings.
	7. Help friends by letting them help you.
	8. Write your feelings in a journal, especially during sleepless hours.
	9. Do things that feel good.
	10. Do not begin hoarding out of fear. It will cause more trouble for everyone.
	11. Do not make any life decisions at this time. They may seem foolish once the crisis is over.
	12. Do not fight flashbacks. Roll with them and talk about them. They will become less painful over time.
	13. Do things that help you feel you have some control over your life.
	14. Listen carefully to traumatized persons.
	15. Do not deny reality, but reduce the addictive listening to radio or watching TV. Avoid reinfecting yourself by watching video of the tragedy over and over.
Child: Mimic puppets and shape new behaviors. **Adolescent**: Learn from role modeling and shape new behaviors.	Role-play situations that create acute stress, and role-model new solutions. In children, use puppets to role model appropriate behavior.

SHORT-TERM BEHAVIORAL GOALS: CHILD/ADOLESCENT

THERAPIST'S INTERVENTIONS

Child: In play therapy, learn to gain control over feelings.

Adolescent: Learn to gain mastery over your feelings.

Child: Develop a more positive attitude through play.

Adolescent: Learn how self-hypnosis and focusing on what you want will help relieve stress.

Use hypnosis to help patient master anxieties (see Behavioral Techniques, Chapter 6). Use puppets and guided imagery with children.

With parents' permission, teach adolescent self-hypnosis to use between sessions to reduce anxiety.

Communicate life story to therapist.

Have patient relate the story of his/her life, use puppets with child.

Express suppressed feelings in a non-threatening environment.

Play *The Talking, Feeling, Doing Game* to understand underlying processes in a non-threatening way (see Therapeutic Games, Chapter 7).

Understand how trauma may have contributed to existing disorder.

Explore patient's background for other traumas that may have exacerbated acute stress.

Discuss personal coping mechanisms developed to handle anxieties.

Investigate with patient possible patterns of withdrawal (freeze) used to avoid anxiety.

Understand how you misinterpreted events.

Explore for misinterpretations of environmental events, and correct them.

Recognize and relate how family impacts the problem.

Explore familial impact on the problem.

Understand ways family anxiety can exacerbate your anxiety.

Teach patient that family anxiety is contagious and can reinfect the patient rather than help reduce his/her anxiety.

SHORT-TERM BEHAVIORAL GOALS: CHILD/ADOLESCENT	THERAPIST'S INTERVENTIONS
Child: Learn self-nurturing techniques. **Adolescent**: Recognize the patterns of your disorder and the possibility of changing how you deal with it.	Discuss the patterns of patient's acute stress disorder, and focus on solutions. Have children play *The Positive Thinking Game*, or *The Ungame* to teach positive self-talk (see Therapeutic Games, Chapter 7).
Learn new relaxation technique.	Teach belly breathing to help control anxiety (see Behavioral Techniques, Chapter 6).
Shift focus from problem to accomplishment.	Ask patient to describe accomplishments of the past week to shift focus from a weak despondent model to a more powerful self-actualization one.
Feel more confident as self-esteem improves.	Compliment patient to provide positive reinforcement whenever possible.
Child: Learn to reduce anxiety by confronting your feelings. **Adolescent**: Read the assigned material and discuss new ways to deal with acute stress disorder.	Have adolescent read *The Anxiety and Phobia Workbook* and discuss it with you. Have child read or have parent read to him/her *Don't Be Afraid, Tommy* or *Linda Saves the Day* (see Resources, Chapter 8).
Child: Learn how famous people have overcome their problems. **Adolescent**: Learn how to work through fears.	Assign adolescent to read *Smart Guide to Relieving Stress* and child to read or have parent read to him/her *Anybody Can Bake a Cake* (see Resources, Chapter 8).
Read about various techniques for getting a good night's sleep.	Assign adolescent to read and child to read or have parent read to him/her *All I Want is a Good Night's Sleep* (see Resources, Chapter 8).

SHORT-TERM BEHAVIORAL GOALS: CHILD/ADOLESCENT

Apply stress reduction techniques in everyday activities and report results to therapist.

Child: Communicate problematic feelings to develop new skills or options.

Adolescent: Learn how fear and stress can be transformed into power and action.

Learn to advocate for yourself.

Understand that you can deal with acute stress. Discuss separation anxiety and dependency. Bring treatment to an end.

THERAPIST'S INTERVENTIONS

Provide positive reinforcement for applying newly learned techniques. Praise attempts and reward success.

Have adolescent read *Conquer Anxiety, Worry and Nervous Fatigue: A Guide to Greater Peace* (see Resources, Chapter 8).

Instruct patient in the technique of self-advocacy to help him/her feel empowered.

Develop treatment termination plan and implement it.

TREATMENT PLAN

ACUTE STRESS DISORDER

SHORT-TERM BEHAVIORAL GOALS: FAMILY	THERAPIST'S INTERVENTIONS
Improve communications among family members to reduce familial anxiety.	Conduct family sessions to reduce alienation, improve communication skills, and enhance understanding of the impact of the trauma on the entire family.
Identify unsatisfied needs and attempt to get help.	Explore if and how basic needs are being met (i.e., food, clothing, shelter, safety, etc.) and, if necessary, refer to FEMA. Explain "second disaster" to family and teach them how to deal with overloaded agencies.
Identify outside resources that can provide temporary support during crisis.	Identify if there are members of the extended family who can provide temporary practical and emotional support.
Each family member shares his/her reaction to the trauma.	Explore individual reactions to the trauma. See how each family member felt before and after the critical incident.
Identify your response to disaster so proper interventions can be customized to help survivors. Family understands responses may vary.	Investigate the individual responses of family members to disaster: fight (get angry, seek vengeance), flight (run away), or freeze (which constricts energy and makes one feel helpless with imploded anger, depression, or post-traumatic stress disorder). (See appropriate treatment plan, Chapter 3.)

SHORT-TERM BEHAVIORAL GOALS: FAMILY	THERAPIST'S INTERVENTIONS
Explain how you feel internally in order to identify and reduce traumatic biological response.	Help family create a climate for healing. Have family members talk about how they feel "inside" (shaky, trembling, etc.).
If there has been a death in the family, understand the normal stages of grieving and what is expected of each other.	Teach the Stages of Grief using either the Kubler-Ross Model: Denial, Anger, Bargaining, Depression, and Acceptance (Kubler-Ross, 1997) or the Phoenix Model: Impact, Chaos, Adaptation, Equilibrium, and Transformation (Jozefowski, 1999).
Share your unique reactions to the critical incident and understand how other family members are reacting.	Have each family member explore his/her feelings and response to the incident to provide a chance to vent their sorrow, which can be cathartic.
Identify how each family member copes with the disaster.	Discuss individual methods of coping with traumatic stress.
Identify irrational thoughts related to trauma.	Explore irrational methods of coping with trauma with all family members.
Identify your unfinished business with the deceased and psychodynamically work through relevant issues that remain unresolved.	Use role-playing with an empty chair representing the deceased. Ask family members to express what they would like to have said to the deceased. Include any unfinished business they would like in order to have closure.
Discuss blame and guilt you feel, and vent your concerns.	Investigate for feelings of blame or guilt and provide the opportunity for family members to vent their feelings.

SHORT-TERM BEHAVIORAL GOALS: FAMILY	THERAPIST'S INTERVENTIONS
Learn to reduce stressors to the critical event.	Teach rational alternatives:

Teach rational alternatives:

1. Help child structure time in a better way; keep busy.

2. Teach patient to realize he/she is not crazy. It's normal to feel that way under stress.

3. Talk to others about your feelings.

4. Understand that attempting to numb the pain with drugs, alcohol, or food just complicates the problem.

5. Reach out and connect with others.

6. Don't suppress your feelings.

7. Help friends by letting them help you.

8. Write your feelings in a journal, especially during sleepless hours.

9. Do things that feel good.

10. Do not begin hoarding out of fear. It will cause more trouble for everyone.

11. Do not make any life decisions at this time. They may seem foolish once the crisis is over.

12. Do not fight flashbacks. Use TRT after teaching self-help (see Chapter 6).

13. Do things that help you feel you have some control over your life.

14. Listen carefully to traumatized persons.

SHORT-TERM BEHAVIORAL GOALS: FAMILY	THERAPIST'S INTERVENTIONS
	15. Do not deny reality, but reduce the addictive listening to radio or watching TV. Avoid reinfecting yourself by watching video of the tragedy over and over.
Family members realize they can find hope through growth and adaptation.	Educate family about the phase of adaptation. Help them realize that they have a chance at a new way of life, which can be the birthplace of hope and transition.
Family members are empowered by realizing through trial and error they can take on new roles and grow.	Assist family to establish equilibrium by taking on new roles and planning a new life even in times of crisis.
Stay in the here and now to reduce stress.	Teach members to reduce stress by staying in the here and now.
Recognize the uselessness of worry.	Reassure family members that worry is useless since the things we worry about seldom happen and the things we do not worry about may well come to pass (see the Atom Bomb story in Chapter 1).
Strengthen yourself by developing a new, productive role.	Help each family member build self-confidence through actual realistic achievements.
Develop your individual SMART action plan to get through the crisis.	Develop a SMART action Plan: Small, Measurable, Achievable, Realistic, Timelined goals (see Change, Behavioral Techniques, Chapter 6).
Realize you have the power to make important changes, even if they seem small.	Help family members recognize they have an opportunity to do some things differently.

SHORT-TERM BEHAVIORAL GOALS: FAMILY	THERAPIST'S INTERVENTIONS
Recognize that major change is the result of small steps taken one at a time.	Help family members identify and prioritize achievable goals.
Identify your transformation.	Have each family member identify ways in which they have been transformed since the tragedy, or the progress they have made toward transformation.
Read and discuss these books to enhance your understanding of grief.	If a family member has died in the disaster, assign reading of *The Phoenix Phenomenon: Rising From the Ashes of Grief* and *Living Beyond Loss: Death in the Family* (see Resources, Chapter 8; also see bereavement plan, Chapter 3).
Make use of community resources.	Refer family to available community group.
Reduce negative communication.	Develop a system of positive reinforcement to help family members interact better and reduce scapegoating.
Work together to develop a treatment termination plan.	Discuss termination issues, and agree on a plan to terminate treatment.

POST-TRAUMATIC STRESS DISORDER

Post-traumatic stress disorder (PTSD) is characterized by development of typical stress symptoms following experience of an event that involves potentially severe personal injury or loss of life. The symptoms may also be triggered by witnessing such a life-threatening event involving another person, especially a close friend or relative, or by watching it on television. The individual's response to the event includes intense fear and helplessness or complete immobility. In the latter case, the individual freezes and involuntarily enters an altered state of consciousness, which eventually binds the person's psychic energy.

Other symptoms include the persistent re-experience of the event, persistent avoidance of stimuli associated with the event, the numbing of general responsiveness (emotional anesthesia), or increased arousal (hypervigilance). Traumatic events are not limited to terrorist attacks and may include violent personal attack, physical or sexual attack, mugging, robbery, severe auto accidents, natural disasters, or being diagnosed with a life-threatening illness. In children, the response to trauma may include disorganized or agitated behavior. The symptoms must persist for more than a month and cause significant distress or impairment in important areas of functioning. Studies show that children whose parents do not overreact fare better in treatment. In children, traumatic events may include sexual experience that is developmentally inappropriate without threat of injury or death.

When a patient experiences a flashback, he or she feels it is happening in the here and now, and there is nothing they can do when it comes over them. It can happen anywhere; at home, work, in the street. They panic and feel as though they are going crazy or out of control. They often cannot go to school or work. I have discovered in my work with patients that Trauma Release Technique (TRT) is extremely effective in reducing the effects of PTSD and returning patients to their normal levels of functioning.

The National Institute of Mental Health (NIMH) (www.NIMH.com) estimate that 5.2 million Americans between the ages of 18 and 54 suffer from post-traumatic stress disorder. About 2 million of that number was added to the PTSD ranks from 1994 to 2000. Although the statistics for 2001 are still incomplete, a significant increase is expected as a result of the 9/11 terrorist attacks. It is suggested that approximately 30% of Vietnam veterans experienced post-traumatic stress disorder after the war.

At an April 2002 conference in Rockland County, New York, Hospice 2002 claimed that 99% of the Oklahoma City bombing victims suffered post-traumatic stress disorder one week after the disaster, 65% after two weeks, and 65% after one month. New cases of PTSD were emerging nine months after the tragedy. A study reported in December 2002 by

Mount Sinai Hospital in New York City concluded that most people involved in the Twin Towers crash continued to suffer from post-traumatic stress disorder. When one is involved with a traumatic event, the psychological scars turn into biological or physical symptoms. What was once a psychological problem is felt in the body. Every cell has a memory, and the way these psychological scars can be healed is by tuning into the "voices" of our bodies. Levine (1997) argues that these psychological scars can be reversed. This treatment plan will attempt to integrate some of his innovative work with more established theories that focus solely on the mind and ignore the body in the healing process.

There is a feeling of helplessness within the bodies of trauma victims. They feel there is no safe place to retreat, and can even dissociate from their bodies. What you think is what you feel, and when traumatized, you think and feel terror both in mind and body.

BEHAVIORAL SYMPTOMS

POST-TRAUMATIC STRESS DISORDER

- Persistent reexperience of the traumatic event as a recollection or a dream
- Flashbacks or feelings of reliving the event
- Displays altered regulation of affect (persistent dysphoria, suicidal ideations, self-injury, inhibited explosive anger, or compulsive or inhibited sexual activity)
- Immobile, frozen state of consciousness
- Intense distress at cues that are reminiscent of the event or some aspect of it
- Other alterations in consciousness (amnesia or hyperamnesia, dissociative states, depersonalization or derealization, intrusive memories, reliving experience as if it is happening now – flashbacks)
- Alterations in self-perception (lack of initiative, sense of paralysis or helplessness, sense of stigma or self-blame, guilt, feels completely estranged from others (no one can help)
- Avoids people, places, activities, and thoughts associated with the event, or keeps replaying event in an altered state
- Unable to remember an important aspect of the event
- Diminished interest in usual activities
- Alterations in relations with others (withdrawn, isolated, persistent distrust, disruptions in intimate relations, repeated failure at self-protection
- Restricted range of feelings
- Has increased sense of limited future

- Has problem falling asleep or maintaining sleep
- Unable to concentrate
- Sense of hopelessness and despair, loss of meaning, inability to sustain faith
- Is easily startled

OBJECTIVES OF TREATMENT

POST-TRAUMATIC STRESS DISORDER

Select one or more:

- Educate patient about the disorder
- Offer a reparative experience through connection with bodily feelings, insight, and empathic attunement
- Reduce freeze reaction
- Reduce flashbacks
- Reduce pervasive anxiety and worry
- Help patient remember what has happened and undergo appropriate mourning
- Help patient develop better coping skills
- Wake patient from symptomatic trance and reorient him/her to current reality
- Eliminate stressors associated with the traumatic event
- Eliminate or reduce intrusive flashbacks
- Diminish symptoms associated with the event (restlessness, fatigue, difficulty concentrating, irritability, somatization, sleep disturbance)
- Educate patient to realize it is normal to respond abnormally in times of crisis
- Restore a sense of control
- Reduce irrational beliefs
- Teach patient Trauma Release Technique
- Promote socialization and reconnection
- Reduce alienation
- Restore patient and family to level of functioning before the event
- Help patient find a survivor statement or mission to restore power
- Help patient resolve trauma and develop awareness that it is never complete

TREATMENT PLAN

POST-TRAUMATIC STRESS DISORDER

SHORT-TERM BEHAVIORAL GOALS: ADULT	THERAPIST'S INTERVENTIONS
Patient feels a sense of empathic attunement or understanding and begins to develop a therapeutic alliance through connection.	Offer patient a reparative experience through connection and empathic attunement.
Feel permission to talk about the "crazy" way you are feeling.	Establish a safe environment to help patient recover. Help patient realize it is normal to feel abnormal in times like these.
Identify ways you responded to the traumatic event in order to feel more grounded.	Encourage patient to tell his/her story, (how it sounded, how it smelled, how his/her body felt during the event). Any gaps in the story baseline can be recovered at a later time.
Identify the bizarre and debilitating residue trapped in his/her nervous system.	Explore for "freeze response" (undischarged residual energy). Educate patient about responses to traumatic events. (In the fight or flight responses to trauma, we are able to discharge negative energy through action. In the freeze response, the energy gets trapped, leading to PTSD and other problems such as depression, psychosis, generalized anxiety disorder, and others.)
Understand that PTSD is not a disease, but a dis-ease within the body that can be healed.	Help patient understand that when involved in trauma, psychology becomes biology. What you think is what you feel in your body.

SHORT-TERM BEHAVIORAL GOALS: ADULT

THERAPIST'S INTERVENTIONS

Identify alterations in your affect.

Explore alterations in patient's affect as a result of the trauma (dysphoria, suicidal ideations, flashbacks, self-injury, inhibited or explosive anger, or compulsive or inhibited sexual activity).

Understand possible need for hospitalization. Join in suicide pact with therapist not to take any action without first contacting therapist.

Check out patient's suicidal ideations, and evaluate for hospitalization if necessary. If patient has a suicide plan in place, consider immediate hospitalization. If no plan exists, explain that it is okay to think about suicide as long as you don't act on it. Enter into suicide pact with patient which he/she agrees not to take any action without first contacting you.

Get comparative experiential sense of how traumatization feels.

Describe for patient how it feels to be traumatized (like a car coming at you at 90 miles an hour and you can't get out of the way). As actor Rod Steiger has explained it (Levine, 1997, p. 59), trauma is a "greasy yellow, jelly fog that permeated [into] my body... into my heart, my spirit, and my soul... It took over, robbing my life." According to Levine (1997, p. 63), "Therapists rarely, if ever, talk about healing the soul, and the disconnection between the body and soul is one of the most important effects of trauma."

SHORT-TERM BEHAVIORAL GOALS: ADULT	THERAPIST'S INTERVENTIONS
Learn to access instinctual reactions and create shields that can reflect and heal them.	In order to heal the soul, gently slide the patient into trauma and ask what he/she is feeling inside his/her body in addition to his/her thoughts. If patient becomes hyperaroused, slow down the process until the patient is ready to talk about it.
Become aware of the diagnosis and what to expect from yourself and your family members.	Educate the patient and the family about PTSD. It often helps to explain the statistics regarding PTSD in other critical events to reduce alienation and feelings of weirdness.
Realize that it is normal to feel abnormal in times of traumatic stress.	Help patient to understand that it is normal to act and feel abnormal in times of traumatic stress.
Understand what is happening, and learn to remove your attention from internal feelings to present-day reality.	If patient is committing self-injury, investigate inner experience and interrupt the hidden meaning. Sometimes, when a person is dealing with an untenable experience, he/she may dissociate. Physical pain feels better than the emotional pain. Self-injury becomes a way to remove oneself from the current problem. O'Hanlon (2000, p. 165) comments that, "The unconscious mind is sometimes smart about things it is dumb to be smart about."
Investigate new ways of coping. Remove yourself from the internal locus of feeling and bring yourself into the here and now. Contract with therapist to refrain from self-injury. Understand possible need for hospitalization.	Explore new ways to cope with the current situation. Contract with patient to refrain from self-injury until the next session. Explain possible need for hospitalization if self-injury continues.

SHORT-TERM BEHAVIORAL GOALS: ADULT	THERAPIST'S INTERVENTIONS
Use a doll as a safety net. The doll eventually can become a symbol of comfort, security, and connection essential to your recovery.	Suggest alternative behaviors (i.e., use of a doll as a safety net). O'Hanlon (2000), in the treatment of a case of self-mutilation, suggested the patient cut a Raggedy Ann doll instead of herself, then sew up the cuts. The doll became a safety net for the patient who eventually recovered.
Identify the personal meaning of the traumatic event.	Explore pre-trauma factors that may have influenced the manner in which patient responded to the event.
Undergo treatment of other disorders related to PTSD.	Evaluate patient for anxiety and other problems related to PTSD and treat (see appropriate treatment plan).
Recognize fears and feelings of negative self-blame over the event.	Evaluate patient's fear and negative self-blame over the traumatic event.
Learn to reach beyond automatic cognitive reactions in viewing the problem.	Expand patient's perspective beyond limited cognitive reactions.
Undergo medical evaluation.	Address patient's medical needs; refer to physician as appropriate.
Become aware that other trauma victims have similar reactions.	Reduce patient's alienation by explaining statistics of other critical events as they relate to police officers, firefighters, and others with PTSD.
Identify and review past traumas.	Investigate for past traumatic events in patient's life and how the patient dealt with them, since they may heavily influence his/her current reactions.

SHORT-TERM BEHAVIORAL GOALS: ADULT	THERAPIST'S INTERVENTIONS
Identify whether family and friends are supportive or not.	Determine if patient has supportive friends and family who can act as a powerful resource for healing. Lack of support can have dramatic impact on recovery.
Cooperate with the "flooding" technique.	If you are trained in hypnosis, use the flooding treatment or Trauma Release Technique developed by the Veteran's Administration for PTSD (see Trauma Release Technique, Behavioral Techniques, Chapter 6). **Note: make absolutely sure that patient is ready to deal with the trauma.** Timing is important. First, apply hypnosis techniques and eventually teach patient self-hypnosis to empower him/her and reduce anxiety. Don't be impatient.
Learn how to deal with stressors.	Teach patient the dynamics of anxiety: not permanent, not dangerous, reduced by confrontation. Exposure can generate growth.
Patient is treated for sleep disorders.	Investigate for sleep problems associated with PTSD and treat (see appropriate treatment plan).
Energy bound-up in distorted beliefs is released.	Review belief systems and challenge distorted beliefs to release bound-up energies. Focus on the experience, not the interpretative meaning.
Identify cognitive distortions.	Weigh patient reactions against evidence-based reality.
Begin to get a better sense of self.	Continue to use the "felt sense" to help patient get to know himself/herself as a biological and spiritual being.

SHORT-TERM BEHAVIORAL GOALS: ADULT	THERAPIST'S INTERVENTIONS
Read assigned self-help books.	Assign patient to read *I Can't Get Over It*, *Life After Trauma: A Workbook for Healing*, and *Waking the Tiger: Healing Trauma* (see Resources, Chapter 8).
Expand your coping skills.	Coach patient in developing new coping strategies for dealing with the problem.
Meet with other people who are experiencing similar difficulties and share solutions for dealing with the effects of trauma.	Refer patient to self-help group.
Discuss termination plan, resolve related issues, and terminate treatment.	Develop a termination plan and resolve related issues of separation and dependency before terminating treatment.

TREATMENT PLAN

POST-TRAUMATIC STRESS DISORDER

SHORT-TERM BEHAVIORAL GOALS: CHILD/ADOLESCENT	THERAPIST'S INTERVENTIONS
Child: Connect with therapist via play therapy. **Adolescent**: Connect in non-threatening therapeutic interaction. Patient feels a sense of empathic attunement or understanding and begins to develop a therapeutic alliance.	Engage patient in a therapeutic alliance through empathic attunement to enhance the outcome of treatment.
Through connection, feels that it is acceptable to talk about the "crazy" way he/she feels.	Establish a safe environment for recovery by helping patient realize that it is normal to feel abnormal at times like this.
Learn more about the diagnosis and develop realistic expectations of self.	Educate the patient about the diagnosis, and discuss the symptoms so he/she has an idea of what to expect.
Identify ways you responded to the traumatic event.	Encourage patient to tell his/her story of what it sounded like, smelled like, and how his/her body felt during the event.
Identify the bizarre and debilitating residue trapped in your nervous system.	Explore for "freeze" response (undischarged residual energy). Note: We are used to the "fight" or "flight" responses, which normally discharge negative energies. However, with the less recognized "freeze" response, the energy is trapped, leading to post-traumatic stress disorder (PTSD) and other problems (depression, psychosis, generalized anxiety disorder, dissociation and others).

SHORT-TERM BEHAVIORAL GOALS: CHILD/ADOLESCENT	THERAPIST'S INTERVENTIONS
Understand that PTSD is not a disease, but a dis-ease.	Help patient understand that in trauma, psychology becomes biology. PTSD is not a disease, but a dis-ease within the body that can be healed.
Describe alterations in your affect since the traumatic event.	Explore alterations in patient's affect (dysphoria, suicidal ideations, self-injury, inhibited or explosive anger, compulsive or inhibited sexual activity).
If actively suicidal, accept hospitalization. If you have no plan in place, enter into suicide pact with therapist.	If patient is suicidal, check out whether he/she has a plan in place or not. Alert parents immediately and discuss possible hospitalization. If there is no plan in place, indicate it is okay to think about suicide from time to time, but not to act on it. Make suicide pact with patient in which he/she agrees not to act until after talking with you. If patient refuses pact, consider hospitalization. Advise parents.
Child: Describe the physical sensations of going through the trauma. Be reassured you can heal.	Use puppets with child to explain how they felt after the trauma. Have puppets talk to one another and to the child describing how it felt. Reassure child he/she will get better. Ask adolescent to describe his/her feelings.
Adolescent: Get an experiential sense of how it feels to be traumatized.	
Learn to access instinctual resources and therefore create shields that can reflect and heal the trauma.	In order to help heal the soul, gently glide patient into the trauma. With child, have puppets describe what they are feeling including bodily sensations as well as thoughts. Move slowly and carefully.

SHORT-TERM BEHAVIORAL GOALS: CHILD/ADOLESCENT	THERAPIST'S INTERVENTIONS
Understand what is happening and agree to contract with therapist not to self-injure without first contacting therapist.	If patient is committing self-injury (cutting self, pulling hair out, etc.) use puppets to encourage child to explain how much emotional pain they are in. (Sometimes, physical pain can be preferable to emotional pain.) Make contract with child/adolescent to call you before deliberately injuring self.
Use Raggedy Ann doll as a safety net. When you get the urge to injure self, cut the doll instead, then sew it up again. Doll becomes a symbol of security and connection.	Suggest using Raggedy Ann doll as a safety net. When experiencing the urge to injure self, cut the doll instead. Sew it up again.
Understand what is happening and shift your attention from internal feelings to the present. Understand need for hospitalization if required for self-protection.	If self-injury continues, explain that it is an ineffective way to remove oneself from the current problem. Investigate new coping strategies: bring yourself into the here and now; remove yourself from the internal locus of feeling. Discuss possible hospitalization for self-protection.
Child: Use puppets to help identify the meaning of the traumatic event.

Adolescent: Identify the personal meaning of the traumatic event. | Using puppets with the child, discuss pre- and post-trauma factors that influence the way you view the trauma. Discuss with adolescent his/her view of the trauma. |
| Comply with medical and psychiatric referrals if required. | Address any medical and psychiatric issues, and refer for appropriate care. |

SHORT-TERM BEHAVIORAL GOALS: CHILD/ADOLESCENT	THERAPIST'S INTERVENTIONS
Identify and evaluate your existing support network.	Evaluate whether patient has supportive parents or members of his/her extended family who can help get them through the trauma.
Cooperate with the Trauma Release Technique.	With parental permission, and assuming you are trained in hypnosis, use the Trauma Release Technique to deal with PTSD and transform the traumatic memory. TRT is similar to "flooding," but uses hypnosis to help reduce symptoms of anxiety and hyper-arousal before reducing the flash-backs and traumatic memories (see Hypnosis and Trauma Release Technique, Behavioral Techniques, Chapter 6).
Identify sleep problems and undergo treatment if necessary. Learn that you can control nightmares and other sleep disorders.	Investigate for sleep disorder and treat if necessary.
Understand how traumatic event was misinterpreted.	Investigate possible misinterpretation of traumatic event.
Learn new coping strategies and solutions.	Develop new coping strategies or alternate solutions.
Recognize underlying feelings of anger or depression and express appropriately.	Explore for underlying feelings of anger or depression.
Explain your beliefs about the trauma. Reframe distorted beliefs. Energy bound up in distorted beliefs is released.	Using puppets with child, discuss his/her beliefs about the trauma. Focus on the experience and not the interpretation. Challenge and reframe distorted beliefs.

SHORT-TERM BEHAVIORAL GOALS: CHILD/ADOLESCENT	THERAPIST'S INTERVENTIONS
Begin to develop a better sense of self.	Continue to use the "felt self" to help patient get to know himself/herself as a biological and psychological self.
Recognize physical cues and use appropriate cognitive strategies to deal more effectively with anxiety.	Teach patient to recognize physical signs of anxious arousal to use as cues, and train in cognitive strategies to avoid flashbacks or panic attacks.
Learn from role-modeling and shape new behaviors.	Role-play situations that create stress and role-model new solutions for dealing with them (see Behavioral Techniques, Chapter 6).
Use hypnosis to master anxiety.	If trained in hypnosis, and with parental permission, use hypnosis to help patient gain mastery over anxieties. Help patient to realize that hypnosis eventually becomes self-hypnosis. The therapist is only a set of training wheels to be discarded once the patient is able to use the hypnosis without assistance (see Behavioral Techniques, Chapter 6).
Learn new ways to handle stressors.	Teach patient Mindfulness to help deal with stress (see Behavioral Techniques, Chapter 6).
Understand anxiety and realize that avoidance only increases it.	Teach patient the dynamics of anxiety: not dangerous, not permanent, avoidance increases it.
Communicate life story to therapist.	Have patient relate the story of his/her life.
Teach resiliency skills.	Play *Bounce Back* to understand underlying processes in a non-threatening way (see Therapeutic Games, Chapter 7).

SHORT-TERM BEHAVIORAL GOALS: CHILD/ADOLESCENT	THERAPIST'S INTERVENTIONS
Discuss personal coping mechanisms developed to handle anxiety.	Investigate with patient possible patterns of withdrawal used to avoid anxiety.
Recognize and relate how family impacts the problem.	Explore familial impact on the problem.
Learn positive self-talk.	Teach patient positive self-talk to interrupt negative patterns.
Learn new breathing technique for dealing with anxiety.	Teach belly breathing to control anxiety (see Behavioral Techniques, Chapter 6).
Learn new relaxation techniques and how to avoid stress.	Assign patient to read, and have parent read to child, *The PTSD Workbook* (see Resources, Chapter 8).
Child: Read or have parent read to you assigned material and discuss with therapist. **Adolescent**: Read assigned material and discuss with therapist.	Assign adolescent to read and parent to read to child *Cool Cats, Calm Kids* and *Everything You Need to Know About Stress* or *The Worry Control Workbook* and have patients discuss with you (see Resources, Chapter 8).
Determine a "wellness date."	Discuss with patient and have him/her establish a date by which the PTSD will be cured. **Caution**: make sure the patient is willing to set a date. The arrangement can create performance anxiety. Make child aware that the date can be revised if necessary.
Shift focus of attention from problem to accomplishment.	Ask patient to describe accomplishments of past week.
Feel more confident as self-esteem improves.	Compliment patient to provide positive reinforcement whenever possible.

SHORT-TERM BEHAVIORAL GOALS: CHILD/ADOLESCENT	THERAPIST'S INTERVENTIONS
Child: Imitate puppets in creating an anchor to interrupt flashback. **Adolescent**: Create anchor to use at home, even after treatment, to bring you back to the present.	With child, have puppets teach ways they can create a safety net through use of breathing exercises and create an anchor (place thumb and pointer finger together) to awaken child from flashback and bring him/her into the here and now. Teach anchoring technique to adolescent.
Communicate problematic feelings to develop new skills or options.	Recommend strenuous aerobic exercise to help release frustrations.
Report results to therapist.	Provide positive reinforcement when patient reports back that he/she has challenged anxiety-provoking situations. Praise attempt and reward success.
Child: Learn how to deal with fears. **Adolescent**: Learn new coping skills to deal with the trauma.	Have parent read to child *Sometimes I'm Afraid* or *Don't Worry, Dear* and adolescent to read *Feel the Fear and Do It Anyway* (see Resources, Chapter 8).
Learn methods that can be used to advocate for yourself.	Instruct patient in the techniques of self-advocacy.
Understand that you can deal with these issues and bring treatment to an end successfully.	Develop a treatment termination plan, and explain issues of separation anxiety and dependency.

TREATMENT PLAN

POST-TRAUMATIC STRESS DISORDER

SHORT-TERM BEHAVIORAL GOALS: FAMILY	THERAPIST'S INTERVENTIONS
Improve communications among family members to reduce familial anxiety.	Conduct family sessions or refer for family therapy to reduce anxiety and improve communication skills within the family.
Family members share their feelings surrounding the trauma and their responses to it. Work together to deal with the issues. "Identified" patient is less alienated. Other members can help even if they just sit and listen.	Have family members explain their personal view of the trauma and its impact on each one of them. If other siblings were involved, see individually and collectively or refer for treatment. Explore how each family member can help self and others.
Feel permission to talk about the "crazy" way you feel.	Normalize feelings by helping members realize that it is normal to feel abnormal when dealing with trauma.
Identify any bizarre and debilitating residue trapped in your mind (soul) or body.	Explore for "freeze" response to trauma to help discharge negative energy. How is family acting differently?
Understand that PTSD is not a disease, but a dis-ease that can be felt within the body and can be healed.	Help family recognize that, in trauma, psychology becomes biology and is felt in your body as well as your mind.
Identify your response to the disaster.	Determine family's response to the traumatic event (fight, flight, or freeze, which constricts energy and makes us feel helpless with imploded anger, depression, and PTSD (see appropriate treatment plan).

SHORT-TERM BEHAVIORAL GOALS: FAMILY	THERAPIST'S INTERVENTIONS
Shift focus from problem to possible solutions.	If possible, have family imagine a future without the problem, and suggest actions that can be taken now to make that future possible.
Identify feelings of being out of control, and unable to soothe yourself, which creates a contagious fear that runs through the entire family.	Determine if family is caught in a double-bind (i.e., urged by the government to remain calm, but at the same time to stay alert to the continuing threats of terrorism).
Recognize that in dealing with children your actions speak louder than words.	Educate parents in the ways that children learn (imitation, identification, introjection). Teach them to recognize and correct incongruities between what they say and what they do.
Identify how you feel inside (shaky, trembling, etc.) as a guide for relieving biological reactions to trauma.	Help family create a climate for healing. Although difficult, it is similar to learning the customs of a new country. Guide them in shifting from thought to sensation. How do they feel inside their bodies? Sometimes, giving families permission to feel reduces pressure not to feel and it will go away. It's like letting the pressure out of a steam cooker.
Identify changes in your affect since the trauma.	Explore changes in affect as a result of the trauma.
Recognize that it may be normal to sometimes think about suicide as long as you don't act on the thought.	Inform family members that people under stress sometimes think about suicide, which is okay as long as they don't act on the thought.

SHORT-TERM BEHAVIORAL GOALS: FAMILY

THERAPIST'S INTERVENTIONS

Individual family members who may be suicidal recognize possible need for hospitalization. Patients with no actual plan in place commit to suicide pact with therapist and/or individual for treatment.

Identify suicidal family members and take appropriate action (hospitalization) for suicidal ideations with an active plan, Without a plan, make a suicide pact with therapist.

Get an experiential sense of how it feels to be traumatized.

Describe to family members how it feels to be traumatized.

Develop awareness of how your personal theory influences your cognition of the problem.

Explore family theory of the problem.

Learn to reach beyond automatic cognitive reactions in viewing the problem.

Expand family perspective beyond limited cognitive reactions.

Recognize the impact of your fears on other family members.

Help members realize the impact of their fears on other members of the family.

Help reduce unnecessary anxieties in those around you.

Teach family members that children need to play and have fun without concern about impending dangers. Adolescents need to know that all reasonable measures possible are being taken by the adults to assure their safety.

Begin to practice living in the here and now. The past is over and the present is the only time we have to learn, act, change, and heal.

Explain the theory of probability. Teach family members to stay in the here and now (not past or future) and focus on outcomes, not problems. Keep things in perspective. Explain the Atom Bomb story (see Chapter 1) and assign adult family members to read *Full Catastrophe Living* (see Resources, Chapter 8).

SHORT-TERM BEHAVIORAL GOALS: FAMILY	THERAPIST'S INTERVENTIONS
Learn techniques to reduce flashbacks and control anxieties.	If family members are willing and therapist is appropriately trained, use hypnosis to reduce anxiety within the family. The anxiety is contagious and so is the opposite effect. Ask one member to volunteer to learn relaxation techniques and proceed from there. Other family members can watch the technique (see Hypnosis, Behavioral Techniques, Chapter 6).
Family members reduce addictive news reports that tend to reinfect their fears and reinforce their anxieties.	Encourage family members to remain informed about world events, but to reduce the addictive listening to radio, watching television news, and reading newspaper accounts of the traumatic event and imminent terrorist activities.
Identify self-injury in family member. Shift attention from internal feelings to present day reality. Understand possible need for hospitalization to curtail or prevent self-injury.	Identify self-injury by family member as a response to the trauma, and explore the inner experience to interrupt the meaning of the act. In dealing with an untenable experience like trauma, people tend to dissociate, and physical pain of self-injury seems preferable to emotional pain.
Find alternate ways to cope with the present situation.	Explore with family members new ways to cope with the current situation (bring yourself into the here and now).
Identify ways in which you can be useful.	Identify any safety nets family members might use instead of self-injury. Warn against "secondary gains."
Release energy stored in distorted familial belief system.	Investigate family belief system and challenge and reframe distorted beliefs.

SHORT-TERM BEHAVIORAL GOALS: FAMILY	THERAPIST'S INTERVENTIONS
Shift focus from problem to possible solutions.	Ask family members to envision a future without PTSD and suggest actions they can take now to help make that future a reality.
Think about what treatment outcome would look like. Each family member explains in turn what he/she would like.	Ask each family member what he/she might want to say about each other when treatment is completed.
Family members realize they have the power to make important changes, even if they seem small.	Help family recognize they have an unusual opportunity to do some things differently.
Map out a realistic plan for change and a new direction.	Develop a SMART plan: Small, Measurable, Achievable, Realistic, Timelined goals (see Change, Behavioral Techniques, Chapter 6).
Family members are empowered. They realize they can create positive change one small step at a time.	Help family members to prioritize achievable goals.
Enhance your understanding of your condition and earn how other families have dealt with similar situations.	Assign homework reading: *Making Families Work and What to Do When They Don't, Whose Life Is It Anyway?* or *The PTSD Workbook* (see Resources, Chapter 8).
Reduce negative communication.	Develop a positive reinforcement system for family members to react better with each other and eliminate scapegoating.
Make use of available community resources.	Refer family to available resources in the community.
Family works together to develop a treatment termination plan.	Discuss termination issues and develop plan to terminate treatment.

BEREAVEMENT

Grief and bereavement are normal reactions to the death of a loved one, and become psychopathic only when the timing and intensity of the grief becomes debilitating.

When death is the result of a critical incident, such as the 9/11 terrorist attacks, the response is usually overwhelming. Addressing the psychological needs of the survivors to mitigate long-term suffering requires special skills, since each terrorist act opens up the wounds of people who have lost loved ones. In the early stages of bereavement, most people are in denial, numbed out, or in an altered state of consciousness. Ironically, in the Impact Stage (Jozefowski, 1999, p. 55) it is normal to feel abnormal. Bereavement as a result of catastrophe is far different from bereavement due to death by natural causes. When grievers start to feel the reality of their loss, they begin to yearn and search for their loved ones. They deny reality. Their loved ones can't really be dead; they must be hurt or lost. Maybe we can still find them. A good example is the case of the police officers and firefighters in the 9/11 disaster who refused to stop looking for their buddies.

Symptoms of bereavement may include anger, depression, sleep disorders, eating disorders, or substance abuse. Unfortunately, there are no simple cookbook answers for helping grievers. However, it is important to "be there," help normalize reactions, and encourage the expression of feelings when people are ready to talk. After 9/11, some people were not ready to talk about it for years. It all depends on the circumstances and the individual. It is important to meet the person or patient where he/she is. Someone who is unfamiliar with therapy can be as harmful or more harmful than no therapy at all.

Although children from infancy through the early years of childhood may experience tremendous losses, they may not understand the concept of death. From ages three through five they deny death or begin to accept it as something that happens to older people. It isn't until ages six through nine that they begin grappling with the concept. Pre-adolescents see death as a finality, while adolescents may question the meaning of life. Those who make it into adulthood psychologically alive continue to modify their ideas. However, we are all confronted by death in the aftershock of a tragedy.

The duration of bereavement and how it is expressed may vary widely in different cultural groups. The bereavement symptoms are accepted as normal by most cultures as long as they don't get out of hand or last too long. Symptoms may be similar to major depressive disorder, and include sadness, insomnia, poor appetite, and weight loss. These symptoms are usually accepted as normal unless they persist for more than two months. Then a diagnosis of major depressive disorder may be appropriate. Certain symptoms may be helpful in differentiating bereavement from depression. Bereavement may include guilt about one's actions or lack of action at the time of death, thinking that he or she too should have died, as well as auditory or visual hallucinations of the deceased. Other psychological symptoms may include unrelated guilt, preoccupation with feelings of worthlessness, marked psychomotor retardation, prolonged functional impairment, other hallucinatory experiences, bizarre behaviors, and suicidal or homicidal thoughts.

A diagnosis of acute stress disorder (ASD) may be appropriate within the first month following the disaster, while a diagnosis of post-traumatic stress disorder requires symptoms that last at least two months.

In some instances, a traumatic incident can trigger a brief psychotic reaction or somatization in the victim. If a person is suffering from psychological symptoms prior to the trauma, the incident will more than likely exacerbate the underlying symptoms. When a child has died, parents often feel that no one can help or understand the complex ramifications of their tragedy.

BEHAVIORAL SYMPTOMS

BEREAVEMENT

- Denial or numbness
- Major persistent anger or depression
- Intense emotional feelings (rage, anger, screaming)
- Inability to fall asleep or stay asleep
- Nightmares or night terrors
- Distressing recollections of the event
- Loss of, or increase in, appetite
- Separation anxiety
- Hyperarousal or exaggerated startle response
- Adjustment disorders
- Serious impairment in activities of daily living
- Helplessness or hopelessness
- Guilt over being a survivor
- Constant anxiety or panic attacks
- Hears voice of, or sees transitory images of, the deceased
- Somatization
- Acts out in various ways including substance abuse

OBJECTIVES OF TREATMENT

BEREAVEMENT

Select one or more:

- Educate patient about dealing with bereavement in catastrophes
- Identify patient response: fight, flight, or freeze
- Help patient understand it is normal to feel abnormal in times like these
- Help patient realize there are four categories of response: emotional, cognitive, biological, and behavioral
- Help mourners through the grieving process
- Reduce pervasive anger, guilt, anxiety, and worry
- Help family regain internal and external control
- Diminish fear responses to improve quality of life
- If children are involved, teach parents about concepts of death at different ages
- Help patient understand he/she needs to take time to grieve
- Resolve feelings of despair and hopelessness
- Diminish symptoms of anxiety or survivor guilt
- Eliminate sleep disturbances and nightmares
- Teach strategies to reduce stressors to critical events
- Demonstrate appropriate communication skills (active listening, questioning, mirroring, paraphrasing)
- Restore normal eating patterns
- Reduce addictive news watching to preclude reinfecting self
- Encourage compliance with educational programs and referrals
- Teach patient the Phoenix Model of grieving (Impact, Chaos, Adaptation, Equilibrium, and Transformation).
- Reframe irrational beliefs
- Promote socialization, reduce alienation
- Develop personal rituals to ensure safety and empowerment
- Help patient rise from the ashes of grief
- Develop discharge plan for coping with everyday life

TREATMENT PLAN

BEREAVEMENT

SHORT-TERM BEHAVIORAL GOALS: ADULT	THERAPIST'S INTERVENTIONS
Collaborate with therapist to reduce overwhelming stressors.	Attempt to establish a therapeutic alliance with patient to help deal with the overwhelming stressors resulting from traumatic event.
Identify the circumstances of the death and your reaction to it.	Identify the nature of the death and how it affects patient.
Patient is treated for other grief reactions to death.	If patient exhibits other symptoms associated with death – acute stress disorder (ASD), post-traumatic stress disorder (PTSD), depression, etc. – treat individually (see appropriate treatment plan and integrate with this plan).
Realize it is normal to feel abnormal under the circumstances.	Explore how patient is responding and help him/her understand that it is normal to feel abnormal at a time like this.
Take the time to mourn.	Encourage patient to take the time to mourn rather than repress memories of the death or traumatic event.
Identify your style of dealing with death.	Explore how patient deals with death – overtly or covertly?
Identify underlying death anxieties.	Investigate patient's underlying death anxiety.
Identify your religious beliefs.	Explore patient's religious beliefs and their relation to death.

SHORT-TERM BEHAVIORAL GOALS: ADULT	THERAPIST'S INTERVENTIONS
Learn the stages of death, and understand that mourning is normal and important.	Educate patient about the stages of death (denial, anger, bargaining, depression, and accommodation) to help understand normal grieving.
Realize that it is okay to express your reactions.	Encourage patient to express pain and grief reactions to loss.
Realize that death anxiety is universal and can lead to other problems.	Educate patient that death anxiety is universal and denial of it can lead to further problems.
Become aware of childhood concepts of death.	Teach patient age-appropriate childhood concepts of death.
Recognize fears and feelings of self-blame.	Evaluate patient's fears and negative self-blame related to the death.
Learn to reach beyond automatic cognitive reactions in dealing with death.	Expand patient's perspective beyond automatic cognitive reactions.
Confront thoughts of unrealistic or exaggerated consequences.	Confront distorted reactions to trigger situations.
Learn to self-soothe rather than to catastrophize	Help patient develop coping mechanisms that are soothing rather than frightening (staying in the here and now, not the past or future). Although this may be difficult, help patient to realize that what he/she worries about often does not happen.
Enter treatment for other crisis-related disorders.	Evaluate patient for other disorders related to the disaster (see appropriate treatment plan).
Become aware of how your personal theory influences your cognition.	Explore patient's theory of the crisis.

SHORT-TERM BEHAVIORAL GOALS: ADULT	THERAPIST'S INTERVENTIONS
Learn how to better deal with anxiety.	Teach patient the dynamics of anxiety: not dangerous, not permanent, avoidance only increases it.
Understand that certain tasks are necessary for you to continue to live.	Teach patient that grief is not a passive state. The ability to move beyond it involves adaptation to a world without the deceased.
Treat your sleep problems.	Evaluate and treat sleep problems and nightmares (see appropriate treatment plan).
Help yourself move through a transitional period toward greater development.	Teach patient the phases of the Phoenix Model: Impact, Chaos, Adaptation, Equilibrium, Transformation.
Identify the Phoenix stage you are in.	Help patient determine where he/she is in the Phoenix Model and what to expect in the next phase.
Understand your need to maintain stability, establish security measures, and reach out to others.	During the Impact Stage, help patient to understand the need for food, shelter, sleep, safety, security, and preliminary belonging. Guide patient in developing a support system.
Recognize the need for physiological stability while acknowledging and expressing grief and resisting isolation.	During the Chaos Stage, the major task is to maintain physiological stability while talking about grief and staying connected.
Understand that during times of crisis and fear, there can be no growth.	The following Adaptation Stage is aimed at normalization. Create a realistic outline to live in today's world while encouraging the expression of feelings.

SHORT-TERM BEHAVIORAL GOALS: ADULT

Identify the changes you must make in order to generate a new way of living without your loved ones.

Realize you are accountable for your actions.

Become familiar with the steps in the development of Equilibrium.

THERAPIST'S INTERVENTIONS

Help patient evaluate changes in his/her lifestyle, relationships with others, and self.

Help patient see he/she can use the pain of loss to push forward.

Teach patient the nine steps in developing Equilibrium (Jozefowski, 1999):

1. **Rehearsing** – trying out new behaviors

2. **Integration** – new pieces of self are interwoven with the old

3. **Taking Risks** – override old fears by facing new challenges leading to self-actualization and realistic self-confidence

4. **Beliefs** – evaluate old beliefs, discard any that carry the potential for suffering, and develop new, healthier ones

5. **Forgiveness or Creative Attunement** – forgiveness encourages healing while anger binds you to the traumatic act

6. **Spirituality or Soul-searching** – some people find a life purpose in religion, while others search inside themselves

7. **Grief Revisited** – this is not a regression, but a normal reaction that may emerge on the anniversary of the death, a birthday, or a wedding day

SHORT-TERM BEHAVIORAL GOALS: ADULT	THERAPIST'S INTERVENTIONS
	8. **The End of Mourning** – face the challenge, begin to become familiar with your new life, and choose to move on
	9. **Transformation** – in the Fifth phase of the Phoenix Model, honor your missing loved one by creating meaning in your life and continuing on the path of self-actualization.
Assist in developing a termination plan and bring therapy to an end.	Develop termination plan. Resolve remaining dependency and separation issues, and terminate.

TREATMENT PLAN

BEREAVEMENT

SHORT-TERM BEHAVIORAL GOALS: CHILD/ADOLESCENT	THERAPIST'S INTERVENTIONS
Develop a therapeutic relationship to help get through the loss of a loved one.	Engage patient in an age-appropriate therapeutic relationship to enhance the outcome of treatment.
Identify how you are trying to cope with the death.	Investigate how the patient is attempting to deal with the death.
Express how the loss has affected you.	Determine what effect the loss has had on the patient.
Realize that you can look to others for support.	Explore and identify available support systems. Can members of the extended family help the patient adjust to the "emotional shockwave."
Understand that children mourn death differently from adults.	Educate child or adolescent about how children mourn. (The mourning process in children is not linear and is repeated as the child matures and understands death from a more sophisticated perspective.) They may experience sadness, denial, guilt, anger, or shame, and may reexperience the mourning at every milestone of life.
Understand that it is normal to feel sad at times like these.	In the Sadness Stage, help child to recognize that it is not unusual to feel depression, withdraw from friends, and abandon playful activities. They may want to stay in bed, lose interest in usual activities, and take unnecessary risks. Younger children may not understand that death is final, and may need to be repeatedly reminded.

SHORT-TERM BEHAVIORAL GOALS: CHILD/ADOLESCENT	THERAPIST'S INTERVENTIONS
Recognize that it is permissible to play while grieving.	Most children have a limited capacity to tolerate grief. In the Denial Stage, teach child it is okay to seek relief in play.
Understand parent has died, even if you do not want to believe it.	If the death involves a parent especially a parent of the same gender, recognize that the normal development process of identification has been interrupted. As a result, child may remain stuck in the Denial Stage.
Identify guilt feelings as a result of the death.	Explore patient's feelings of guilt related to the death, especially if a parent died suddenly.
Understand that insecurity is a normal childhood reaction to death and reduce the need to "act out" your anger and confusion.	Explore patient's anger or confusion to reduce "acting out" since children's emotions about death are often confusing and overwhelming.
Discuss your feelings with other children to reduce the stigma of shame.	Refer to a group where other children have lost loved ones in order to reduce the stigma of shame children often feel when a close family member has died.
Realize that it is okay to preserve the image of your lost loved one. The attachment will lessen over time as the child grows up.	Children rarely reach the Acceptance Stage since they may need to preserve the lost person's presence to get through the milestones of growing up. Assure them that they can hold on to the attachment until they feel ready to give it up.
Use therapist as a role model to experience death of a loved one.	Share with patient how you experienced the loss of a loved one (first death, first funeral, etc.).

SHORT-TERM BEHAVIORAL GOALS: CHILD/ADOLESCENT	THERAPIST'S INTERVENTIONS
Get a better understanding of the loved one's death.	With younger children, use puppets to have a pretend conversation about death. The deceased can even be represented by a puppet to make the experience more real and explain the details of what happened.
Adolescent has final conversation with the deceased, discovering details of the death and saying last words.	With older children or adolescents, role-play a conversation using an empty chair to represent the deceased. Provide the patient an opportunity to ask questions and say final words to the deceased.
Feel respected and understood and express what happened, rather than your feelings.	If patient is reluctant to talk about death, "don't push the river." Instead, respect the patient's defense of denial and empathize with the pain of losing a loved one. Go beyond denial by becoming more concretized and ask about details of the death and funeral. If child still refuses to talk, respect the defense and provide a sound holding environment until he/she is ready.
Regard your feelings as normal.	Investigate what life has been like for the child after the death and normalize what patient says he/she is feeling (i.e., it is okay to feel angry, other children feel angry, sad, and guilty in these circumstances).
Learn about funerals and what to expect.	If funeral has not yet taken place, teach patient what to expect.
Realize that you can choose to view the body or not as you see fit.	Many children are afraid of a dead body. Let patient know it is his/her choice to view the body or not.

SHORT-TERM BEHAVIORAL GOALS: CHILD/ADOLESCENT	THERAPIST'S INTERVENTIONS
Identify irrational beliefs about death.	Explore patient's irrational beliefs about death.
Reframe beliefs about fears and anxieties using evidence-based reality.	Discuss beliefs and develop rational alternatives.
Explain your involvement or lack of involvement in the funeral ceremonies.	If funeral has transpired, explore with patient how it was handled. Was the patient excluded to avoid upsetting him/her? Was the patient included in the process to realistically involve him/her in mourning the death?
Use relaxation techniques and guided imagery to gain control over feelings	With parental permission, teach patient relaxation techniques and guided imagery to master anxieties. (See *Behavioral Management Guide: Essential Treatment Strategies for Adult Psychotherapy* or *Behavioral Management Guide: Essential Treatment Strategies for the Psychotherapy of Children, Their Parents, and Families.*)
Undergo treatment for sleep problems.	Investigate for symptoms of a sleep disorder, nightmares, insomnia, or night terrors (see appropriate treatment plan).
Recognize that human beings are not perfect and reduce stressors imposed on yourself.	Remind patient that human beings are not perfect.
Identify the impact of your loss on your schoolwork.	Explore for indications of academic problems related to the death and treat accordingly (see appropriate treatment plan).

SHORT-TERM BEHAVIORAL GOALS: CHILD/ADOLESCENT	THERAPIST'S INTERVENTIONS
Recognize that others also feel bad when a loved one dies and that talking about it is helpful.	Investigate for feelings of low self-esteem related to the loss.
Identify your reactions to the death of a sibling.	If a sibling has died, explore how the surviving child is dealing with the loss. Does survivor blame himself/herself or feel guilty?
Understand there can also be physical responses to loss.	Explore for any physical responses such as hyperactivity or somatization (tightness in the chest, stomach pains, fatigue, etc.).
Understand anxiety and realize that avoidance makes it worse.	Teach patient the dynamics of anxiety: not dangerous, not permanent, confrontation can promote change.
Communicate your life story to the therapist.	Have patient relate the story of his/her life.
Express suppressed feelings about saying final goodbye to a loved one.	Play *The Goodbye Game* to dispel myths and false ideas about death (see Therapeutic Games, Chapter 7).
Discuss personal coping mechanisms developed by you to handle death.	Investigate with patient possible patterns of social withdrawal or overactivity as a way of dealing with the death.
Recognize and discuss your family's impact on the problem.	Explore the family's impact on the problem. Are they supportive? Do they talk about the death? Pretend it never happened?
Learn positive self-talk.	Teach patient positive self-talk to interrupt negative patterns.

SHORT-TERM BEHAVIORAL GOALS: CHILD/ADOLESCENT	THERAPIST'S INTERVENTIONS
Identify the changes you must make to generate a new way of life without the deceased loved one.	Help patient evaluate changes in his/her lifestyle, relationships with others, and self.
Realize that you are accountable for your actions.	Urge patient to see he/she has choices that can push him/her forward.
Shift focus from the problem to accomplishments.	Ask patient to describe accomplishments of the past week.
Feel more confident as self-esteem improves.	Compliment patient at every opportunity to provide positive reinforcement for accomplishments.
Read assign books to gain further information about dealing with loss.	Assign patient to read or have read to him/her *When Someone Dies* (see Resources, Chapter 8).
Learn how to avoid hazards and grow through bereavement.	Assign older adolescent to read *Facing Change: Falling Apart and Coming Together Again in the Teen Years* (see Resources, Chapter 8).
Learn to advocate for yourself.	Teach patient the techniques of self-advocacy.
Understand you can deal with these issues and bring treatment to an end.	Discuss separation anxiety and dependency, and terminate treatment.

TREATMENT PLAN

BEREAVEMENT

SHORT-TERM BEHAVIORAL GOALS: FAMILY	THERAPIST'S INTERVENTIONS
Improve communication among family members to reduce familial anxiety.	Conduct family sessions to reduce alienation, improve communication skills, and enhance understanding of the trauma on the entire family.
Identify unsatisfied needs and get help.	Determine if basic needs are being met (food, clothing, shelter, safety, etc.) and, if necessary, refer family for (FEMA). Discuss "secondary trauma" and frustration of bureaucratic red tape.
Identify outside sources that can lend temporary support during the grieving process.	Identify if there are members of the extended family who can provide additional support.
Each family member shares his/her reactions to the loss.	Explore individual reactions to the trauma. Learn how each family member felt before and after the loss.
Demonstrate boundaries, alliances, triangles, and emotional currents that may exacerbate the problem.	Use family sculpturing to explore boundaries, alliances, triangulation, and emotional currents (see Behavioral Techniques, Chapter 6).
Validate your feelings of overwhelming helplessness as a result of the traumatic death.	Provide a haven for mourning by validating the patients' feelings, confusion, paralyzing fear, and anger over the death of a loved one.
Each family member identifies his/her reaction to the loss.	Explore individual reactions to the death. Determine how each member felt before and after the death.

SHORT-TERM BEHAVIORAL GOALS: FAMILY	THERAPIST'S INTERVENTIONS
Share your view of the deceased and how he/she died in order to verbalize your sorrow.	Have each member share his/her view about the deceased and the death to give words to their sorrow, which can be cathartic.
Share ideas about coping with other family members and the therapist.	Discuss methods of coping.
Understand that it takes courage to create meaning out of the tragic death.	Help patients realize that the task of finding meaning in the death of a loved one will take extraordinary courage.
Become aware of the normal stages of grieving and what to expect from each other.	If the rest of the family is unaware of the stages of grief, explain both the Kubler-Ross Model: Denial, Anger Bargaining, Depression, and Acceptance (Kubler-Ross, 1997) and the Phoenix Model: Impact, Chaos, Adaptation, Equilibrium, and Transformation (Jozefowski, 1999).
Explain how you are attempting to deal with the death.	Explore the ways in which the family is trying to deal with the death. Are they mourning silently or trying to share feelings with one another?
Provide opportunity for children to participate.	Encourage parents to include children in funeral or memorial activities to provide an opportunity to say goodbye to the deceased and gain support from other family members.
Realize that children mourn differently at different ages.	Educate parents and other adults about children's concept of death, and become aware that children mourn differently at different ages.

SHORT-TERM BEHAVIORAL GOALS: FAMILY	THERAPIST'S INTERVENTIONS
Identify your irrational thoughts and beliefs related to the death.	Explore irrational thoughts and feelings over the death. Do they feel guilty? Do they blame each other?
Develop rational alternatives.	Reframe irrational beliefs using evidence-based reality.
Work through remaining issues psychodynamically with the deceased.	Use role-playing with an empty chair representing the deceased. Ask each family member to talk to the deceased and resolve any unfinished business they may have.
Explore ways in which the family can grow out of loss.	Have family imagine a future without their loved one and suggest actions they may take now to help grow, even in the middle of loss.
Recognize hidden blame in order to work it out.	Explore for hidden blame among family members and resolve it.
Identify possible survivor's guilt, learn that it is normal, and resolve it.	Investigate for survivor's guilt and explain that is a normal part of the grieving process.
Realize you can find hope through growth and adaptation.	Educate family about the phases of adaptation and help them realize that their old life has ended. Help them to let go and recognize this process as the birthplace of hope.
Become empowered by the realization that through trial and error you can take on new roles and grow.	Assist family to establish a new equilibrium by taking on new roles and planning a life without the deceased.
Identify the changes you must make to generate a new way of being without the deceased loved one.	Help family evaluate the changes needed in their lifestyle, relationships with others, and themselves.

SHORT-TERM BEHAVIORAL GOALS: FAMILY	THERAPIST'S INTERVENTIONS
Realize that you are accountable for your actions and have individual choices to make in order to get beyond the loss.	Help family members see that they each have choices that can push their lives forward.
Learn the phases of Equilibrium.	Teach family the nine steps in developing Equilibrium (Jozefowski, 1999):

1. **Rehearsing** – trying out new behaviors

2. **Integration** – new pieces of self are interwoven with the old

3. **Taking Risks** – override old fears by facing new challenges leading to self-actualization and realistic self-confidence

4. **Beliefs** – evaluate old beliefs, discard any that carry the potential for suffering, and develop new, healthier ones

5. **Forgiveness or Creative Attunement** – forgiveness encourages healing while anger binds you to the traumatic act

6. **Spirituality or Soul-searching** – some people find a life purpose in religion, while others search inside themselves

7. **Grief Revisited** – this is not a regression, but a normal reaction that may emerge on the anniversary of the death, a birthday, or a wedding day

8. **The End of Mourning** – face the challenge, begin to become familiar with your new life, and choose to move on

9. **Transformation** – in the Fifth phase of the Phoenix Model, honor your missing loved one by creating meaning in your life and continuing on the path of self-actualization.

SHORT-TERM BEHAVIORAL GOALS: FAMILY	THERAPIST'S INTERVENTIONS
Strengthen yourself by developing new and productive life roles.	Help each family member to build self-confidence through realistic self-actualization.
Develop a SMART plan.	Develop a SMART action plan (O'Hanlon, 2000): Small, Measurable, Achievable, Realistic, Timelined Goals (see Change, Behavioral Techniques, Chapter 6).
Recognize you have the power to make important changes, even if they now seem small.	Help family members to see that they have the power to do some important things differently.
Family members are empowered and recognize they can create positive change.	Ask family members to relate what they have accomplished in the past week.
Identify individual transformation.	Have each family member explain ways in which he/she has transformed since the death of their loved one.
Read the assigned books to enhance your understanding of grief.	Read *The Phoenix Phenomenon: Rising from the Ashes of Grief.* Also recommended: *Living Beyond Loss: Death in the Family* (see Resources, Chapter 8).
Make use of available community resources.	Refer family to available bereavement group in the community.
Reduce negative communication.	Develop a system of positive reinforcement to improve interactions and reduce scapegoating.
Work together to develop a treatment termination plan.	Discuss termination issue of dependency and separation anxiety, develop termination plan and terminate treatment.

4
EXISTING DISORDERS
AFFECTED BY TRAUMA

In addition to the major disorders caused by trauma and presented in Chapter 3, there are other existing disorders that may be exacerbated by a traumatic event. These disorders existed at the time of the traumatic event and were worsened by it. They are covered here under the general category of Anxiety Disorders.

ANXIETY DISORDERS

Statistical analyses of the 9/11 event are still under way. However, according to the National Institute of Mental Health (NIMH) (http://www.nimh.gov), more than 19 million Americans aged 18 to 54 had existing anxiety disorders when the Twin Towers crumbled. Anxiety disorders usually coexist with depression, eating disorders, and substance abuse. Many people have more than one anxiety disorder. Among these disorders are panic disorder, specific phobia, social phobia, generalized anxiety disorder, obsessive-compulsive disorder, and separation anxiety disorder.

Panic Disorder

The essential feature of panic disorder is the persistence of panic attacks and worry about the possible indications or consequences that may occur. The attacks are not associated with a situational trigger such as post-traumatic stress disorder, and at least two panic attacks are required to justify a diagnosis. They may appear suddenly, with or without agoraphobia. The frequency and severity of panic attacks may vary greatly, but they have been commonly described as feeling like a car is coming at you at 90 miles an hour with no way to escape. The age of onset is usually between adolescence and the mid-30s, but this might have changed since the 9/11 disaster.

Transient tachycardia and moderate elevation of blood pressure may occur during a typical attack. Some victims feel like they are going "crazy," have some life-threatening illness, or are losing control. Concerns about the next attack may often be associated with avoidant behavior. For example, one patient was afraid that if she suffered a panic attack, she would faint. That, in turn, meant she couldn't drive her car, which created a problem in getting to work, which was not accessible by public transportation. An extremely social person before her panic attacks, she applied for disability and became a comparative recluse.

Many individuals who suffer from panic attacks report constant or recurring feelings of anxiety associated with specific situations or events. Many of them somatize and go from doctor to doctor hoping to find an organic cause for their problem. People with this disorder are prone to problems with employment and personal relations. They may become demoralized and ashamed, and abandon normal activities. They may be absent from work and frequently visit hospital emergency rooms for treatment.

Panic attack sufferers usually have multiple disorders. Approximately 50% to 60% of people suffering panic attacks also develop depressive disorders. A subset of this group turns to substance abuse to self-medicate, using the substance as a self-soothing salve. Some 15% to 30% of panic attack victims also report agoraphobia, 8% to 10% report obsessive-compulsive disorder, 10% to 20% report specific phobia, and 10% of them complain of generalized anxiety disorder. Many of them had separation anxiety as children.

First-degree biological relatives of panic attack victims have a four to seven times greater chance of developing panic disorder. There are indications it may be contagious. After treating a patient with this disorder for a considerable period of time, I often feel my own anxiety rising in response to our sessions.

Specific Phobia

Specific phobia involves the persistent, excessive, and unreasonable fear of objects or situations, which provoke an immediate anxiety response known as a panic attack. In children, anxiety may be expressed by crying, tantrums, clinging, or freezing. Although adults or adolescents may realize that the fear is excessive or unreasonable, children clearly may not. Usually, the feared object or situation is avoided, but sometimes may be endured under duress. For children under 18 years of age, the phobia must significantly interfere with the individual's daily schedule and persist for more than six months to qualify for a diagnosis of specific phobia. There are five general types of specific phobia: animal, natural environment, blood injection, situational, and other. Such fears are common in children, but the level of impairment is usually insufficient to justify a diagnosis. Fear of animals is common and usually is transitory.

Social Phobia

Still another common phobia is social phobia, marked by the persistent fear of social situations in which evaluation by others is possible. The individual is afraid of acting in an embarrassing or humiliating manner and often reacts to social interaction with panic attack. Usually, the victim recognizes the fear as unreasonable and excessive.

Onset of this disorder typically appears in the mid-teens after a childhood of shyness. Children appear excessively timid in unfamiliar settings and shrink away from contact with people they do not know. Characteristically, they do not participate in group play or other social activities, and may cling to, or need to remain close to, a familiar adult. Such children do poorly in school, may be school-phobic, and avoid age-appropriate social activities. Mutism may exist in extreme cases. When onset is in adolescence, social phobia leads to a decreased ability to function academically. Some studies show that the phobia is more prevalent in girls than boys.

Generalized Anxiety Disorder

Generalized anxiety disorder (GAD) is characterized by excessive anxiety and worry about various events and activities that persists for at least six months. In children, the anxiety and worry are accompanied by at least one other major symptom such as restlessness, irritability, fatigue, difficulty concentrating, muscle tension, or disturbed sleep. The duration and intensity of the anxiety and worry is usually out of proportion with the likelihood of the anticipated or feared event. Children with this disorder tend to worry about their competence, or the quality of their performance, in routine school activities, sporting events, or at home. They may be insecure, overly conforming, and perfectionist, and are often overanxious in seeking approval and reassurance. It is common for individuals with generalized anxiety disorder to also suffer from depression or other anxiety disorders.

Obsessive-Compulsive Disorder

Obsessive-compulsive disorder (OCD) is marked by persistent, time-con-suming obsessions or compulsions that cause significant distress or impairment in the activities of everyday life. Obsessive characteristics are: inappropriate and intrusive ideas, thoughts, impulses, and images that cause anxiety or distress. These may take the form of thoughts about contamination, repeated doubts, the need for a specific pattern of order, sexual imagery, aggressive impulses, or rigid adherence to rules, rituals, or routines. Compulsions are repetitive behaviors or mental acts designed to relieve anxiety or distress, or to prevent a dreaded event. Common compulsions include washing and cleaning, counting, checking, and other repetitive actions. Most patients with obsessive-compulsive disorder have a weak internal locus of control. They believe they can take care of themselves and control what happens in their lives. Unexpected events will push them into further crisis as they attempt to develop further compulsions or obsessions to compensate.

Although most adults realize that the obsessions or compulsions are excessive or unrealistic, children may not have the cognitive ability to make the judgment that their thoughts and behaviors are out of contact with reality.

Separation Anxiety Disorder

Separation anxiety disorder involves excessive anxiety over being sepa-rated from home or from a major attachment figure. The anxiety must occur before age 18 and persist for at least four weeks to qualify for the diagnosis. The anxiety is beyond that considered appropriate for the child's development level.

Adolescents with this disorder fear traveling by themselves and may be reluctant to go to school, camp, visit a friend's house, or go on errands alone. This can lead to decrease in major academic activities and social withdrawal. They may display clinging behavior and shadow a parent around the house.

They typically have difficulty at bedtimes, and nightmares focus on feared destruction of the family by catastrophe. If separation is immi-nent, physical complaints may include headaches, nausea, palpitations, dizziness, or feeling faint. Children with this disorder may be demand-ing, intrusive, and in need of constant attention. Their demands often lead to parental frustration and resentment, and conflict within the family.

Although usually considered a disorder of childhood and adoles-cence, separation anxiety disorder often accompanies the child into adulthood, where it can easily be misdiagnosed.

BEHAVIORAL SYMPTOMS
ANXIETY DISORDERS

PANIC DISORDER

Symptoms develop quickly and reach a peak in a few minutes.

- Palpitations, pounding heart, increased pulse
- Perspiration
- Trembling or shaking
- Shortness of breath
- Feeling of smothering or choking
- Chest pain
- Nausea
- Dizziness
- Derealization or depersonalization
- Fear of losing control, going crazy, or dying
- Numbness, tingling
- Chills or hot flashes

AGORAPHOBIA

- Anxiety over being in a situation or place where escape may be difficult or impossible, or where a panic attack may be embarrassing
- Anxiety over being in a situation or place where help may not be available in case of a panic attack
- The situation or place is avoided with duress or endured with the support of a companion

SPECIFIC PHOBIA

- Excessive and unreasonable fear of an object or situation
- Immediate anxiety when exposed to object or situation
- Excessively clingy
- Throws tantrums or cries a great deal
- Freezes (unable to act)
- Fails to recognize unreasonable nature of the fear
- Avoids or endures the object or situational trigger
- The distress interferes with the patient's daily life activities

SOCIAL PHOBIA

- Persistent fear of social interactions where evaluation by others is possible
- Fear of acting in social situations in an embarrassing or humiliating way
- Exposure to social situations gives rise to panic attacks
- Patient recognizes the fear as excessive or unreasonable
- Feared social situations are avoided or endured under duress
- The fear and duress interfere significantly with the patient's life
- The fear and duress are unrelated to drugs, medication, or a general medical condition

GENERALIZED ANXIETY DISORDER

- Feels restless
- Fatigues easily
- Has difficulty concentrating
- Is often irritable
- Displays muscular tension
- Has difficulty getting to sleep or staying asleep
- Complains of multiple physical ailments
- Symptoms impair patient's daily activities

OBSESSIVE-COMPULSIVE DISORDER

Obsessions
- Irrational or exaggerated perception of what is dangerous
- Overreaction to external events
- Poor internal locus of control
- Intrusive, inappropriate thoughts, impulses, or images that cause anxiety or distress
- Suppresses these stimuli by ritualized thought or action
- Recognizes the stimuli as the products of his/her own mind (children may not)

Compulsions
- Acts out repetitive physical or mental tasks to reduce or eliminate distress or to prevent a dreaded event
- The behavior is not connected in a realistic way with the event
- Patient recognizes the obsessions or compulsions as excessive or unrealistic (may not be true of children)

- The obsessions and compulsions are time-consuming, cause distress, and interfere with the patient's daily activities
- Unrealistic or rigid adherence to rules, rituals, and routines

SEPARATION ANXIETY DISORDER

- Excessive, inappropriate anxiety when separated from home or major attachment figure
- Persistent fear of losing major attachment figure, or of harm coming to the figure
- Persistent worry that a catastrophic event will result in separation from attachment figure
- Reluctance or refusal to leave home or go to school for fear of separation
- Fear of being alone
- Fear of going to sleep without closeness of attachment figure
- Repeated nightmare focused on separation by catastrophe
- Somatization in anticipation of imminent separation
- Symptoms persist for four weeks or more
- Symptoms cause significant distress or impairment in academic and social functioning

OBJECTIVES OF TREATMENT

ANXIETY DISORDERS

- Diminish excessive fear of object or situation
- Decrease anxiety when exposed to object or situation
- Eliminate need to avoid or endure object or situation
- Eliminate interference with patient's activities of daily life
- Reduce alienation and promote socialization
- Reduce irrational beliefs
- Restore patient to optimal level of functioning
- Reduce pervasive anxiety and worry
- Diminish shyness
- Diminish fear of social situations
- Reduce frequency of panic attacks
- Eliminate school phobia
- Reduce and eliminate fear of embarrassment in social interactions
- Eliminate need for avoidance of social interactions
- Encourage compliance with educational programs and referrals
- Reduce irrational beliefs
- Promote socialization
- Diminish symptoms of anxiety (restlessness, fatigue, difficulty concentrating, irritability, somatization, sleep disturbance)
- Teach patient to focus on outcomes, not possibilities
- Ameliorate obsessive thoughts, impulses, and images that cause anxiety or distress
- Develop a stronger internal locus of control
- Educate patient about Double-Bind Theory
- Educate patient about full catastrophe and the power of living in the here and now
- Teach patient the contagion of fear
- Reduce irrational beliefs, fears of loss, catastrophe
- Reduce fear of being alone
- Encourage school attendance, reduce alienation
- Eliminate nightmares, establish normal bedtime routine

TREATMENT PLAN

ANXIETY DISORDERS

SHORT-TERM BEHAVIORAL GOALS: ADULTS	THERAPIST'S INTERVENTIONS
Collaborate with therapist to reduce overwhelming stressors.	Attempt to establish a therapeutic alliance with patient to help deal with the overwhelming stressors.
Identify the nature of your anxiety disorder. Is it ongoing or did it just occur?	Investigate history of patient's anxiety disorder. Is it acute or chronic?
Learn that anxiety is not dangerous or permanent.	Teach patient the dynamics of anxiety.
Identify family history of the disorder.	Explore family history of the disorder. Is it a family coping style in which the anxieties of other family members impinge on the patient? Is family ritualistic or superstitious?
Explain the events and situations that trigger your anxiety.	Explore the cues that result in panic attacks and anxiety in the patient.
Examine irrational beliefs, and reframe them using evidence-based reality.	Identify and reframe irrational beliefs.
Identify your internal locus of control.	Explore control. Does patient feel in control of his/her life or are external events in control of patient's life?
Do you feel double-bound by the national response to terrorism?	Explain Double-Bind theory. Does patient feel helpless and hopeless as result of terrorism?
Realize that fears and anxieties block reason and lead to ritualistic behaviors.	Educate patient about anxiety and fears.

SHORT-TERM BEHAVIORAL GOALS: ADULTS	THERAPIST'S INTERVENTIONS
Understand that the usual responses to trauma are pathological. At least with fight or flight, you discharge pent-up energy while the freeze response results in immobility and helplessness, which exacerbate anxiety-driven disorders.	Discuss fight, flight, or freeze theory with patient.
Understand that you cannot ward off anxiety by adherence to rules, rituals, and routines.	Help patient to recognize that rigid adherence to rules, rituals, and routines will not reduce anxiety. Warn him/her that changing behaviors can create anxiety.
Learn the nature of obsessive-compulsive disorder and the impact of critical incident events or fears of bio-chemical warfare and how they impinge on an already compromised ego.	If patient has OCD, instruct him/her on the nature of anxiety and how critical incident events can exacerbate anxiety and create further problems. Explain that rituals or obsessions often are actually unconscious wishes to ward off bad things or thoughts and prevent them through "magical thinking."
Understand that therapy can control or reduce your symptoms and make your life more enjoyable.	Soothe patient by reassuring him/her that therapy can help control or reduce symptoms to make their lives more livable.
Comply with psychiatric referral.	If appropriate, refer patient for psychiatric evaluation and possible medication.
Follow medical regimen if prescribed.	Instruct patient on importance of regular medical schedule.
Complete homework assignments.	Assign homework to monitor rituals used to control anxiety.

SHORT-TERM BEHAVIORAL GOALS: ADULTS	THERAPIST'S INTERVENTIONS
Recognize and correct cognitive distortions.	Analyze and correct cognitive distortions.
Using relaxation techniques, act out ritual in imagined situation, and gradually reduce the frequency and repetition of the ritual.	Use relaxation technique or hypnosis to gradually reduce the frequency and repetition of ritualized actions. Provide audiotape for patient's home use.
Use diaphragmatic breathing to help relaxation.	Teach patient belly breathing for relaxation (see Behavioral Techniques, Chapter 6).
Read assigned books.	Assign to read *Becoming Stress-Resistant* or *Waking the Tiger: Healing Trauma* (see Resources, Chapter 8).
Feelings of isolation and hopelessness are diminished.	Encourage a collaborative relationship with patient to provide a safe environment for healing.
Start living in the here and now and focus on outcomes.	Explain the probabilities: auto accidents kill 400,000 people a year; anthrax has harmed comparatively few.
Recognize that worry is not productive and is usually misplaced. Understand the power of the here and now. The past is over and the future isn't here yet. The now is all we have to learn and heal.	Relate the Atom Bomb story (see Chapter 1).
Restrict addictive news reports that reinforce your fears and anxieties.	Encourage patient to be knowledgeable, but to reduce his/her addictive listening or viewing of the news.
Review termination plan and discuss separation and dependency issues and terminate treatment.	Address issues of separation and dependency and terminate treatment.

TREATMENT PLAN

ANXIETY DISORDERS

SHORT-TERM BEHAVIORAL GOALS: CHILD/ADOLESCENT	THERAPIST'S INTERVENTIONS
Child: Join with therapist in play therapy. **Adolescent**: Enter non-threatening therapeutic interaction geared to appropriate developmental age.	Engage child in play therapy, adolescent in non-threatening therapeutic relationship.
Identify how you found out about the critical incident and how parents and teachers helped you deal with it.	Explore how patient found out about the critical incident.
Relate the story of your life to the therapist.	Have patient relate the story of his/her life. Use puppets to help child.
Learn about the diagnosis and develop realistic expectations of self.	Educate patient about the diagnosis, and discuss symptomatology.
Does your family help soothe your fears, or do they add to your anxiety?	Determine how patient's family is dealing with everyday life since the incident.
Identify automatic thoughts and behaviors.	Explore patient's automatic thoughts and behaviors, and correct cognitive distortions.
Become aware of cognitive distortions, and replace them with evidence-based reality.	Reframe cognitive distortions with evidence-based reality.
Realize that therapy will help you learn to control your obsessions and compulsions.	In cases of obsessive-compulsive disorder, explain that rituals or obsessions are actually magical thinking in the form of unconscious wishes designed to ward off bad deeds.

SHORT-TERM BEHAVIORAL GOALS: CHILD/ADOLESCENT	THERAPIST'S INTERVENTIONS
Recognize that double messages can lead to ritualistic behavior and feeling that there is no other solution.	Explore for double-binds. Use puppets with child.
Have open discussions with responsible others to soothe fears and anxieties. Avoid overanxious people.	Teach patient that overanxious people can create an unhealthy climate for healing.
Become aware of ways to reduce stress during critical incidents or disasters.	Teach patient ways to reduce stressors to the critical incident:

1. Structure time; keep busy.

2. Don't label yourself "crazy." It's normal to feel "crazy" under stress.

3. Talk to friends and family.

4. Understand that attempting to numb pain with drugs, alcohol, or excessive food just causes problems.

5. Reach out and connect with others.

6. Show feelings.

7. Help others and let them help you.

8. Adolescents: Start journal to record feelings, especially during sleepless hours.

9. Do things that feel good.

10. Don't start hoarding out of fear. It creates more problems for everyone.

11. Do not fight flashbacks. Talk about them. Realize they will become less painful over time.

SHORT-TERM BEHAVIORAL GOALS: CHILD/ADOLESCENT	THERAPIST'S INTERVENTIONS
	12. Do things that help you feel you have some control over life.
	13. Listen carefully to other traumatized persons.
	14. Do not deny reality, but reduce the addictive time spent listening to radio or watching TV to avoid reinfecting yourself.
Understand that it is okay to have fun, even in critical times.	Point out to children that play is good for them and they should not feel guilty that they are having fun.
Learn to stay in the here and now.	Help patients learn to stay in the here and now and not focus on possibilities (i.e., anthrax has harmed relatively few people compared with automobiles).
Identify and track ritualized actions you use to ward off anxiety.	Identify and monitor patient's ritualized actions.
Understand anxiety and realize that avoidance does not work.	Teach patients the dynamics of anxiety: not dangerous or permanent; avoidance increases anxiety.
Psychodynamically work through the stressors that lead to anxiety-provoking behaviors.	Role-play stressful events that lead to ritualized actions. Explore more appropriate behaviors.
Learn that it is okay to express feelings.	Reward/praise patient for expressing his/her feelings appropriately.
Recognize underlying feelings of anger or depression and express appropriately.	Explore for underlying feelings of anger or depression and treat if necessary (see appropriate treatment plan).

SHORT-TERM BEHAVIORAL GOALS: CHILD/ADOLESCENT	THERAPIST'S INTERVENTIONS
Understand the different responses to trauma.	Discuss with patient the fight, flight, or freeze reactions to trauma.
Work through the traumatic events, discharging pent-up feelings in a safe environment.	Using play therapy for child and psychodrama for adolescent, work through the traumatic event/s. Point out distinctions between fear, terror, and excitement. Become a safe container for the child, metabolizing the child's poisonous feelings and feeding them back to him/her in a more digestible form.
Realize that others also feel bad and overcome the feeling.	Investigate for feelings of low self-esteem related to anxiety disorder.
Begin to see possible solutions.	Discuss effective ways to deal with obsessions and compulsions.
Identify irrational beliefs, reframe irrational thoughts, and develop rational alternatives.	Discuss irrational beliefs and develop rational alternatives.
Learn to use relaxation techniques or guided imagery to gain control.	If trained in hypnosis, and with parents' permission, use hypnosis with children to reduce obsessive-compulsive behaviors (see Behavioral Techniques, Chapter 6).
Express suppressed feelings in a non-threatening environment.	Play *The Talking, Feeling, Doing Game* to understand underlying processes in a non-threatening way (see Therapeutic Games, Chapter 7).
Explore patterns of withdrawal you use to avoid anxieties.	Explore with patient his/her patterns of withdrawal used to avoid anxieties.
Recognize and express how family impacts the problem.	Explore familial impact on the problem.

SHORT-TERM BEHAVIORAL GOALS: CHILD/ADOLESCENT	THERAPIST'S INTERVENTIONS
Learn diaphragmatic breathing to control anxiety.	Teach patient belly breathing to control anxiety (see Behavioral Techniques, Chapter 6).
Recognize that thinking affects feelings, and replace cognitive errors with positive thinking.	Use *The Talking, Feeling, Doing Game* to show patients how to identify negative feelings and replace them with positive thinking (see Therapeutic Games, Chapter 7).
Learn to communicate, control, and accept feelings.	Use the game *Your Journey Through the Land of Feelings* to help younger patient accept his/her feelings and release frustrations (see Therapeutic Games, Chapter 7).
Shift focus of attention from problem to accomplishment.	Ask patient to describe accomplishments of past week.
Feel more confident as self-esteem improves.	Provide positive reinforcement for patient whenever possible.
Understand that aerobic exercise produces endorphins that reduce stress.	Recommend aerobic exercise to reduce stress.
Attempt to use new control skills in school.	Urge patients to use new control skills in the classroom.
Report results to therapist.	Provide positive reinforcement, praise attempt, reward success.
Learn positive problem solving and how other people have overcome obstacles.	Assign adolescent to read *The OCD Workbook* (see Resources, Chapter 8).
Learn to reduce stress and use healthy self-esteem to keep the monsters away.	Assign adolescents to read and parents to read to younger children *Anybody Can Bake a Cake*; *Don't Pop Your Cork on Mondays!* or *Don't Feed the Monster on Tuesdays!* (see Resources, Chapter 8).

SHORT-TERM BEHAVIORAL GOALS: CHILD/ADOLESCENT	THERAPIST'S INTERVENTIONS
Learn to advocate for yourself.	Instruct patient in the techniques of self-advocacy.
Deal with separation and dependency issues and terminate treatment.	Address termination issues and bring therapy to an end.

TREATMENT PLAN

ANXIETY DISORDERS

SHORT-TERM BEHAVIORAL GOALS: FAMILY	THERAPIST'S INTERVENTIONS
Improve communication among family members.	Conduct family sessions or refer for family therapy to reduce anxieties and/or alienation and improve communication skills.
Identify family's communicative styles and methods of soothing or creating further anxieties for each other.	Explore where each family member was during the critical incident. Did they try to comfort each other or did they create further chaos?
Understand that depression and anxiety are contagious.	Teach family members Contagion Theory: Just as soothing is contagious, so are depression and anxiety.
Describe your cognitive reactions to the critical event.	Explore the thoughts of each family member about the incident.
Describe any symptoms of distress.	Investigate the psychological or physical symptoms of each family member as a result of the incident.
Become aware of ways to reduce stress during the critical incident or disaster.	Teach patient ways to reduce stressors to the critical event:

Teach patient ways to reduce stressors to the critical event:

1. Structure time; keep busy.

2. Don't label yourself "crazy." It's normal to feel "crazy" under stress.

3. Talk to friends and family.

4. Understand that attempting to numb pain with drugs, alcohol, or excessive food just causes problems.

5. Reach out and connect with others.

SHORT-TERM BEHAVIORAL GOALS: FAMILY

THERAPIST'S INTERVENTIONS

6. Show feelings.

7. Help others and let them help you.

8. Adolescents: Start journal to record feelings, especially during sleepless hours.

9. Do things that feel good.

10. Don't start hoarding out of fear. It creates more problems for everyone.

11. Do not fight flashbacks. Talk about them. Realize they will become less painful over time.

12. Do things that help you feel you have some control over your life.

13. Listen carefully to other traumatized persons.

14. Do not deny reality, but reduce the addictive time spent listening to radio or watching TV to avoid reinfecting yourself.

Identify nature of the disorder in the family.

Investigate history of anxiety in the family. Is it acute or chronic?

Identify cultural impact to reduce possible negative effects and increase positive customs.

Explore cultural impact on patient.

Understand underlying dynamics that contribute to behaviors related to anxiety.

Explore and clarify underlying dynamics that lead to anxiety disorder.

Identify whether you feel in control or out of control.

Explore family's locus of control.

SHORT-TERM BEHAVIORAL GOALS: FAMILY	THERAPIST'S INTERVENTIONS
Understand the meaning of rituals and become more hopeful about reducing or eliminating them.	Explain that rituals or obsessive behavior are actually unconscious wishes to ward off bad thoughts and happenings.
Practice living in the here and now, and focus on outcomes, not possibilities, to reduce contagious anxieties in family members.	Help family stay in the here and now and focus on outcomes instead of possibilities.
Understand the power of here and now. The present is the only time we have to learn and heal.	Explain the Atom Bomb story (see Chapter 1) to reinforce here and now thinking.
Realize that repetitive news reports are reinfecting your fear and anxiety.	Encourage family members to remain knowledgeable, but to reduce and limit radio and television news coverage.
Understand Double-Bind theory. Stay focused in the here and now to reduce helplessness and hopelessness.	Teach family the dynamics of the "Double-Bind." Stress the need to stay in the here and now to control exaggerated response.
Understand how children mourn and allow them the space to do so.	Understand how children learn (imitation, identification, introjection, internalization). What they do is more important than what they say.
Recognize that fears and anxieties block reason and lead to ritualistic or obsessive behaviors.	Point out the impact of fear and anxiety on reason.

SHORT-TERM BEHAVIORAL GOALS: FAMILY	THERAPIST'S INTERVENTIONS
Become aware of the classical response to trauma: fight, flight, or freeze.	Explain the classic responses to trauma: fight, flight, or freeze. In the first two responses, pent-up energy is discharged. The freeze response leads to helplessness and immobility, exacerbating Obsessive-Compulsive Disorder (OCD) or developing post-traumatic stress disorder.
Understand that rigid adherence to rules, routines, or rituals will not ward off anxieties.	Help patient to see that rigid adherence to rituals will not fend off anxiety. Warn him/her that changing behavior might create new anxieties.
Learn more about Obsessive-Compulsive Disorder to help develop better coping strategies.	Assign family members to read *The OCD Workbook* or *Stop Obsessing: How to Overcome Your Obsessions and Compulsions* (see Resources, Chapter 8).
Enhance your skills at overcoming needless worry and anxiety.	Assign family members to read *Becoming Stress-Resistant, Waking the Tiger: Healing Trauma*, or *Conquer Anxiety, Worry, and Nervous Fatigue* (see Resources, Chapter 8).
Work out conflicts psychodramatically. Try to understand and share.	Role-play family dynamics. Have members switch roles.
Demonstrate boundaries, alliances, triangles, and emotional currents.	Explore family boundaries using Family Sculpturing(see Chapter 6).
Identify internal and external barriers that lead to maladaptive behaviors.	Investigate internal and external barriers to a better future.
Identify resources that will help reduce family stress.	Investigate available community resources that may facilitate change.

SHORT-TERM BEHAVIORAL GOALS: FAMILY	THERAPIST'S INTERVENTIONS
Create a SMART plan.	Create a SMART action plan: Small, Measurable, Achievable, Realistic, Timelined Goals (see Change, Behavioral Techniques, Chapter 6).
Shift focus from problem to possible solutions.	Have family imagine a future without these problems and suggest actions to make it a reality.
Realize you have the power to make important changes.	Help family members realize they have the power to make significant changes.
Enhance understanding of how to improve ways family works together.	Assign members to read *Making Families Work and What to Do When They Don't* (see Resources, Chapter 8).
Make use of available community resources.	Refer family to community resources.
Reduce negative communication.	Develop a system of positive reinforcement to improve family interaction and eliminate scapegoating.
Work together to develop a treatment termination plan.	Discuss termination and bring therapy to a close.

DEPRESSION

According to the National Institute of Mental Health (NIMH) (http://www.nimh.nih.com), 18.8 million adults throughout the world suffer from depression, more than half of them in the United States. The disorder may appear early in life, especially in people born in the last decade, and has become the leading cause of disability in America. Nearly twice as many women as men are likely to experience depression with onset in their late twenties. More than 30,500 people committed suicide in 1987, the latest year for which data are available. The highest suicide rate was found in men over age 85. Although women attempt suicide three times more than men, four times as many men as women actually succeed. The suicide rate among young people has increased dramatically over the past few decades.

People suffering from depression are up to four times more likely to have a heart attack than others. Once a child experiences depression, he or she is at risk for another depressive episode within the next five years. Late-life depression affects about a million Americans, only 10% of whom will ever receive treatment. Americans over age 65 are more likely to commit suicide than any other age group.

Depressed people (NIMH, 2002) show a high prevalence for self-injury, threats to and loss of life, somatic complaints, increased sick leave, decline in immune functioning, inappropriate guilt reactions, sleep disruption, illness relapse, and mental health problems including post-traumatic stress disorder, anxiety, and substance abuse. Chronic problems may include troubled interpersonal relations as well as financial, environmental, and ecological worry and stress. Depressed children may also display various problems such as separation anxiety and anti-social behavior.

Major Depressive Disorder

Major depressive disorder is characterized by one or more depressive episodes without a history of manic, mixed (depressive-manic), or hypomanic episodes. If such episodes occur, the diagnosis should be revised to bipolar disorder. Major depressive disorder may be preceded by dysthymic disorder, and may coexist with other mental disorders. Statistics on the prevalence of depression as impacted by the events of 9/11 have yet to be compiled. Accordingly, it is difficult to estimate how terrorism, economic decline, or the stock market slump may have affected the prevalence of the disorder.

We don't usually regard depression as positive, but it can be a wake-up call that forces us to turn inward and consider thoughts, images, and emotions that may have escaped our full attention. Crises and depression can either become a perpetual state of mourning, or they can push us to a new level of personal growth.

BEHAVIORAL SYMPTOMS

MAJOR DEPRESSIVE DISORDER

- Depressed mood (as observed by others)
- Diminished interest or pleasure in almost all activities
- Social withdrawal
- Significant weight loss or gain
- Insomnia or hypersomnia
- Psychomotor agitation or retardation
- Irritability
- Somatic complaints
- Fatigue, loss of energy
- Feelings of worthlessness, excessive guilt
- Diminished ability to think or concentrate
- Recurrent thoughts of death
- Recurrent suicidal ideations with or without a plan
- Attempted suicide

Dysthymic Disorder

About 40% of adults meet the criteria for dysthymic disorder, which normally begins in childhood. Dysthymia has fewer symptoms and is less severe than major depression. It is differentiated from a normal, non-clinically depressed mood by the intensity and pervasiveness of the symptoms that are in excess of those considered normal reactions to the difficulties of life. Patients must have experienced depressed mood for at least two years and display at least two of the symptoms listed below in order to meet the requirements for this diagnosis.

Dysthymia occurs equally in boys and girls and usually impairs school performance, work, and interpersonal relations. However, in adulthood, women are two to three times more likely to suffer from the disorder than men. People with this disorder typically display low self-esteem, are cranky and irritable, and tend to be pessimistic. Patients with dysthymia are vulnerable to major depression. Studies have shown psychotherapy to be an effective treatment.

BEHAVIORAL SYMPTOMS

DYSTHYMIC DISORDER

- Pervasive, depressed mood
- General loss of interest
- Feelings of helplessness, hopelessness
- Fatigue
- Irritability, excessive anger
- Decreased activity, productivity, effectiveness
- Poor concentration
- Low self-esteem
- Insomnia, hypersomnia
- Difficulty making decisions
- Excessive, inappropriate guilt
- Poor appetite
- Overeating
- Thoughts of suicide or death

OBJECTIVES OF TREATMENT

DEPRESSIVE DISORDERS

- Educate patient about the disorder
- Determine family history of the disorder
- Help patient develop better coping skills
- Reduce persistent depression, pervasive anxiety, and worry
- Eliminate suicide plans, control suicidal ideations
- Eliminate feelings of worthlessness, guilt, anger
- Reduce feelings of worthlessness, hopelessness
- Encourage compliance with educational programs and referrals
- Improve energy level
- Reduce irrational beliefs
- Restore interest in former pleasurable activities
- Promote socialization, reduce alienation
- Restore patient and family to optimum level of functioning

TREATMENT PLAN

DEPRESSIVE DISORDERS

SHORT-TERM BEHAVIORAL GOALS: ADULT	THERAPIST'S INTERVENTIONS
Collaborate with therapist in development of a treatment plan.	Establish therapeutic alliance to enhance outcome of treatment.
Help therapist understand your development of major depression.	Assess problem with patient, and record a comprehensive history of his/her development of major depression.
If actively suicidal, hospitalize immediately to preclude harm to self.	If patient is actively suicidal, hospitalize immediately.
Enter into "suicide pact" with therapist. Undergo immediate evaluation to determine possible need for hospitalization.	If patient has suicidal ideations, but no active suicidal plan, evaluate immediately to determine need for hospitalization.
Become aware of the diagnosis and what to expect.	Educate patient about the diagnosis. Explain chronicity and contagion of depression.
Realize that anger is a pitfall.	Inform patient that family members often become angry with the depressed patient, mainly because they feel helpless to do anything about it.
Identify ways the traumatic event changed your life.	Explore the ways in which the traumatic event has impacted the patent's life and family relations.
Develop awareness of how your personal theory influences cognition of the problem.	Explore patient's theory of the problem and how it developed.

SHORT-TERM BEHAVIORAL GOALS: ADULT	THERAPIST'S INTERVENTIONS
Identify other problems associated with depression.	Investigate other problems that may be associated with depression (sleep disorders, somatization, eating disorders, guilt, worthlessness, fatigue).
Recognize fears and feelings of negative self-blame related to the problem.	Evaluate fears and negative feelings of self-blame for disorder.
Learn to reach beyond automatic cognitive reactions in viewing the problem.	Expand patient's perspective beyond limited cognitive reactions.
Be evaluated for medical problems and treated if necessary.	Refer patient for medical evaluation and treatment if necessary.
If sexual abuse is confirmed, have patient placed in protected environment and treated.	Evaluate and rule out sexual abuse (see *Behavioral Management Guide: Essential Treatment Strategies for Adult Psychotherapy*).
Identify existing triggers that may contribute to depression.	Investigate patient's underlying feelings and identify issue that may cause or contribute to depression.
Realize that the more mindful you are, the less apt you are to lose personal power.	Help patient find something that will help get him/her through the day.
Shift focus from the problem to possible solutions.	Have patient imagine a future without the problem and suggest possible actions to make that future possible.
Learn diaphragmatic breathing as relaxation technique.	Teach belly breathing to assist patient in relaxation (see Behavioral Techniques, Chapter 6).

SHORT-TERM BEHAVIORAL GOALS: ADULT	THERAPIST'S INTERVENTIONS
Realize that depression does not arise out of logic, but the way you experience the world.	Help patient understand that logical thinking does not yield knowledge of the empirical world.
See your problem outside of yourself and try to envision a solution.	If trained in hypnosis, help patient change his/her inner world by becoming aware of his/her bodily sensations. Attempt to visualize the problem on an external screen and then add a solution.
Learn creative options for building the life you want.	Assign patient to read *Creative Visualization* or *I Can See Tomorrow* (see Resources, Chapter 8).
Realize that worry is a useless emotion and only exacerbates depression.	Explain the Atom Bomb story (see Chapter 1) to help patient reduce worry.
Realize you can change cognitions and learn to focus on what you want, rather than on the depression.	Guide patient in understanding that what you focus on expands. If you focus on your depression, it will expand.
Discuss a treatment termination plan and resolve related issues.	Develop a treatment termination plan, discuss issues of dependency and separation anxiety, and terminate.

TREATMENT PLAN

DEPRESSIVE DISORDERS

SHORT-TERM BEHAVIORAL GOALS: CHILD/ADOLESCENT	THERAPIST'S INTERVENTIONS
Engage child in play therapy. Enter non-threatening therapeutic interaction with adolescent geared to developmental age.	Engage patient in age-appropriate therapeutic relationship.
Learn about diagnosis and develop realistic expectations of self.	Educate patient about the diagnosis and discuss symptomatology so he/she can adjust self-expectations.
Understand symptoms related to this disorder.	Explore ways in which depression manifests itself (e.g., feelings of worthlessness, guilt, irritability, somatization, fatigue, etc.), and clarify underlying dynamics.
Identify the ways in which the traumatic event has changed your life.	Explore the impact of the traumatic event on the patient's life.
Realize that human beings are far from perfect, and reduce the stressors imposed on yourself.	Remind patient that human beings are not perfect. Reduce self-imposed stressors.
If actively suicidal, comply with hospitalization for self-protection.	If patient is actively suicidal, hospitalize immediately. Call 911 or ambulance. Do not leave patient unattended.
Willingly enter into "suicide pact" with therapist to report all suicidal ideations and active plans. Agree to inform therapist of your intent before taking any action.	If patient is not actively suicidal, but has suicidal ideations, implement a "suicide pact" in which he/she agrees to inform you before taking any action.

SHORT-TERM BEHAVIORAL GOALS: CHILD/ADOLESCENT	THERAPIST'S INTERVENTIONS
Child: Understand family climate and where to go for support. **Adolescent**: Assess family climate and identify who is most supportive.	Evaluate family climate and identify who may be most supportive for the patient. Use puppets with child if necessary.
Realize that others also feel bad and overcome those feelings. Discuss feelings with therapist and what you can do about them.	Investigate for feelings of low self-esteem related to depression.
Understand how trauma may have contributed to the existing disorder.	Explore patient's background for trauma that may have exacerbated the depression.
Recognize existing triggers that cause or contribute to depression.	Explore feelings and issues that may lead to depression.
Recognize and express feelings of anger and rage.	Probe for feelings of self-anger and rage.
Through role-playing, better understand your relationships with others and develop improved communications.	Use role-playing to clarify patient's relationships and communication style.
Child: Begin to see possible solutions. **Adolescent**: Replace negative self-talk.	With child, use puppets to discuss how the child deals with negative feelings. With adolescent, replace negative self-talk with positive affirmations.
Understand the dynamics of anxiety.	Teach patient about anxiety: It is not permanent, not dangerous, and avoidance makes it worse.
Communicate life story to therapist.	Have patient relate his/her life story or play *Life Stories* (see Therapeutic Games, Chapter 7).

SHORT-TERM BEHAVIORAL GOALS: CHILD/ADOLESCENT	THERAPIST'S INTERVENTIONS
Express suppressed feelings in a non-threatening environment.	Play *The Talking, Feeling, Doing Game* to understand underlying processes in a non-threatening way (see Therapeutic Games, Chapter 7).
Understand how trauma may have contributed to existing disorder.	Explore patient's background for trauma that may have exacerbated the disorder.
Recognize and relate how family impacts the problem.	Explore familial impact on the problem.
Understand how others react to your depression.	Inform patient of how families and friends often get angry with depressed people and that depression is contagious.
Learn new techniques for handling depression.	With parental permission, use hypnosis, visualization, or relaxation techniques to coach child in new ways to handle triggers of depression. If appropriate, provide audiotape for home use and reinforcement.
Read self-help books to enhance your new skills.	Assign patient to read or have someone read to him/her *The Adolescent Depression Workbook* or *When Nothing Matters Anymore* to enhance his/her understanding and coping skills (see Resources, Chapter 8).
Diminish need to "hide out" because of guilt/anger over having this disorder.	Gradually build patient's confidence to a level where avoidance behavior is no longer a rational response.

SHORT-TERM BEHAVIORAL GOALS: CHILD/ADOLESCENT	THERAPIST'S INTERVENTIONS
Participate in recreational activities with others.	Review with patient past interests in recreational activities (sports, exercise, cards, chess, etc.) and urge patient to join external exercise or recreational group to renew patterns of contact and communication with others.
Learn methods that can be used to advocate for yourself.	Instruct patient in the technique of self-advocacy.
Understand that you can deal with these issues and bring treatment to an end successfully.	Develop a treatment termination plan, and explain issues of separation anxiety and dependency.

TREATMENT PLAN

DEPRESSIVE DISORDERS

SHORT-TERM BEHAVIORAL GOALS: FAMILY	THERAPIST'S INTERVENTIONS
Improve communication among family members to reduce familial anxiety.	Conduct family sessions or refer for family therapy to reduce anger and/or alienation, and improve communication skills.
Demonstrate boundaries, alliances, triangles, and emotional currents that may exacerbate the anxieties.	Explore family boundaries using sculpturing, a useful technique for understanding triangulation, alliances, and emotional currents (see Behavioral Techniques, Chapter 6).
Explain how depression impacts your life and suggest strategies for dealing with it.	Explore with each family member how depression affects them and possible strategies for dealing with it.
Shift focus from problem to possible solutions.	Have family imagine a future without the problem and suggest actions that can be taken now to make that future possible.
Other family members are treated.	Determine if other family members have depressive disorders and treat or refer for treatment (see appropriate treatment plan).
Understand that it is normal but counterproductive to get angry with depressed family member.	Explain dynamics of depression cycle: depression triggers anger in others, which, in turn, exacerbates the depression.
Family members realize they have the power to make important changes, even if they seem small.	Help family to realize they have an opportunity to do some things differently.

SHORT-TERM BEHAVIORAL GOALS: FAMILY	THERAPIST'S INTERVENTIONS
Learn new ways to deal with unpleasant feelings.	Encourage social behaviors to develop family cohesiveness.
Family members are empowered. They recognize that they can create positive change.	Ask family members to relate what they have accomplished in the past week.
Realize that major change is the result of small steps taken one at a time.	Help family to identify and prioritize achievable goals.
Focus on strengths rather than on weaknesses.	Have each family member identify strengths they see in the other members.
Enhance understanding of depression and learn how other families have dealt with this disorder.	Assign homework reading of *Making Families Work and What to Do When They Don't* (see Resources, Chapter 8).
Make use of available community resources.	Refer family to available resources in the community.
Read monograph to develop ideas of what to do together to reduce alienation.	Encourage family outings to reduce alienation. Have members read *Museum Visits and Other Activities for Family Life Enrichment* (see Resources, Chapter 8).
Reduce negative communication.	Develop a system of positive reinforcement with family to interact better with each other and reduce scapegoating.
Family works together to develop a treatment termination plan.	Discuss termination issues, and develop plan to terminate treatment.

DISSOCIATIVE DISORDERS

Roger Simon (*U.S. News and World Report*, November 12, 2001, p. 14) reported that the events of September 11 had unleashed a "host of new devils." It created a city of people walking round in altered states of consciousness. In response to President Bush's suggestion that we go on with our normal lives, late-night television host David Letterman joked that he went home and sat around in his underwear drinking malt liquor. But the reactions of most people to the disaster of 9/11 to were not quite as casual. They slipped into dissociative states that are usually marked by a disruption in the functions of consciousness, perception, memory, or identity. For them, going on about their normal lives was impossible. This disorder can be gradual or sudden, chronic or transient. Dissociative symptoms may also be found in acute stress disorder, posttraumatic stress disorder, and somatization.

The events of September 11 unleashed many new problems, including depersonalization (persistent or recurrent feelings of being detached from one's body), dissociative amnesia (forgetfulness, significant stress, or impairment in daily activities), and other dissociative disorders such as derealization. It produced a new kind of "normalcy" in which people were more frightened than ever before. That fear exacerbates these illnesses.

BEHAVIORAL SYMPTOMS

DISSOCIATIVE DISORDERS

- Derealization without depersonalization
- Persistent or recurrent feeling of being detached from one's mind or body
- Reality testing remains intact
- Excessive age-appropriate inability to recall important personal information not explainable as simple forgetfulness
- Significant stress or impairment in the activities of daily living

OBJECTIVES OF TREATMENT

DISSOCIATIVE DISORDERS

- Educate patient about the disorder
- Help patient develop better coping and comforting skills
- Reduce pervasive anxiety and worry
- Identify environmental stressors, and help patient and family develop new techniques for living in this stressful world
- Reduce acute symptomatology
- Reduce associated depression, anxiety, and mood swings
- Teach patient to live in the here and now
- Help reduce irrational beliefs
- Help patient accept the trauma that may have led to the dissociation
- Reduce depersonalization
- Encourage compliance with referrals and educational programs
- Educate patient in self-hypnosis to reduce outside stressors
- Reduce alienation, promote socialization
- Restore patient and family to optimum level of functioning
- Develop discharge plan for coping with everyday life in a world filled with fear

TREATMENT PLAN

DISSOCIATIVE DISORDERS

SHORT-TERM BEHAVIORAL GOALS: ADULT	THERAPIST'S INTERVENTIONS
Collaborate with therapist in development of a treatment plan.	Establish therapeutic alliance to enhance outcome of treatment.
Help therapist understand your development of dissociative disorder and other associated emotional problems.	Assess problem and record a comprehensive history of the development of dissociative disorder and explore accompanying emotional problems (anxiety, depression, mood swings).
Help identify other symptoms associated with the disorder.	Explore with patient the symptomatology of the disorder, such as amnesia, derealization, depersonalization, identity confusion or alternation, insomnia, and time lapse in consciousness.
Identify triggers that touch off dissociation.	Investigate known triggers that result in dissociation.
Understand what you can do to help yourself.	Teach patient how stress triggers dissociation. What patient most needs are connection, comfort, communication, and cooperation.
Reduce time devoted to watching or listening to news broadcasts.	Suggest patient go on a "news diet" to preclude bring reinfected traumatically.
Become aware of the diagnosis and what to appropriately expect.	Educate patient about the diagnosis and how a stress-free environment aids healing.

SHORT-TERM BEHAVIORAL GOALS: ADULT	THERAPIST'S INTERVENTIONS
Accept diagnosis and use available resources to live more comfortably with it.	Help patient overcome denial.
Help identify trauma or abuse that may have led to dissociative disorder.	Explore for trauma or abuse in patient.
Enter treatment for psychological problems, if appropriate.	Evaluate patient for other psychological problems and treat or refer for treatment if appropriate. (See *Behavioral Management Guide: Essential Treatment Strategies for Adult Psychotherapy*.)
Learn how to stay in the here and now.	Teach patient mindfulness: 1. Stay in the here and now; the past is over and the future is uncertain. 2. You can control your mind rather than have your mind control you.
Develop awareness of how your personal theory influences cognition of the problem.	Explore patient's theory of the problem.
Recognize fears and feelings of negative self-blame related to the problem.	Evaluate fears and negative feelings of self-blame.
Learn to reach beyond automatic cognitive reactions in viewing the problem.	Expand patient's perspective beyond limited cognitive reactions.
Learn to deal with sleep problems.	Investigate for sleep problems and teach patient how to deal with them.
Learn a range of comforting techniques.	Read *All I Want is a Good Night's Sleep* (see Resources, Chapter 8).

SHORT-TERM BEHAVIORAL GOALS: ADULT	THERAPIST'S INTERVENTIONS
Confront thoughts of exaggerated and unrealistic consequences – "what-ifs?"	Guide patients in confronting distorted reactions to trigger situations.
Identify cognitive distortions.	Weigh the reactions against evidence-based reality.
Restructure distortions with evidence-based consequences.	Reframe distortions with reality-based reactions to stressors.
Learn how to deal with stressors more effectively.	Teach patient how to build a stress-free environment in an age of terrorism.
Develop new skills while learning more about this disorder.	Assign patient to read *The Stranger in the Mirror: Dissociation, the Hidden Epidemic* (see Resources, Chapter 8).
Learn how to build a positive mission statement.	Explain how mission statement can bring wholeness to detached parts of patient's personality: i.e., "I am safe today; today is going to be okay."
Learn distraction techniques to deal with dissociative episodes.	Teach patient distraction techniques to help cope with dissociative episode (i.e., play cards, go for a bike ride, etc.).
Learn positive self-talk to fight off destructive thoughts and urges.	Teach patient to counter destructive thoughts and urges with positive self-talk drawing on successful experiences from the past.
Interact with other patients who are experiencing similar difficulties and share solutions for coping with the problem.	Refer patient to self-help group.

SHORT-TERM BEHAVIORAL GOALS: ADULT	THERAPIST'S INTERVENTIONS
Learn proven techniques for further relieving your fears and anxieties.	Assign to read *Smart Guide to Relieving Stress* or *Healing Fear* (see Resources, Chapter 8).
Discuss a treatment termination plan, and resolve related issues.	Develop a treatment termination plan and discuss issues of separation, anxiety, and dependency.

TREATMENT PLAN

DISSOCIATIVE DISORDERS

SHORT-TERM BEHAVIORAL GOALS: CHILD/ADOLESCENT	THERAPIST'S INTERVENTIONS
Engage in age-appropriate therapeutic alliance or collaborative approach to enhance outcome.	Engage patient in an age-appropriate therapeutic relationship.
Learn about diagnosis and develop realistic expectations of self.	Educate patient about the diagnosis and discuss symptomatology so that he/she can adjust self-expectations.
Comply with medical and psychiatric recommendations.	Refer patient for medical and psychiatric evaluations.
Relate feelings about medical and psychiatric evaluations.	Discuss with patient his/her feelings about medical and psychiatric evaluations.
Understand need for hospitalization during times of crisis and resolve any fears.	Evaluate need for hospitalization, and resolve patient fears of hospital.
Understand dangers of mixing medication and street drugs or alcohol.	Instruct patient of dangers of mixing prescribed medication with other drugs or alcohol.
Understand importance of building a stress-free zone to enable healing.	Help patient to build a stress-free zone inside and outside of therapy to assure that healing will take place.
Learn and practice self-comforting skills.	Teach quiet, self-comforting skills such as belly breathing and others (see Behavioral Techniques, Chapter 6).

SHORT-TERM BEHAVIORAL GOALS: CHILD/ADOLESCENT	THERAPIST'S INTERVENTIONS
Learn to build positive dialogues with self to reduce fears created by traumatic events.	Teach patient to develop an inner voice to counter fear, rage, and depression.
Confirm sexual abuse and undergo appropriate treatment.	Investigate for sexual abuse and, if positive, treat immediately. As a mandated reporter, inform appropriate authorities.
Expand understanding of sexual abuse by reading self-help book.	If appropriate, assign patient to read *Everything You Need to Know About Sexual Abuse* (see Resources, Chapter 8).
Transfer to a secure environment to escape continued abuse.	If sexual abuse continues, have patient removed from home to a protected environment.
Discuss feelings to diminish amnesia.	Help patient to share feelings and memories to reduce amnesia.
Develop internal response system to prevent trauma response and reduce derealization.	Teach patient how to distinguish between past and present to avoid derealization.
Learn relaxation techniques or hypnosis to reduce stressors.	With parental permission, use hypnosis to work through fears that lead to dissociation (see Behavioral Techniques, Chapter 6).
Learn to stay in the here and now.	Teach patient "mindfulness" by staying in the here and now. The past is gone and the future is unpredictable.
Replace destructive thoughts with positive self-talk.	Teach patient to counter destructive thoughts with positive self-talk drawing on past successful experience.

SHORT-TERM BEHAVIORAL GOALS: CHILD/ADOLESCENT	THERAPIST'S INTERVENTIONS
Replace irrational beliefs with evidence-based rational thought.	Explore and confront patient's irrational belief system. Point out consequences if irrational beliefs and reframe them.
Learn to cultivate a wise mind.	Teach patient to integrate his/her emotional and rational minds to develop wisdom.
Learn new ways to comfort self.	Assign to read or have someone read to him/her, *Homecoming: Reclaiming and Championing Your Inner Child* (see Resources, Chapter 8).
Learn to live with dissociative identity disorder.	Assign older adolescents to read *The Stranger in the Mirror: Dissociation, the Hidden Epidemic* (see Resources, Chapter 8).
Recognize underlying feelings of anger or depression and express appropriately.	Explore for underlying feelings of anger or depression and treat (see appropriate treatment plan).
Undergo treatment for sleep problems.	Investigate for sleep problem and treat accordingly (see appropriate treatment plan).
Learn techniques to promote sleep.	Read or have read to you, *Can't You Sleep, Little Bear?* (see Resources, Chapter 8).
Develop a repertoire of self-comforting skills.	Have patient build a repertoire of skills for daily comfort.
Realize that others also feel bad, and overcome that feeling.	Investigate for feelings of low self-esteem related to anxiety.
Understand anxiety and realize that avoidance does not help.	Teach child the dynamics of anxiety: Not dangerous, not permanent; exposure can promote change.

SHORT-TERM BEHAVIORAL GOALS: CHILD/ADOLESCENT	THERAPIST'S INTERVENTIONS
Understand how trauma may have contributed to existing disorder.	Explore patient's background for trauma that may have exacerbated the disorder.
Discuss personal coping mechanisms developed to handle the disorder.	Investigate with patient possible patterns of withdrawal used to avoid anxieties.
Shift focus of attention from problem to accomplishment.	Ask patient to describe accomplishments of past week.
Feel more confident as self-esteem improves.	Compliment patient at every opportunity to provide positive reinforcement for positive accomplishments.
Develop exercise routine to help release frustrations.	Recommend routine exercise to help release frustrations.
Communicate problematic feelings and develop new options.	Explore problematic feelings and help patient develop new alternatives.
Learn methods that can be used to advocate for yourself.	Instruct patient in the technique of self-advocacy.
Explore separation and dependency issues and bring treatment to an end.	Develop a treatment termination plan, and resolve issues of separation and dependency.

TREATMENT PLAN

DISSOCIATIVE DISORDERS

SHORT-TERM BEHAVIORAL GOALS: FAMILY	THERAPIST'S INTERVENTIONS
Improve family communications to reduce family anxiety.	Conduct family sessions or refer for family therapy to reduce alienation and improve communication skills.
Become aware of the symptoms and what you can do to help.	Educate family about the diagnosis and symptoms of the disorder.
Demonstrate boundaries, alliances, triangles, and emotional currents that may exacerbate the disorder.	Explore family boundaries using sculpturing, a useful technique for understanding triangulation, alliances, and emotional currents (see Behavioral Techniques, Chapter 6).
Identify your feelings toward the problem.	Explore the perceptions of each family member regarding the problem and investigate for possible anger, scapegoating, or rejection.
Shift focus from problem to possible solutions.	Have family imagine a future without the problem and suggest actions that can be taken now to make that future possible.
Understand the importance of a "stress-free zone" to control dissociation.	Help family members understand that stress and anxiety trigger dissociation, and brainstorm ideas for creating a "stress-free zone" to reduce episodes.
Understand the dynamics of dissociation and how to be supportive.	Teach family members the need for connection, comfort, cooperation, and communication for those who dissociate in response to trauma.

SHORT-TERM BEHAVIORAL GOALS: FAMILY	THERAPIST'S INTERVENTIONS
Work with other members to find solutions.	Develop a SMART plan (Smart, Measurable, Achievable, Realistic, Timelined goals) to deal with the problems (see Behavioral Techniques, Chapter 6).
Think about what treatment outcome would look like. Explain what changes you would like to see in other family members when treatment is completed.	Ask family members to think about what they might want to say about each other when treatment is completed.
Family members realize they have the power to make important changes even if they seem small.	Help family members realize they have an opportunity to do some things differently.
Family members are empowered. They recognize that they can create positive change.	Ask family members to relate what they have accomplished in the past week.
Realize that major change is the result of small steps taken one at a time.	Help family identify and prioritize achievable goals.
Enhance understanding of condition and see how other families have handled similar problems.	Assign homework reading *Making Families Work and What to Do When They Don't* (see Resources, Chapter 8).
Make use of available community resources.	Refer family to available resources in the community.
Reduce negative communication.	Develop a system of positive reinforcement with family to interact better with each other and reduce scapegoating.
Family works together to develop a treatment termination plan.	Discuss termination issues, and develop plan to terminate treatment.

5
EATING DISORDERS AND SUBSTANCE ABUSE

The stress response is an unavoidable consequence of life today that can lead to many physical and psychological dysfunctions (for further information see http://www.stress.org).

Traumatized people use a variety of methods in an attempt to reduce their anxieties. These methods are often bizarre and self-destructive, ranging from self-mutilation and unusual sexual practices to binging and purging and drug and alcohol abuse (van der Kolk, McFarlane, and Weisaeth, 1996).

Since trauma-induced hyperarousal interferes with the normal capacity to put experience into words, it is likely to result in the discharge of tension by other means. Under chronic stress, many people seek relief in self-medication, food, drugs, and alcohol. It is claimed that drugs are selected for their specific psychotropic effects. Heroin may be used to mute feelings of rage and aggression, cocaine to mask depression and alcohol, to reduce sleep disturbance, nightmares, and symptoms of PTSD. This trauma-induced drug abuse usually goes undiagnosed and untreated because trauma patients find it easier to talk about their trauma symptoms than their addictions. The night after 9/11 many New York City bars were jammed to capacity in a bizarre, manic response to the tragedy.

Anorexia is associated with control and superiority. In order to avoid the feelings triggered by the trauma of 9/11, an anorexic would use food in a futile effort to control his or her body, and thus feel superior which, in turn, would reduce anxieties. ("If I can control my body, I can ward off unwanted feelings.") In the same way, people with bulimia use food to stuff down their feelings. They can almost go into a trance state while eating without being aware of how much they have consumed. Some will purge themselves afterward. In a similar manner, alcoholics and drug abusers use their favorite substances to avoid their anxieties.

Therapists may have great difficulty in treating addictions since most addicts do not want treatment. Giving up drugs, alcohol, or overeating leads back to the very anxiety they are trying to avoid in the first place.

TRAUMA AND WEIGHT

by Martin Tesher, MD, CCFP, ABFP, Family Physician

Weight changes are almost always related to some kind of trauma. The exceptions are weight changes due to a medical problem (i.e., glandular disorder), or disease.

For this discussion, there are two kinds of trauma: physical and psychological. Let's take a look at the easy one first. Physical trauma can be divided into trauma that prevents, inhibits, or discourages eating; and trauma that inhibits or prevents physical activity.

Trauma that interferes with your desire to eat, such as an abdominal injury sustained in a fight or accident, will make the person feel ill. Even the thought of food might be unpleasant. People who are suffering from acute pain usually do not have an appetite except for water. There is also trauma leading to physical difficulty in eating (i.e., broken jaw, hand, or arm.) These traumas lead to weight loss, which in most cases is transient as long as the disability is not permanent.

Trauma that inhibits or prevents physical activity includes the physical handicap and its psychological implications. Exercise in some form is important for good physical and psychological health and essential for anyone wanting to maintain or lose weight. In weight control, the function of exercise is not just to burn calories, but also to increase the body's metabolism so it will need and use up more calories even at rest. Exercise has psychological benefits as well. You feel less lethargic and more energetic so that the need for food for energy is reduced. In addition, exercise increases the body's production of endorphins, which have the effect of elevating your mood and making you feel happier and more energetic. This effect reduces one's need and desire to eat or drink, which, in turn, causes some degree of weight loss.

In people who suffer from a broken limb or debilitating disease, their ability to exercise is significantly inhibited, thus opening the door to weight gain or difficulty in shedding excess pounds.

Psychological trauma is more complicated and difficult to diagnose and treat. There are both positive and negative psychological traumas. Positive trauma is less common and usually lasts for a shorter period of time. Examples might include winning the lottery, getting a promotion, or becoming pregnant. In contrast, negative trauma can be recent or old and may last for a short time, but could have long-lasting effects. These traumas include situations such as the death of a loved one, loss of a job, significant environmental damage to your home, or divorce.

Old or chronic trauma can be caused by the effects of a dysfunctional family of origin, emotional or physical abuse, and sometimes genetic factors such as the effect of ADHD, which may cause low self-esteem, or bipolar disorder, which can cause "brain pain" due the constantly changing moods.

Psychological trauma leaves people stressed and unhappy. In babies, the natural instinct for gratification and relaxation is sucking, a reflex that matures in adulthood to the use of one's mouth. Thus, people almost always respond to psychological trauma with the increased intake of calories in the form of food and drink to make them feel better. These people end up being overweight and/or obese (a Basal Metabolic Index of 33 or more). Occasionally, people will react in the reverse fashion and reject food, becoming thin. This excludes anorexia and bulimia, although bulimics are not always overweight or thin.

Why do people tend to eat more when they are traumatized psychologically? Many people use food for solace when unhappy. Some use food to hide from the view of those who traumatized them earlier (when they were thin). Others use food and/or drink to reduce anxiety and stress.

As a physician, the only way I can successfully treat a patient with a weight problem is to find out why they became overweight or underweight in the first place.

On rare occasions, weight problems are the direct result of some medical disease or glandular problem. Without fail, if the weight gain is not caused by some physical trauma that prevents them from performing their usual activities or exercise, it is the result of psychological trauma usually of long standing.

BEHAVIORAL SYMPTOMS

SUBSTANCE ABUSE AND EATING DISORDERS

- Increased need for the substance of choice to reach desired effect and reduce anxiety
- Diminished effect with continued use of the same amount of the substance
- Characteristic withdrawal syndrome
- Same or related substance taken to avoid withdrawal symptoms
- Substance taken in larger amounts or over a longer period of time
- Persistent desire or unsuccessful effort to reduce or control use, or to recover from substance use
- Inordinate amount of time spent to obtain, use, or recover from substance use
- Important social, occupational, or recreational activities are abandoned or reduced
- Substance abuse continues despite knowledge of a persistent related physical or psychological problem
- Repeated substance use leading to failure to fulfill major work, home, or school obligations
- Repeated substance use in physically dangerous situations
- Recurrent substance use and related legal problems
- Continued substance use despite resulting social or interpersonal problems

BEHAVIORAL SYMPTOMS

ANOREXIA NERVOSA

- Body weight is significantly (85%) below normal
- Intense fear of gaining weight or becoming fat
- Clings to the shelter of childhood
- Amenorrhea – absence of three consecutive menstrual cycles
- Denies seriousness of low body weight
- Restricts calorie intake, obsessed with low-calorie, low-fat foods
- Overeats and purges by vomiting or use of laxatives, enemas, or diuretics
- Uses excessive exercise to control weight
- Feels superior to others because of food control
- Extremely self-critical, needs to be perfect

BEHAVIORAL SYMPTOMS

BULIMIA NERVOSA

- Recurrent binge eating
- Feeling of loss of control during binge
- Inappropriate use of vomiting, laxatives, or diuretics
- Overexercising
- Exhibits low self-esteem
- Overconcern with body weight and fatness
- Extremely self-critical
- Depressed and/or anxious
- Difficulties with family of origin
- Poor interpersonal skills

OBJECTIVES OF TREATMENT

SUBSTANCE ABUSE AND EATING DISORDERS

- Educate patient about the disorder
- Determine family history of the disorder
- Confront denial of substance abuse
- Recognize and accept abuse as a disease
- Refer to group: Alcoholics Anonymous, Narcotics Anonymous, or Rational Recovery Group
- Evaluate and reduce idiosyncratic beliefs related to food and weight
- Help patient develop better coping skills
- Reduce preoccupation with food and promote weight gain
- Sustain sobriety
- Help patient understand how traumatic events can exacerbate anxiety and lead to eating disorders
- Eliminate purging and compulsive exercise
- Identify traumatic events that may lead to eating problems
- Understand self-sabotaging behavior
- Reduce/eliminate shame/guilt
- Identify people, places, and things that trigger abuse
- Understand how traumatic events can trigger abuse
- Mitigate need for perfection
- Decrease need to control environment and be superior
- Prevent relapse
- Restore patient to optimal level of functioning

TREATMENT PLAN

EATING DISORDERS AND SUBSTANCE ABUSE

SHORT-TERM BEHAVIORAL GOALS: ADULTS	THERAPIST'S INTERVENTIONS
Agree with therapist on target problems.	Create treatment plan, and agree on target problems.
Join in treatment relationship.	Cultivate a therapeutic alliance or collaborative relationship to build trust and enhance treatment outcome.
Discuss underlying dynamics and possible causes of the disorder.	Encourage patient to discuss feelings about self and clarify underlying dynamics that have created or contributed to the problem.
Identify ways in which trauma has played a role in the disorder.	Explore ways in which trauma may have exacerbated anxieties leading to current dysfunctional behavior.
Understand how you are self-medicating to avoid dealing with fears.	Explain how trauma is often felt in the body as anxiety and how the patient is self-medicating to avoid dealing with the fears.
As appropriate, accept hospitalization or enter into "suicide pact" agreeing to inform therapist of ideations and plans and to provide prior notification before any self-destructive action.	Assess possible homicidal or suicidal effects of addictive behavior. If actively suicidal, hospitalize immediately. If patient has suicidal ideations, but no specific plan, enter into "suicide pact."
Identify genesis of substance abuse in family of origin.	Explore distressed thinking or denial, and assess patient's cognitive and intellectual functioning, which contribute to the problem.

SHORT-TERM BEHAVIORAL GOALS: ADULTS	THERAPIST'S INTERVENTIONS
Give up your denial and be freed up to work on the problem.	Help patient overcome denial by looking at the facts of addictive behaviors and the problems they have caused.
Work on underlying issues that contribute to substance dependence.	Evaluate patient for possible dual diagnosis and treat other symptoms (e.g. anxiety, trauma, post-traumatic stress disorder, depression, social phobia, etc. (see appropriate treatment plan).
Understand patterns of stress that lead to addictions.	Explore patterns of addictions and their relationship to life stresses.
Attend Narcotics Anonymous or Alcoholics Anonymous and obtain a sponsor, or attend a Rational Recovery Group meeting.	Refer patient to 12-step program or to alternate Rational Recovery Group.
Understand process you must undergo to get clean.	Explain mourning process, and help patient mourn substance of choice.
Recognize and learn how to avoid potential triggers for relapse.	Identify triggers (person, place, or thing) that may cause backsliding or relapse.
Maintain a daily journal to monitor feelings rather than act them out.	Assign patient to keep a daily journal of his/her feelings and reactions.
Learn new techniques for dealing with self-destructive urges.	If trained in hypnosis, teach patient hypnosis to cope with feelings. Provide audiotape for home use (see Behavioral Techniques, Chapter 6).
Recognize family triggers and avoid enablers.	Investigate family conflicts, and identify enablers who aid in patient's addiction.

SHORT-TERM BEHAVIORAL GOALS: ADULTS	THERAPIST'S INTERVENTIONS
Replace ritualistic behavior with more rational response.	Examine ritualistic behaviors related to addictions, and offer patient more rational responses.
Realize the destructive effect of addiction on the quality of your life.	Explore and identify the effects of addiction on patient's social, familial, occupational, and other relations.
Improve family relations.	Conduct family sessions or refer to family therapist (see family plan).
Become more knowledgeable about the disorder.	Assign books on addictive behaviors as homework: *Fat is not a Four-Letter Word, Bulimia: A Guide for Family and Friends,* or *The Addiction Workbook.* (see Resources, Chapter 8).
Develop understanding that the disorder is not your fault, but must constantly be worked on to control it.	Review issue of shame and guilt that may cause or contribute to addictive behavior.
Make commitment to someone else to reduce addiction.	Instruct patient to enter into a formal contract or commitment with someone else in favor of abstinence.
Develop alternate behaviors to substance abuse.	Discuss possible alternate behaviors to addiction.
Diminish anger and aggression toward self and others.	Guide patient in releasing anger and aggression toward self and others.
Make use of support systems when you feel substance use triggers being activated.	Help patient create and use support systems and resources in the environment to maintain sobriety or healthy life style.
Explore possible mood disorders that may exacerbate anorexia.	Evaluate possible mood disorders that may contribute significantly to anorexia (see appropriate treatment plan).

SHORT-TERM BEHAVIORAL GOALS: ADULTS	THERAPIST'S INTERVENTIONS
Maintain daily journal of eating patterns, feelings, triggers, and reactions. Discuss with therapist.	Assign patient to keep daily journal of eating patterns and reactions. Discuss regularly with him/her.
Explore irrational beliefs about becoming fat.	Examine patient's beliefs about fatness and its consequences.
Replace distorted beliefs with rational thinking about weight and appropriate body size.	Provide rational approach to weight and body size.
Identify family and societal obsessions with thinness.	Investigate family and societal issues that reinforce pathological eating patterns.
Learn to gain control over your mind.	Help patient realize he/she can control his/her mind rather than being controlled by it. Show how the rational mind can mediate the emotional mind to develop a wise mind.
Learn to reduce anxiety by living in the here and now.	Teach patient mindfulness, how to live in the here and now without ruminating.
Realize that security is a myth.	Help patient realize that there is no such thing as "security." We never had security and we never will. Trying to avoid insecurity through addiction is futile.
Reduce tension by going on a "news diet."	If listening to or watching the news creates anxiety, put the patient on a "news diet" of less than one-half hour a day to stay informed while reducing addictive exposure.
Recognize an underlying need for perfection and where it started.	Address the need for perfection and its origins.

SHORT-TERM BEHAVIORAL GOALS: ADULTS	THERAPIST'S INTERVENTIONS
Live more comfortably within self. Accept lower self-expectations as good enough.	Teach patient that "good enough" is acceptable.
Recognize secondary gains (control, attention, feelings of superiority, avoidance of adulthood) and replace them with new coping skills.	Point out the secondary gains of food control, and replace with new coping skills.
Realize that relapse is not a trigger to give up, but a warning that you have to work harder at sobriety.	Help patient regard a relapse as a "red flag," indicating they must work harder.
Diminish and eliminate purging behavior.	Evaluate purging behavior, and replace with new ways to cope.
Gain confidence in role-playing sessions.	Conduct role-playing exercises to help patient deal with persons, places, and things that trigger addictions.
Apply role-playing experience to external environment.	Guide patient in bringing his/her new skills into the real world.
Become aware of your negative or ambivalent feelings toward others.	If necessary, identify patient's lack of empathy for others.
Be armed with alternate behaviors to help prevent relapse.	Teach patient alternate constructive behaviors to prevent relapse.
Discuss and resolve treatment termination issues with therapist. Agree on termination plan.	Resolve issues of dependence and separation anxiety, and agree on a treatment termination plan.
Attend support group.	Refer patient to active support group.

TREATMENT PLAN

SUBSTANCE ABUSE AND EATING DISORDERS

SHORT-TERM BEHAVIORAL GOALS: CHILD/ADOLESCENT	THERAPIST'S INTERVENTIONS
Join in treatment. Improve outlook and reduce isolation and anger.	Cultivate therapeutic alliance or collaborative relationship with patient to build trust and enhance treatment outcome.
Resolve fears. Understand and accept possible need for hospitalization.	Explain possible need for hospitalization to treat withdrawal symptoms and provide detoxification with supervision.
Enter into "suicide pact," agreeing to inform therapist of suicidal or homicidal ideations and plans before taking action. If actively suicidal or homicidal, agree to hospitalization.	Assess possible homicidal or suicidal effects of substance use. If actively homicidal or suicidal, hospitalize and notify parents. If patient has ideations but no active plan, enter into "suicide pact."
Explore denial and understand factors contributing to substance abuse.	Explore patient's level of distressed thinking or denial, and assess his/her cognitive and intellectual functioning that contributes to addiction.
Understand that relapse may occur, but you can return to abstinence.	Normalize possible relapse, and help patient regard it as a learning opportunity to develop new techniques to restore abstinence.
Face problems caused by your substance abuse. Take responsibility for the consequences of addiction.	Help patient look at the facts of addiction and the resulting problems.
Recognize how you are self-medicating to avoid fears.	Explain how trauma is often felt in the body as anxiety and how patient is self-medicating to avoid dealing with fears.

SHORT-TERM BEHAVIORAL GOALS: CHILD/ADOLESCENT	THERAPIST'S INTERVENTIONS
Identify ways trauma has affected addictions.	Explore how trauma has exacerbated addiction.
Work out underlying issues that contribute to substance abuse.	Evaluate patient for dual diagnosis, and treat other symptoms (anxiety, depression, PTSD, etc.; see appropriate treatment plan).
Become aware of patterns of stress that lead to substance abuse.	Explore past patterns of substance abuse and their relationship to life stress.
Recognize that substance abuse can quickly become dependency and addiction.	Educate patient about the potential dangers of drug dependency.
Seriously examine and question your addiction.	Provide feedback on negative consequences of addiction.
Explore feelings about change.	Explore patient's ambivalence, fears, and other feelings about change.
Cooperate with therapist in formulating a plan of action.	Explore obstacles while organizing an action plan so patient can see it develop in small, achievable steps.
Actively develop new behaviors.	Encourage, support, and reinforce any positive new behaviors.
Understand the process you must go through to "get clean."	Explain the mourning process, and help patient mourn his/her addiction.
Recognize and avoid potential triggers for relapse.	Identify persons, places, and things that may cause backsliding and relapse.
Maintain daily journal to monitor feelings rather than act out on them.	Assign patient the responsibility of keeping a daily journal of his/her feelings and reactions.
Recognize family triggers for substance abuse and avoid family enablers.	Investigate family conflicts, and identify enablers who promote patient's substance abuse.

SHORT-TERM BEHAVIORAL GOALS: CHILD/ADOLESCENT	THERAPIST'S INTERVENTIONS
Attend Narcotics Anonymous, Alateen, or Alcoholics Anonymous and obtain a sponsor, or attend a Rational Recovery Group.	Refer patient to a 12-step program (Narcotics Anonymous, Alcoholics Anonymous, Alateen, or Rational Recovery Group. Do not send anorexic patients to Overeaters Anonymous, since it reinforces this addiction.)
Replace ritualistic behavior with more rational response.	Investigate ritualistic behaviors related to addictions and teach patient more realistic behaviors.
Reduce anxiety by living in the here and now.	Teach patient mindfulness (living in the here and now without rumination).
Recognize that addictions do not eliminate insecurity.	Help patient to understand that security is a myth. We never had it and never will. Trying to avoid feelings of insecurity through addiction is fruitless.
Go on a "news diet" to restrict tension-producing radio and television broadcasts.	If listening to or watching the news creates anxiety, put the patient on a "news diet," restricting radio and television news to one half-hour a day to stay informed, but to reduce anxiety.
Learn how to begin to develop a wise mind.	Explain how the patient can gain control over his/her mind rather than have the mind control him/her. See how the rational mind can control an emotional mind to become a wise mind.
Learn to soothe self and regulate emotions rather than resort to addiction.	Use hypnosis, relaxation techniques, or creative visualization to help patient learn to reduce stressors that lead to addictive behaviors (see Behavioral Techniques, Chapter 6).

SHORT-TERM BEHAVIORAL GOALS: CHILD/ADOLESCENT	THERAPIST'S INTERVENTIONS
Realize the destructive effects of addictive behavior on the quality of your life.	Explore the destructive effects of addiction on the patient's social, familial, occupational, and academic relationships.
Become more knowledgable about your addiction.	Assign reading of books on addictions (see Resources, Chapter 8).
Learn effective techniques for dealing with destructive urges.	Teach patient self-hypnosis to cope with destructive feelings. Provide audiotape for home use (see Behavioral Techniques, Chapter 6).
Understand that this disorder may not be your fault, but needs to be worked at constantly to maintain recovery.	Review issues of shame and guilt that may cause or contribute to substance abuse.
Develop a SMART plan to deal with recovery.	Help patient develop a SMART action plan: Small, Measurable, Achievable, Realistic, Timelined goals (see Change, Behavioral Techniques, Chapter 6).
Develop alternate behaviors to substance abuse.	Review and select alternate behaviors (exercise, sports, hobbies, etc.).
Reduce anger toward self and others.	Guide patient in diminishing anger toward self and others.
Discuss and resolve termination issues. Help formulate a treatment termination plan.	Resolve separation anxiety and dependency issues. Develop plan for treatment termination.

TREATMENT PLAN

SUBSTANCE ABUSE AND EATING DISORDERS

SHORT-TERM BEHAVIORAL GOALS: FAMILY	THERAPIST'S INTERVETIONS
Improve communication among family members to reduce misunderstandings, anger, and anxiety.	Conduct family sessions or refer for family therapy to reduce anxiety and anger.
Empathize with patient, and help support change.	Help family understand ambivalence and fear of change.
Identify other members of the family who have addiction problems.	Explore familial addictions and identify how other family members deal with chronic stress.
Understand the double-bind that entraps the patient and help in the search for solutions.	Explain Double-Bind theory to family members (abstinence unleashes anxiety, anger, depression, etc., while continued addiction creates physical and psychological problems).
Explore solutions and challenge obstacles to change in order to empower patient to give up addiction.	Explore various solutions to create realistic steps to successful recovery (12-step program, aerobic exercise to stimulate endorphins, hypnosis to raise motivation to abstain, etc.).
Work together to help patient gain abstinence.	Assign family members to read *The Great Brain Robbery* or *The Addiction Workbook* to discover new ways of dealing with the problem (see Resources, Chapter 8).
Demonstrate boundaries and internal family relationships that may exacerbate anxiety.	Explore family boundaries using family sculpturing, a helpful technique for understanding triangulation and family emotional currents (see Behavioral Techniques, Chapter 6).

SHORT-TERM BEHAVIORAL GOALS: FAMILY	THERAPIST'S INTERVETIONS
Identify enablers and enabling behaviors to diminish their effects.	Discuss enabling behaviors with family members to reduce destructive influences.
Shift focus from problem to possible solutions.	Have family members imagine a future without the problem and suggest actions that will make that future possible.
Think about what treatment outcome would look like. Explain what changes you would like to see in other family members when treatment concludes.	Ask family members to think about what they might want to say to each other when treatment comes to an end.
Identify sources of stress.	Explore the possible sources of stress that lead to addictive behavior in the family.
Examine the origins of the stressors.	Question the sources of stress. Are family members trying to please others? Have they taken on tasks they cannot reasonably accomplish?
Identify positive feelings among family members that produce ego strengths.	Explore positive feelings that are refreshing such as outstanding accomplishments.
Explore stress-reducing activities.	Help family members develop ways to replace stressful activities.
Acquire techniques for living in the here and now.	Teach family members to reverse negative ideas and focus on positive outcomes. This may be easier said than done. Focus on past successes with negative outlooks that turned out positively.
Learn self-hypnosis to restructure negative thinking that leads to addictive behaviors.	Teach family members self-hypnosis to experience deep relaxation and focus on their positive goals rather than negative outcomes.

SHORT-TERM BEHAVIORAL GOALS: FAMILY	THERAPIST'S INTERVETIONS
Family members realize they have the power to make important changes, even if they seem small at first.	Show family members their opportunity to do some things differently and make major changes.
Recognize that major change is the result of many small steps taken one at a time.	Help family prioritize achievable goals.
Help identify possible triggers of relapse.	Explore triggers for relapse, and provide support and understanding to patient.
In event of relapse, mobilize to find new solutions.	Teach family members that relapse is normal and should be regarded as a learning tool to uncover new solutions.
Each family member develops a SMART action plan.	Develop a SMART action plan: Small, Measurable, Achievable, Realistic, Timelined goals (see Change, Behavioral Techniques, Chapter 6).
Reduce negative communication.	Develop a system of positive reinforcement within family to reduce scapegoating and improve interactions.
Work together to develop a treatment termination plan.	Discuss termination issues and develop a plan to terminate treatment.

6
BEHAVIORAL TECHNIQUES

Behavioral Techniques attempt to help patients process thoughts and problems in new ways. They include Belly Breathing, Change, Family Sculpturing, Hypnosis, Trauma Release Technique (TRT), Hypnotic Induction, Hypnosis with Children, Mindfulness, Practical Steps for Dealing with Terror, and Personal Power.

BELLY BREATHING

Belly Breathing, sometimes called diaphragmatic breathing, is an effective technique for dealing with anxiety that can be taught to a patient quickly and easily. It helps patients overcome the natural inclination to "freeze" when they feel anxious. It can be used anywhere at any time once the technique has been acquired.

Learning the Technique

In teaching the technique, I ask the patient to lie down on the couch and place a pillow over his/her belly. The patient then breathes in slowly through the nose, letting the air go down through his/her lungs until it reaches the belly. The patient can watch the belly pillow rise, and then slowly exhale the air through the mouth.

When we get anxious, our chest, lungs, and shoulders tighten and our breathing shortens. This breathing technique expands our lung and chest capacity, and relaxes the muscles of the diaphragm, providing an effective tool for coping with any anxiety-provoking situation.

Although most patients master the technique, others may have considerable trouble getting it. I sometimes ask them to silently say the word "calm" with each exhalation and to sense a gentle connection between mind and body described as "inner wisdom."

Belly Breathing is helpful because it can be performed standing up or sitting down, yet helps patients flow rather than freeze.

CHANGE

by Bill O'Hanlon, MS

Step 1: Acknowledge
- Acknowledge people and validate their points of view
- Don't blame or make them wrong
- Get specific: Use action talk (videotalk*) to avoid labeling or generalizing
- Acknowledge concerns (yours and others)
- Acknowledge problems
- Acknowledge what has worked: no need to throw the baby out with the bathwater

Step 2: Find and agree on a direction/mission/vision
- If you don't know where you're going, you'll probably end up somewhere else
- If possible, paint a vivid picture of the future, again in action talk (videotalk)
- Get consensus or at least mutual understanding of that future
- Use possibility talk (expect change, open up possibilities for change, etc.)

Step 3: Acknowledge barriers and identify resources to achieving that future
- What has stopped you or tripped you up in moving toward that future?
- What are the internal barriers (fears, old habits, outdated or unhelpful beliefs you're moving on?
- What are real world barriers (money, lack of consensus, lack of information, actions that haven't been taken) to moving on?
- What or who are the resources available to overcome or resolve the barriers?
- What has worked well in the past?
- Identify patterns of thinking, focus, and action that do not help the situation change

---

*Videotalk means to describe something only in terms of what one could see or hear if watching and listening to a videotape

Step 4: Make an action plan
- Start small
- SMART (Small, Measurable, Achievable, Realistic, Timelined) goals and directions are more likely to succeed

Step 5: Act (Just Do It!)
- Take action, notice results, adjust action if needed
- Break patterns of thinking, focus, and action
- Decide who is going to take what action by when
- Get a promise and arrange to follow up
- Persist until goal is achieved

Step 6: Acknowledge and celebrate progress and success
- Give lots of credit
- Rituals/awards/celebrations to acknowledge milestones achieved and goals met

From "How to Change 101," *Possibilities* newsletter (2001). E-mail by Bill O'Hanlon. Reprinted with permission.

FAMILY SCULPTURING

Family Sculpturing, also referred to as Family Choreography, is a technique for delineating emotional relationships that are always in motion. It depicts transactional patterns such as alliances, triangles, and shifting emotional currents. This adaptable technique can be used with any theoretical modality and modified to implement a variety of goals. Virginia Satir used Family Sculpturing to demonstrate what she called the four most common stances of family members: the accuser, the placatory, the rational one, and the irrelevant one. The technique is also used to change family relationships, create new patterns, and realign the family system.

In practice, after defining or describing the family problem, each family member is asked to arrange family members as he/she experiences them or show a visual picture of the way he or she experiences the problem, to arrange the family members according to their emotional relationship with each member, and to identify their characteristic way of coping with this relationship. The technique can also be used to show how major stressors, such as death or illness, have altered relationships over time. To help move the process along, the therapist might ask questions aimed at shedding light on the traditional patterns. Each member is asked to arrange the other family members as they would like to interact with them. In this way, Family Sculpturing can be used to reveal human relationships within a social, psychological, and physical system and to realign those relationships when necessary. It is a silent motion picture of the family that eliminates the linguistic traps and pattern of attack-counterattack that often mark family sessions.

The therapist might ask questions to shed light on the transactional patterns. Members might also be asked to show the family as they would like to see it. The results can reveal human relationships within a social, psychological, and physical system, and can be helpful in realigning those relationships when necessary.

HYPNOSIS

> *... all knowledge of reality starts*
> *from experience and ends in it.*
> — Albert Einstein

The purpose of hypnotherapy is to provide alternatives for old behaviors to obtain new outcomes. For example, Viktor Frankl, at a conference in Vienna in 1990, told a story of how he survived the Nazi death camp. He was marching under guard along a freezing, barren landscape in Poland without food or water when he fell to the ground. A Nazi guard kicked him and ordered him to get up, but Frankl did not have the energy to stand. As a result, he was beaten and left for dead. As he lay dying, his mind drifted to another place and he imagined himself giving a lecture in Vienna, called, "The Psychology of Death," in which he described how he survived the death camp. These thoughts gave him the energy to get up and continue marching. It was a form of dissociating from his tragic circumstances and focusing on a better outcome. In his mind, Frankl was no longer on the ground, but talking to an imaginary audience and, in the process, creating a sense of a brighter future. All of the time he remained in the Nazi death camp, he worked on his presentation. He finally did give it after his release from prison and went on to write many books dealing with his experience and the meaning of life.

Frankl's experience is reflected in his book, *Man's Search for Meaning* (1976, p. 104): "Everything can be taken from a man but... the last of human freedoms – to choose one's attitudes, in any given set of circumstance, to choose one's way."

Effective therapy is actually hypnotherapy. As most therapists know, the internal world is more negotiable than we realize. People do have the will to choose. Our beliefs about ourselves are fairly well formed by ages 12 to 15. Meta communications (hypnotic trance) invites people to step out of themselves and investigate new resources.

By going into a trance state one can dissociate from everyday life and tap into the unconscious or creative part of the brain – the part that knows how to breathe and send oxygen to the blood cells without using the conscious mind. Hypnotic language can communicate with the part of the brain that forms belief systems. It opens the pathways to changing old beliefs and behaviors to achieve new outcomes.

Hypnosis is an induced altered state of consciousness, or a trance state, in which the individual is more susceptible to suggestion. We are imprinted with mindsets that originate in our families of origin and are incorporated into the unconscious. We organize our personalities and behavior around these imprints. We do not operate directly on the world, but through a map or model of the world, a created representation of what we believe. In hypnosis, the therapist aims at changing, or otherwise influencing, the maps we hold in our minds. All hypnosis is essentially self-hypnosis, which broadens responses and increases cognitive flexibility.

It is a common mistake to believe that the conscious mind is responsible for all thoughts and behaviors, including emotional reactions and decision-making. In reality, the conscious mind possesses few skills and is responsible for very few actions or creative thoughts. It is the unconscious aspects of the mind (Havens and Walters, 1989) that play a major role in the events of everyday life.

Hypnosis is a way to access the untapped power of the mind. In this state of intense relaxation and concentration, the mind is able to focus on positive suggestions that may be carried out at a future time. These subliminal messages can be very powerful. The mind is like an onion. The outer layer, or conscious mind, deals with intelligence, reality, and logic. The inner mind is concerned with emotion, imagination, and memories, as well as the autonomic nervous system, which automatically controls our internal organs (how we breathe, send oxygen to our blood cells, or walk without thinking about it). The internal mind is on autopilot, reacting to dictates of the pleasure principle. It seeks pleasure and avoids pain.

We often use unconscious suggestions in everyday life: e.g. "I can't stop smoking. If I do, I will gain weight." Newspaper and television advertising attempt to persuade, and their repetition reinforce suggestion.

Hypnosis can create positive changes and create new mantras through creative visualization while in a trance. Whatever your mind can conceive, within reason, your mind and body can achieve. Hypnosis can help to build self-esteem and confidence, control eating problems, stop smoking, eliminate sleep dysfunctions, reduce anxiety, control fears, manage stress, help master public speaking, control pain, improve sports performance, and promote health. It is particularly effective in releasing emotional and physical trauma.

Hypnosis can be a highly effective therapeutic tool in dealing with almost all disorders. When patients have slipped into trance after induced relaxation, they can return to the scene of the trauma where, from a safe vantage point, they can bring back traumatic memories that have been repressed (see Trauma Release Technique). Trance is a day-dream state that people slip into and out of all day without knowing it. You are in a trance when you listen to music or think about something else while you drive and arrive at your destination without knowing how you got there. Trance states like these are actually a state of passive, inner-focused awareness. Patients in trance are able to pay attention to their unconscious minds, which can be sources of healing information and guidance. It is important to explain to the patient the Law of Reverse Effect: If you try to will yourself to sleep, it will not come. If you will yourself to have an erection or an orgasm, it will not work. The same is true of hypnosis. The trick is to just let it happen. I reassure patients by telling them there is no way to do it incorrectly. It is the opposite of school, where we are taught to memorize in order to learn. Here, you don't even have to pay attention.

Unfortunately, many people fear hypnotherapy because of the stigma of ridicule and embarrassment that surrounds "stage hypnosis," in which volunteer subjects are made to waddle like ducks or generally make fools of themselves. Such displays only give credence to the super-sensitivity of a few people to the awesome power of suggestion. These "volunteers" are carefully selected by the stage hypnotist before the show begins. However, the majority of people are poor subjects for stage hypnosis. The volunteers chosen are either very gullible, so exhibitionistic as to crave the attention of an audience, or just plain "shills," planted by the hypnotist to assure success.

Hypnotherapy works differently. Most patients respond cooperatively to ideas of relaxation or guided visualization because they feel their self-control is not threatened. There is nothing magical about it. Hypnosis is a technique that simply allows them to focus on what they want, instead of what they do not want. In time, patients come to regard the hypnotherapist as a set of "training wheels" that can be discarded when they learn the technique of hypnosis for themselves. It is important to explain to the patient what will take place before the session, to determine what they want to work on, and to set reasonable goals. Some patients will need help in doing this, thus the therapist must be ready to provide some suggestions. According to Erickson, the master hypnotherapist, trance is "the state in which openness to change is most likely to occur" (Rosen, 1982, p. 27).

Erickson would get the patient's attention, model the patient's feelings, and provide intriguing or attractive solutions that effectively reduce feelings of anger, helplessness, and passivity. Each clinician must find the induction techniques that work best for him or her, and are consistent with his or her personality, rhythm, feeling, and response to the patient. An induction is not a set of words or phrases; it is the communication of ideas.

Erickson (Rosen, 1982, p. 46) felt that the therapist's job is to bring back the (patient's) real self, which had been distorted. He tells the story of the wandering horse to help him with that task. When Erickson was a young boy, a horse with no identifying mark wandered into his family's yard. Erickson returned the horse to its owners by letting the horse decide which way he wanted to go. "I didn't know – but the horse did. All I did was keep him on the road," he said.

That is the therapist's job: to keep the patient on the road to recovery. Christopher Bollas (Rosen, 1982, p. 52) regards hypnosis as "a kind of communication, in which we are receptive to the intelligence and 'emotional breeze' of the other."

Each hypnosis session should be uniquely designed for where the patient is and where he or she wants to go. After these sessions, patients usually feel better and do better. They are obviously more relaxed. One patient even arrived with a heart monitor and upon completion of the session found her blood pressure significantly reduced. I always ask for feedback at the end of the session. Most patients say they feel lighter or somewhat removed from their problems. Each time a patient comes to a hypnosis session, I modify what I say in an effort to meet the patient where he or she is at that moment in time.

Nevertheless, this technique is not for all patients. It may take many sessions to develop the trust to undergo this exercise. It is best to go slowly, let the patient know that this is a team effort, and that he or she is in control.

Hypnosis is an induced altered state of consciousness, or a trance state, in which the individual is more susceptible to suggestion. People are imprinted with mindsets that originate in their families of origin and are incorporated into the unconscious. We organize our personalities and act around these imprints. We do not operate directly on the world, but through a map or model of the world, a created representation of what we believe. In hypnosis, the therapist aims at changing, or otherwise influencing, the maps we hold in our minds. All hypnosis is essentially self-hypnosis, which can broaden responses and increase cognitive flexibility.

The following is a typical session. Prior to hypnosis, I always discuss with patients their hopes, dreams, and specific intensions for this session. The patient is asked to lie down or sit up, and is given the option of closing his/her eyes or keeping them open. Most patients willingly close their eyes. If not, it is a signal to proceed slowly and cautiously, continually checking to assure that the patient is comfortable. If they like, I provide patients with an audiotape of the session so they can practice the technique at home. The tape serves as a transitional object and reassures patients of what I have said. They can listen to it without the therapist present. I caution all patients against listening to the tape while driving. Trance and transportation do not mix well.

Patients are asked to focus on their breathing, consciously feeling their breath as it enters their lungs and is expelled. I explain that, with their permission, I would like them to have an experience that meets their needs. They may be surprised at or changed by what they discover. I remind them that they are completely supported by the couch or chair, and it is okay if their conscious mind wanders because I am talking to the back of their mind, the part that motivates their behavior.

As they go deeper into trance, I remind them that their unconscious mind will become more accessible and receptive to new teachings and the discarding of old habits they no longer want. Patients are asked to relax their forehead and feel the stresses of the day fade away. Pay attention to the wave of relaxation as it spreads down to their eyes and into their jaws where tension is often held. Then they are asked to imagine a heavy weight lifting off their shoulders and feel the relaxation going into their bronchial tubes, heart, lungs, and up and down their spine into their abdominal system, buttocks, legs, and feet. This is the induction phase, and a good time to tell a story.

One story of the power of hypnosis comes from Erickson's own life. As a young boy, he contracted polio and was placed in an iron lung to facilitate his breathing. He overheard the doctors tell his mother in June 1919 that he would be dead by morning. Infuriated that they would tell her such a thing, he vowed to beat the polio and get better. Erickson survived the night and went on to steadily improve. Although he could only move his eyes, he spent a great deal of time silently analyzing the hidden messages and intricacies of the conversations of his parents and siblings. He also examined the minute details of the relationship between thinking and healing and their effects on the mind and body. With nothing but the power of his own brain, Erickson eventually cured himself.

The story usually gets the patient's attention, reduces feelings of helplessness and passivity and, in the final step, shows how to reframe the way we look at our own condition. It also builds anticipation and expectation. Pacing is important. The therapist must learn to adjust to the patient's rate of response and to match the patient's breathing pattern. As the therapist becomes more comfortable and experienced with these techniques, the outcome will dramatically improve.

When they are totally relaxed, I suggest that patients go to a special place they have previously visited or where they would like to be, a place to find peace and comfort. A suggestion is made to look around this special place and experience the sounds, smell the fragrances, and feel the sun on his/her body. Here patients can inhale peace and exhale anxiety; inhale clarity and exhale confusion; inhale calmness and exhale anger. I add other specific feelings and emotions to this part of the session that are appropriate to the issues we are dealing with in therapy.

Then I ask patients to imagine a scale or ruler, and on a scale of one to ten (ten being the most relaxed) to indicate where they are. No matter what the response, I let patients know that this number is right for them. If the number is less than five, I ask if they would like to be more relaxed. It is extremely important to respect whatever they say. I suggest that they imagine pouring a liquid into a glass container, and as they pour the liquid, feel themselves becoming more and more relaxed as the container fills up. Patients are then asked to form a mental picture of where they are on the scale. Whatever the number, it is important to give them positive reinforcement. If patients are appropriately relaxed, I anchor the feeling by asking them to put their thumb and index finger together and letting them know that this relaxation can be practiced during the day simply by touching index finger to thumb, taking three deep breaths, and imagining themselves back in their special place. Most of all, hypnosis should be a positive, relaxing, and uplifting experience.

Climbing Magic Mountain

At this point, one technique I like to use is "Climbing Magic Mountain." First, I describe what Magic Mountain looks like and then I have them imagine walking toward this lush, beautiful mountain blanketed by abundant grass, wildflowers, and trees. I ask them to look around and see rainbows of color. I draw their attention to the majestic trees standing high on the mountain, to watch the leaves as they reach the sky. I suggest that when we get to the top they may gain some new insights into their life on earth. I pause here and ask them to project all their hopes, dreams, and goals up to the top of the mountain. (**Note**: The patient's hopes, dreams, and goals must already have been discussed before the session. If the patients are not in touch with their hopes, dreams, and goals, do not use this technique.)

When they have completed this task, I ask them to give me a signal by moving their fingers. This technique is called ideomotor; it brings subconscious thinking to the conscious level and gives me feedback on when to continue. At this point I ask them to visualize a pool, which I call Misery Pool, where patients can bathe or simply drop off whatever problems they are dealing with and watch them sink to the bottom. They can feel the problems draining from their bodies and submerging into the water.

When they are ready to move on, I ask that they signal me again by moving their fingers. As we resume the journey, I again remind them of the beautiful surroundings and the sun gently warming their bodies. The green grass is springy beneath their feet as they allow their subconscious to take more responsibility for guiding and directing their awareness as we ascend the mountain. Some patients prefer to have me at their side, while others want to make the trip alone. They are asked to imagine spheres of light surrounding their bodies: blue for power, gold for wisdom, pink for love, purple for cleansing, white for hope and healing, and green for truth. These colored spheres of light will help glide them easily up the mountainside to the top where I describe the lush scenery, clouds, trees, beautiful flowers, etc. As we resume the journey, I again remind them of the beautiful surroundings and the sun gently warming their bodies. The green grass is springy beneath their feet as they allow their subconscious to take more responsibility for guiding and directing their awareness as we ascend the mountain.

On the mountain top are their hopes, dreams, goals, and intentions. There is a special satchel for them to pack up their hopes and dreams. They can pack all of them or return to the mountain at a later time to complete the job. On the way down the mountain, we come to a footbridge where we can sit and reflect on our experience. When they are ready, we return to the room alert, relaxed, and refreshed.

TRAUMA RELEASE TECHNIQUE

Trauma Release Technique (TRT) should be used only if patients are sufficiently experienced with hypnosis or trained in self-hypnosis. Such expertise may take up to 10, 12, or more sessions. The patients know how to anchor their feelings (see Hypnosis). An essential ingredient in using the technique is a therapeutic alliance between patient and therapist. If the patients do not feel completely safe, the procedure should be put on hold for the future. Patients who dissociate or are psychotic may feel threatened and are inappropriate candidates for this technique.

Clear evidence for the effectiveness of TRT is found in the outcomes of combat veterans who underwent flooding treatment at a Veteran's Administration hospital. Patients who completed this treatment reported dramatic reductions in the intrusive and hyperarousal symptoms of post-traumatic stress disorder (PTSD). They suffered fewer nightmares and flashbacks, combined with a general improvement in anxiety, depression, concentration problems, and psychosomatic symptoms. Moreover, six months after completing the flooding treatment, patients reported lasting improvement in their intrusive and hyperarousal symptoms (Herman, 1997).

TRT differs from flooding treatment inasmuch as it first teaches the patient hypnosis, whereas flooding treatment is a careful exploration of patients' memories of the traumatic event through a prepared script read over and over "with a formal delivery ritual" (Herman, 1997, p. 182) at the completion of therapy. Under hypnosis, as the patients experience the emotional impact of their fears, other recollections usually emerge spontaneously to break the barriers of amnesia. TRT has the ability to use trance logic to help trauma survivors break through the barrier and revalue conflicted aspects of their trauma so they do not reemerge as flashbacks, nightmares, or panic attacks.

Trauma patients tend to be in a state of anxiety that can be exacerbated by introducing new techniques. The challenge (Araoz, 1995, p. 5) is to learn to use suggestions in a "constructive, ego- and health-producing way." He explains that any "thought, belief, mental impression, or image can act as a self-suggestion affecting perception, mood, and behavior."

Trauma is not only felt in the mind, but is remembered by every cell in the body. Hypnotic suggestions (Barber, 1984) can affect the physiological activities of the cells in the human body. If psychology can become biology, hypnotic suggestions can transform a person's thinking, which can, in turn, change biology and activate the miraculous process of self-healing (healing the soul).

In a typical session, the patient should already be familiar with hypnosis and know which "relaxation number" is most comfortable for him or her (see Hypnosis above). There are many inductions that can be used. Once the patient is sufficiently relaxed, there are also a number of different ways to go back in time to the traumatic event. Related traumatic memories (Herman, 1997) have a tendency to become disconnected from their sources and take on a life of their own.

O'Hanlon (2000, p. 165) reminds us that, "The unconscious mind is sometimes smart about things it is dumb to be smart about." When the context is changed, and the patient is in a safe place, we can slowly go back in time to regain the dissociated parts of the mind and make it possible to reduce uncomfortable flashbacks.

When patients are sufficiently relaxed, I sometimes have them imagine they are sitting on a train in front of a giant window. They will see what is happening to them, but they will always remain in the safety of the train. This takes the experience outside the patients' bodies. Another viable technique is to have patients sit inside a movie theatre next to you or, if they are secure, alone. The technique is really a matter of patient choice. If patients prefer the train, we ride together through a tunnel to emerge on the other side in time to witness the traumatic event. If any hyperarousal begins, I take the patients back to their safe relaxation number and start again. They are reassured that there is no way to do this procedure incorrectly.

I ask the patients to describe what they see, and listen for clues in the narration under trance. We move along from present to past, performing the uncovering work with patients, using the trance state for soothing and relaxation, while I closely monitor their facial expressions and body movements. We sometimes stop briefly to re-anchor them in a comfortable place. Patients usually come out of the trance with a lot of affect: sadness, thoughts, and images about what has happened, but with some distance from the traumatic event, and feeling lighter.

At the end of the session, I leave plenty of time for them to reorient themselves and perform intense exploration of what has happened to them. Breaking these barriers reduces the need for flashbacks, nightmares, or lack of affect. Although I usually record these sessions on audiotape, patients may be reluctant to take the tapes home since they may be too traumatic to listen to when they are alone.

I use the coping mechanisms I teach in the hypnotic induction in dealing with many different situations that arise in the lives of my patients. These mechanisms become valuable tools to expand patients' creativity and ingenuity, and improve their lives.

In trauma, the usual response (Herman, 1997) is to banish the event from consciousness or freeze, which breeds a wide variety of symptoms. The atrocities become disconnected from their source in much the same way that aspects of the self become disconnected in multiple personality disorder (they develop lives and personalities of their own or turn into flashbacks and intrusive memories or nightmares). Patients with post-traumatic stress disorder feel as though they are going through the trauma in present time. Like the victims of the World Trade Center attacks, they feel their bodies experiencing it again and again, or they smell the burning rubble, which leads to an overwhelming feeling of helplessness.

Levine (1997, p. 197) explains, "It is common for traumatized individuals to get sucked into the trauma vortex, or to avoid the breach entirely by staying distanced from the region where the trauma occurred." Trance logic or hypnosis has the ability to help survivors regain the disavowed parts of the self. The therapeutic experience (Warren, 1999) is characterized by sound holding, listening, and intervening, which combine empathic relating with cognitive explanation. When the timing is right, sharing the horror of the images can open a virtual floodgate of anguish.

HYPNOTIC INDUCTION

Before using this technique, it is important that you gain some experience in the practice of hypnosis or hypnotherapy. You should begin the initial hypnotic session by relating the nature of trance to a deep state of relaxation. For some patients, the word "trance" is too frightening, and the word "relaxation" is a more comfortable alternative. With relaxation the patient never loses control, while trance seems to imply he or she may not be able to come out of it. I explain that the unconscious part of the mind, or the back of the mind, is the most intelligent part of the psyche. It knows how to control your breathing and how to send oxygen to the body's cells. It even knows how to make you walk without thinking with the front of your mind. That's the conscious part of the mind.

Patients have been in and out of trance states all day long. You are in a trance when you are watching a movie and forget the story line. A good example of a trance state is when you are driving and don't remember how you got to your destination. The back of your mind guided you there automatically, while the conscious part of your mind was thinking about something else. I explain that the powerful unconscious part of your mind can help you to heal by creating a climate of positive expectation.

Sometimes it is helpful to tell a story of how it helped another patient, or how the famous hypnotherapist Milton Erickson used the power of the back of his mind to cure himself of polio. Relaxation (Araoz, 1995, pp. 34–5) "gives the parasympathetic nervous system the chance to take over. Tension, the opposite of relaxation, occurs when the sympathetic nervous system is active longer than necessary to take action or face the threat of danger." Relaxation will bring the bodily symptoms to optimal functioning and help reduce anxieties (fight, flight, or freeze). When we are sufficiently relaxed in a safe environment, we can glide into the memories rather than have them pop into our minds in the form of unexpected flashbacks.

Patients are reassured that they need to do nothing since, in hypnosis, the harder one tries, the more difficult it becomes. It's like trying to sleep. The more you try to force it, the more elusive it becomes. You just have to let it happen. Patients might concentrate on a spot on the ceiling and let their eyelids become heavier and heavier. If they prefer, they can even go into a trance with their eyes open, although most people just close them naturally. We then focus on the rhythm of breathing. Don't rush it, just relax. You might even feel a heavy weight being lifted from your shoulders. Breathe in slowly and, with the next exhalation, release all the air from your lungs. Your arms might get heavy or they might feel so light that you want to raise them. I don't know, but the back of your mind does. Relax. Feel the relaxation spread through your entire body like a wave. It flows down into every cell, every organ. It calms and it heals. Feel the knots in your stomach untie as you breathe in and out.

The patient is then taught the laws of reversed effect: that willpower is ineffective in suppressing memories. As you try harder to force or suppress them, it has an adverse effect. The key is self-suggestion, which operates at the level of unconscious thinking.

You must establish rapport and a cooperative relationship. Timing is critical. Wait for the patient to be ready, and then create a climate of positive energy. Tell the patient that emotions are carriers of energy that have the power to heal and protect.

Patients are then asked to visualize a blackboard containing a relaxation scale with the numbers one through ten, with ten being the most relaxed. Then they are asked to indicate where they are on the scale. If they are located on the low end of the scale, we continue with the relaxation, breathing in and out, releasing darkness and inhaling light, exhaling anxiety and inhaling calm and courage, releasing anger and hatred and inhaling a white healing energy. We continue the cycle until we reach the higher numbers on the relaxation scale.

At this point they are encouraged to describe what they are feeling in their bodies, and are slowly guided in gradually getting in touch with a peaceful, calm. When they are sufficiently relaxed, they are instructed to place their pointer finger and thumb together to "anchor" the feeling. Patients can use the anchoring technique whenever they need to restore this feeling of relaxation in or out of session. It is a reminder that they have some control over how they feel. Usually, two or three relaxation technique training sessions are required before patients are ready to talk about the traumatic experience and experience the flashbacks. Always pace yourself to the patients. It's like dancing; let the patients lead.

When patients have become experienced with relaxation technique you can continue. The difficult part is to come face to face with the horrors on the other side of the amnesic barrier. As they tell their stories, points of hyperarousal may emerge. If these reactions are too strong, it is best to backtrack to the relaxation exercise.

Not until patients are thoroughly relaxed, and the hyperarousal state is diminished, can we continue. We may even have to wait for another session. At this point, patients need to be reassured that hypnosis is not magical. They must be reminded that when we concentrate our attention on a goal (getting rid of the flashbacks) it tends to be realized. Once again, the principle of positive suggestion, such as, "Your unconscious is working hard today, is extremely important. Your mind should take pride in how hard it is working to uncover the trauma and let it go. Your unconscious mind is like a river. We know you can't push a river; you have to flow with it."

To further reinforce positive outcome over time, remind patients of the difficult things they have accomplished in their lives. Once they are sufficiently relaxed, they can return to telling the story as though they were seeing it on a movie screen outside their bodies. It is important for patients to see their experiences and create a fully developed narrative of them. It is like putting together the pieces of a puzzle. Sometimes it can be accomplished without formal hypnotic induction.

"Hypnotic suggestion" (Warren, 1999, p. 7) "is surprisingly powerful. Even a subtle suggestion can reorganize ideas, memories, and fantasies, as well as self and object relations." However, using the flooding treatment with traumatic memories requires a high degree of skill on the part of the therapist and should be done slowly and carefully. Flooding must be preceded by careful preparation and followed by an adequate period of integration, using the trance state for soothing and relaxing patients to enable them to move on to the next stage.

Havens and Walters (1989, p. 90) explain, "hypnotherapy merely sets the stage, and provides an opportunity for change." As previously mentioned, a good technique with patients who have become familiar with hypnosis, or trance states, is to have them imagine they are in a movie theater. The patient is reminded that he or she is not alone. The clinician is sitting next to the patient in the imaginary theater and they are watching a film of the patient's life, starting with the present and going backward in time. The patient describes what is going on as the film travels through the past. During the journey, one must always be on the alert for signs of hyperarousal, which can be countered with one of the relaxation techniques patients have already learned. When the patient is again feeling relaxed, ask the unconscious mind to continue in an attempt to reconstruct the trauma. If the patient cannot do that at this time, use a termination procedure reminding the patient that he or she will only remember what is comfortable. Welcome the patient back from the trip reassuring him or her that as much time can be taken as needed to return. Then address what the patient would like to discuss about the experience. Eventually, you will be able to go back to the movie, and put together the remaining pieces of the puzzle.

Dissociation and Hypnosis

These techniques can have only limited success if the relational aspects of the process are ignored. In working with patients with multiple personalities who are aware of their dissociated personalities, I change the movie to a stage, and have the personalities discuss the different aspects of themselves in order to work toward integration. Before you start, let patients know that dissociation is a normal coping response to trauma designed to reduce anxiety.

The typical session consists of four parts. The first part of the session should be used for discovering the status of the patient. The second part is for hypnosis or relaxation if the patient is ready. In the third part, the patient is helped to come to terms with his/her traumatic memories and mourning as a prelude to reconnect. The fourth part is the termination of the induction. Other sessions can help the patient in plans for the future. "Isolation and helplessness are the core experiences of psychological trauma... Empowerment and reconnection are the core experiences of recovery" (Herman, 1997, p. 197).

Always bring the patient back to his or her safe environment. Ask what number pops into mind on the relaxation scale and get the patient back into a comfortable state. Ask if he or she would like to be more relaxed. If so, return to the blackboard and strive for a higher relaxation number. Then focus again on breathing, reminding the patient that breathing heals, breathing calms, breathing relaxes. There is no rush.

Instruct the patient to take his or her time, concentrating on the rhythm of breathing, the rhythm of his or her body until he or she is comfortable enough to continue. Have the patient look around his/her safe environment and experience how it feels, what it sounds like, how it smells.

Ask if there is anything the patient would like to bring back to remind him or her of the hypnotic experience. Then the patient is given a code word such as "confidence" to remind him or her of the relaxed feeling in the safe environment. The code word can be used before going to sleep, letting his or her dreams work on it or in the morning upon awakening to presage the wonderful day ahead. The code word will also trigger whatever parts of the experience the patient's conscious mind can deal with. Usually, an audiotape of the hypnosis or relaxation experience is recorded for the patient's use at home to reinforce the experience. The patient is told to take as much time as necessary to review in his or her mind the hypnotic experience and indicate when he or she is ready to come to wakeful alertness.

The aim of the session is to help people move from their haunted past to the here and now, becoming capable of responding to life and their fullest potential. The key element of the hypnosis is integration of the unacceptable. The trauma becomes an integrated part of the patient's history so that victims are no longer trapped in their past, but are helped to reestablish control over their lives.

HYPNOSIS SCRIPTS

The following hypnosis scripts were developed for use in my practice. They may give you a better idea of a typical hypnosis session.

Stressless Mountain

Please let me introduce you to a very surprising way of releasing the terrible twins: stress and anxiety. You may be pleasantly amazed or surprised how quickly you can relieve yourself of these debilitating feelings. It is my hope that you use this CD as often as you like but never when you are driving a car or using heavy equipment. Find a nice quiet place and shut the world off for about 20 minutes. Stressless Mountain me in my dreams. I believe your unconscious speaks to you in your dreams, if you learn how to listen to your dreams.

So, begin by turning the world off for about 20 minutes. Find a nice place to sit or lie down. I prefer to lie down because my neck is supported and I can really relax and let go.

So, let's begin. You might want to stare at a spot above your eyes and you might even begin to feel them beginning to blink already and you may want to close your eyes, it is all up to you because I would not want you to go into a trance too quickly or too slowly. So, just let go as you tune in to my voice. You do not have to listen with the front of your mind because I am talking to the back of your mind, the part of your mind that knows how to make you breathe, the part that signals you when you are hungry or thirsty, so just let go and I will lead your unconscious on this stressless trip where you might lose as much of your anxiety, or stress, that you choose to let go of. Remember, you can take everything away from a person except the freedom to choose one's attitude so let me show you how to choose your attitude for a stressless life.

Stress can be all around you but it does not have to be inside you.

Now imagine with me that you are outside, perhaps somewhere in nature, or at the beach, or a lake on a mountain. If you prefer the city, imagine you are in the city, or even in your home, but make sure it is a very peaceful and restful scene – one especially just for you. You can be alone or you can invite someone to be with you – it is all up to you. Feel a warm healing breeze on your body. See in your mind's eye the most beautiful sights around you.

Smell a sweet fragrance and hear the sounds of nature or music soothing you, look around with your mind's eye. Feel yourself sinking down further and further as I count down from seven to one, and as I do, let go of all your worldly concerns. Your breathing becomes slower and more rhythmic... *six*... inhale life-giving oxygen exhale anxiety... *five*... inhale personal growth, exhale anything you want to get rid of... *four*... inhale whatever you want and exhale stress... *three*... inhale peace and exhale darkness... *two*... inhale love and exhale anything else you want to rid yourself of... *one*... let go of all your worldly or material problems for now and take in all your dreams. Now my voice will disappear for about a minute and when it comes back you will be ten times more relaxed.

You are now ready to enter the island of your dreams. The countdown has already transformed you. The part of your brain that sends stress hormones to your body has been shut down. Your immune system is now working automatically to heal your mind and body of any dis-ease. You can already feel a white healing energy surrounding your body, entering your pores, going through the top of your head, balancing your brain, and relaxing your jaw. Feel your jaw becoming loose and limp like a rubber band. Feel the white light going into your sinuses. Around your eyes, feel the little muscles around your eyes relaxing more and more – just let go. Feel the energy going into your heart, lungs, liver, kidneys, gastrointestinal system, buttocks, down your legs into your feet. Feel the white static energy surrounding every dis-eased cell healing and cleansing, healing and cleansing every cell, every tendon, every nerve in your mind and body. Now feel four valves opening at the bottom of your feet and the tips of your toes releasing the terrible twins, stress and anxiety. See them walking off into the sunset together. Feel your body becoming lighter and lighter, almost like floating. Just let go. We are now ready to leave for Stressless Mountain. Remember what you focus on expands. Be the wish you wish to see in the world. You can transform your own life. The answers may come in a dream, or a small voice talking to you inside your mind, or in a flash. I don't know, but the back of your mind knows what is best for you. Remember Einstein only used 12% of his brain and hypnosis is a way of dipping into more of your brain. So now my voice will disappear for about a minute to give you time to prepare to leave for Stressless Mountain.... *Pause*....

We are now ready to leave for Stressless Mountain. Feel the warmth of the sunshine on your body as we walk along the road, hear the sounds of nature around you, smell the fragrance of the flowers, and even taste this special place of yours. We are ready to start up Stressless Mountain where all your hopes, dreams, and goals are. You can go up the mountain alone or you can invite anyone you please.

So let's begin our trip. Notice how beautiful this mountain is. The majestic pine trees along the way, the wild flowers, of all shades of colors, the birds singing, the billowy white clouds floating above your head. See all the pleasant things around you. You have finally found your bliss. We are coming to the top of Stressless Mountain. You feel so at home here. You are so at home here. In order to anchor this feeling, put your pointer finger and thumb together, and anytime you want to recapture this feeling, just touch your pointer with your thumb and you will have this feeling. Remember, as Viktor Frankl has said, you can take away anything from men or women except their freedom to choose their attitude.

It is now time to find a nice comfortable place to sit down. A nice big rock or a comfortable bench, feel the texture of it, visualize the color... just relax into wherever you are sitting. This is your finest moment. Feel it, taste it, see it. Your family and friends are around you applauding you, or if you would rather be alone that is okay too... it all belongs to you. Be the change you wish to be. My voice will disappear so these images become deeply embedded in the back of your mind.... *Pause*.... You may be amazed or surprised at the transformation because all that you ardently want and vividly imagine will happen.

The back of the mind is so sophisticated it can even make it happen in a split second. So, my voice will disappear so these images can become deeply embedded in the back of the mind.... *Pause*.... End.

Library of Personal Power

Helen Keller tells us that when one door closes another one opens. So, find a nice quiet place for yourself and shut the world off for about 20 minutes because we are going on a journey into yourself; a quiet place where no one can disturb you. This is a place where you can leave your worries and stresses behind and find your own personal power that you never thought you had. It is a place deep within you. So, lie back or sit down, whichever you prefer. I am more comfortable lying down so that my neck is supported. Feel your eyes becoming heavier and heavier.... They might even begin blinking and you might even want to close them.... It is all up to you.

So, take a nice long deep breath into your belly and release your breath. You might want to put your hands on your belly and feel it rise and fall. That way you will know you are taking deep belly breaths. Take four or five more deep belly breaths while my voice disappears in order to give you a chance to settle deep down inside yourself and when my voice comes back you will be ten times more relaxed.... *Pause*....

Now, I am talking to the part of your mind known as the unconscious part of your mind, or the back of your mind. So, you can let the front of your mind do whatever it wants. It need not even listen to me. This is the part of your mind that knows how to make you breathe. It is your deep unconscious wisdom system and, in fact, it remembers everything you learned in your entire life. People say Einstein only used 12% of his brain. Hypnosis is a way of tapping into this part of your mind and helping you find your own personal power to reduce that stress and anxiety. This CD will provide you with your own personal tools to rid yourself of those unwanted feelings. Today, we are going on a special trip to your personal library where we can create your future life story. Remember, what you focus on expands. When the cocoon thought it was over, it became a butterfly. I will provide you with the tools that can help you rid yourself of stress and anxiety and achieve mastery over those debilitating feelings. Remember, the mind is the prototype for all computers, only smarter. In the first couple of years of your life, you not only learned to walk, you learned to speak a language, maybe even two. You learned to comb your hair, recognize people in your family – and even family friends who you learned to differentiate from strangers – you learned your way around the immediate neighborhood. You even learned to begin to read and write. So, imagine what you can learn from this CD.

So, let's begin the count down now to your own personal library where you can learn to get rid of stress, which only interferes with your life and your memory process, and learn how to recreate a stressless life where you can learn new life skills without stress to interfere.

First, begin by practicing belly breathing; put your hands or a pillow on your belly, and take four or five deep deliberate breaths. Feel your belly rise and fall, rise and fall, rise and fall. My voice will disappear for a minute, so you can get comfortable with your belly breaths... *Pause*....

Imagine a staircase made of wood, stone, or marble. Any color you wish... as I count down... *one*... going down... relax... focus on your breathing... *two*... feel yourself breathing in life-giving oxygen... *three*... center your focus inwards on yourself as you get closer to your library... *four*... prepare yourself with attitude of quiet and passive attention... *five*... getting ready to step into your very own library... *six*... notice what the building looks like... *seven*... the roof top... the windows... the color of the building... the size and shape of the door.

Outside the library is a bench. Sit down on it. See how comfortable you are, notice the color of the bench. Hear the sounds of nature around you. Notice in front of you is the most beautiful trunk. Open the lid. Fill the trunk with all your stress and anxiety and problems you are willing to get rid of. Remember, we are living in a world of what I call the National Trauma Syndrome. Stress can be all around you but it does not have to be in you. My voice will disappear for about a minute for you to complete this task and when you've finished, wiggle your fingers to let your conscious mind know you have completed this task.... *Pause*.... Close the trunk. Notice that it has a big, red helium balloon attached. It starts lifting the trunk up, up, up to the sky, draining from your body all the stress and anxiety. Feel yourself getting lighter and lighter; almost like floating.

Now, we are ready to enter. Open the door and notice the room... smell the aroma of the room... notice the paintings and books... see the plush, oversized easy chair made especially for you. Feel a sense of peacefulness surround you. Take a nice, easy breath, look around, and notice that there is a leather-bound book with your name on it. Pick up the book. Sink down into the easy chair and start reading the book. My voice will disappear for a couple of minutes while you go through the pages of your life. Then wiggle your fingers to let your conscious mind know you have completed this task.

There is nothing we can do about the past, that was yesterday, that was yesterday, that was yesterday, let it be. Now, I want you to think of your finest moment and if you can't think of one, make one up. Live it... Feel it... Taste it... See it in your mind's eye.... Be it now. Keep that feeling with you and begin to visualize change in your future, a future without stress or anxiety. You are now being surrounded by spheres of light and in the spheres of light is a white glow for healing, blue for power, pink for love, green for abundance, gold for wisdom, and purple for truth. These are your spheres of light. They will go with you from now on. You can always call on them. Remember, you have the power now to choose to change your mental beliefs and you may be amazed or surprised how this CD has already transformed you.

As you are sitting there looking in your life book, see a future of happiness with personal power. See it... hear it... feel it... taste it... focus on it, and, as you do you, become surrounded by a white shield, which will stay with you from now on and all stress will bounce off it and away. As you luxuriate in your library, a new feeling of personal power begins to grow and a new sense of self-esteem and self-worth is yours.

My voice is going to disappear so these images can become deeply imbedded in the back of your mind. If you are using this CD before your bedtime, you may be fast asleep. Sleep... sleep through the night and allow your dreams to work on these images... And when you awake, you will wake refreshed and alert.

And if you are using this CD during the day, take as much time as you need to review what I said, and when you are ready, come back to the room refreshed and alert with your own personal power.... End.

HYPNOSIS WITH CHILDREN

Young children may have difficulty with progressive relaxation through breathing. With parental permission, hypnosis or visualization (see "Hypnosis") may be used to help the child change his or her inner world. Use of the word "hypnosis" may be scary for some children. "Deep relaxation" or "creative visualization" may be more appropriate terms. It is important to keep sessions with children short in order to maintain their concentration.

Ask the child to curl his or her toes, then relax them; to tighten his or her knees, then relax them; next, to make his or her stomach as hard as possible, then relax. This procedure is continued until each muscle group is contracted. Have the child squeeze his or her face as if eating a lemon, or have him or her take an adventure on a magic carpet. Their eyes can be open or closed. Some children may feel uneasy closing their eyes. Always ask their permission to go to a deeper state of relaxation, and assure them that they control the rate at which you proceed.

Children love stories, and you might want to take them to a magic land where they can learn something new. But first they may want to take a bath in the "Misery Pool" and leave all their bad feelings behind. After the bath, they may emerge into the sunshine and be empowered by multicolored spheres of light that surround them. The colors include blue for power, gold for wisdom, pink for love, white for hope and healing, green for cleansing, and purple for truth. The children may call on these light spheres to help them solve problems. Next, have them identify what they left behind in the "Misery Pool," and go to the other side of the Magic Mountain to see their hopes and dreams. Let the children choose which ones they want to bring back with them.

Take as much time as necessary wandering down the mountain and return to the room where they started. If they can't visualize hopes and dreams, they may need more time, and remind them that they can return to the Magic Mountain at another time when they may be amazed at what they see, or perhaps their hopes, dreams, and goals will come to them in their dreams, or they will be surprised very soon.

When working with traumatized children, you might ask them to imagine they are watching their favorite cartoon. Discover a character they consider particularly brave and ask if the familiar cartoon character would be willing to help when they are afraid. This gives children something to hold onto and empowers them in dealing with fear.

If children have completed the induction stage and are relaxed, have them imagine that the cartoon character is with them, watching the traumatic event unfold on television (i.e., the Twin Towers crashing down). If there are signs of hyperarousal in the patients, go back to the induction stage and start again. Do not rush. First you want the children to realize they can control their emotions before you revisit the traumatic event.

When they are sufficiently calm, have them revisit the experience in a movie or on television to break through the amnesic barriers and reduce flashbacks. Have the children verbalize how it feels, smells, sounds, and looks. This technique is a slow, painstaking undertaking and should be applied carefully, always pacing yourself with the children. The idea is to empower the children and reduce flashbacks. The locus of control must remain with the children. If the traumatic event must be revisited, it should be handled in the second part of the session. Otherwise, it is best to postpone it for another time. Intense exploration is done in the third part of the session, while the end of the session should be devoted to allowing the patients to reorient themselves and calm down (Herman, 1997). Remind children at the end of the hypnotic experience that their cartoon hero will always be there when they need it.

This may appear to some people as magical thinking, but it is effective in empowering children to deal with their trauma. It gives the children a chance to heal reverses, repression, and amnesia, and opens the possibility of change with a helpful friend to provide support during fearful times.

MINDFULNESS

1. **Open yourself up to the experience**
   Notice everything
   Stay alert to every thought, feeling, and action without reacting to it emotionally

2. **Verbalize it**
   Add words to what you thought and felt

3. **Enter into the experience**
   Become one with it
   Go inside yourself and watch your thoughts come and go

4. **Act intuitively**
   Integrate your rational and emotional minds to develop wisdom

5. **Practice your skills**

6. **Accept yourself and the experience as they are**

NEURO EMOTIONAL TECHNIQUE (NET)

by Rita Ghiraldini, DC

Emotions are normal reactions to daily interactions. In her experiments with chemical receptors, Candace Pert (1997) established the irrefutable connection between emotions and the body's physiology through the so-called opiate receptors in the cells. Her studies scientifically established the mind-body connection.

Neuro Emotional Technique (NET) addresses the emotional component of disease and pain. Emotions change the physiology/chemistry of the body at the time they happen. Occasionally, emotional trauma in the presence of a neurological or meridian deficit can cause a physiopathological dysfunction in the body that does not resolve of itself. If not completely processed, this altered physiology remains in the body and gets stored in the tissues. The Neuro Emotional Technique is a methodology used to normalize unresolved physical and/or behavioral patterns in the body, bringing about physiological change as a result of a physical intervention. This technique was discovered by Dr. Scott Walker in conjunction with Dr. Debbie Walker.

It makes use of the neuro-mechanisms of speech, general semantics, emotions, acupuncture, and chiropractic principles, laws of the meridian system, cutaneous reflex points, principles of traditional psychology, and more. NET does not treat emotions, but rather the complete mind-body when there is a stuck emotional component. We call these stuck emotions Neuro Emotional Complexes (NECs). It effectively addresses "fixations of emotions" held within the body that can be vulnerable to retriggering under specific conditions relating to the original formation of the NEC (www.netmindbody.com/net_inc_info.html). The end product is a more neurologically integrated and healthier person. Patients report that this quick and easy process is pleasant and often life changing. As part of its diagnostic methodology, it requests of the patient, at times, a neuro-emotional case history to assist in uncovering the presence of an NEC. Once discovered, a correction is made and the treatment cycle is ended. Any case history that reveals a need for psychotherapy is discussed with the patient and an appropriate referral is made.

NET is not psychotherapy. It is used by psychotherapists and health care practitioners of all disciplines in tandem with their other techniques to quickly enhance their patients' results.

The following case histories will better illustrate how NET works.

Case History 1

Female patient, mid-forties, presents to my office with trigeminal neuralgia, which is a very painful condition in the face and head. The trigeminal nerve has three branches that go into the ear, the upper and lower jaw. Many patients with this condition commit suicide because the pain is intolerable. She had tried several types of treatment, and at the time was taking a prescription drug (the usual route for this kind of condition) that was sending her liver enzymes off the charts. She wanted to reduce the drug intake, but it was the only thing that was curbing her pain. I asked her if she would be willing to try NET, to explore the potential underlying emotional cause of her pain. She agreed, and through NET, we uncovered the fixated emotions (NECs) around her father's death. Her pain scale would go from 8 at the beginning of the session, to 2 or 3 at the end of it. A pain scale is used in doctor's offices to assess its severity. It ranges from 1 to 10, one being very little or no pain, and 10 being excruciating pain. After a few sessions with NET, she was able to reduce the drug intake to its minimum dosage as her pain decreased significantly, and her liver enzymes also reduced to slightly above the normal range. I combined her treatment with traditional chiropractic care, and her condition stabilized.

Case History 2

A male patient, early fifties, complains of intermittent lower back pain. He is a chiropractor himself, and had been treated with traditional chiropractic care with good results, but they were not lasting. So he asked me to try NET for his case. During the treatment, we uncovered NECs around his relationship with his father. His intermittent lower back pain has not returned since this session.

In both examples, the NECs uncovered were related to these patients' fathers. This is a coincidence, as the NECs can be related to family, friends, financial matters, the patient, the patient's concept of God, and so on. This technique is always pleasantly surprising, to both the practitioner and the patient.

PRACTICAL STEPS FOR DEALING WITH TERROR

1. Be mindful
Stay in the here and now. Don't live in a flashback or a future that may never come. Sure, you can think about the past and the future, but don't get stuck in them.

2. Life is an adventure
The unchallenged life may not be worth living. We must face up to the challenge and make the most of it. It's time to take stock in yourself, conduct a personal inventory. Get in touch with your strengths and weaknesses. Have you changed since 9/11? Seek and find new ways to transcend the effects of terror.

3. Focus on the solution
What you focus on expands. If you focus on the problem, it will get bigger. So let's stick with the possible solutions.

4. Take the bullets out of the gun
Mentally downgrade outcomes that scare you while remaining prepared for any possibility.

5. It's okay to be afraid
Confront your fear. When it arises, acknowledge it, visualize it, feel it, but don't get frozen in it. Fear is one thing, but letting it control your mind and your life is quite another.

6. Seek stability

The best place to look is in connections with family and friends. Use positive mental images as a backdrop for your daily life. Emotions are carriers of energy with the power to protect and heal. Safe attachment figures can re-set the traumatized part of the brain.

7. Search for meaning

Search for and find new personal meaning in your life. Remember that creative minds always endure.

8. Act out of wisdom, not emotion

The truth may set us free, but probably not before it scares the hell out of us.

Take hold of your mind, and act from your wise mind, not your emotional mind.

9. Remember that life is precious

We create our own humanity. Make the most of life every day.

From *Possibilities* newsletter (2002)
E-mail by Bill O'Hanlon. Reprinted with permission.

PERSONAL POWER SCALE

Fear	1	2	3	4	5	6	7	8	9	10	Power
	○	○	○	○	○	○	○	○	○	○	

This behavioral technique provides immediate feedback of positive reinforcement for persons confronting their fears.

Explain to your patients that the only way out of their fears is through them. Therefore, every time they confront what they are afraid of, they have the power to change their painful feeling (fear, anxiety, distress, etc.). Using the figure above, have your patient mark where he or she is with a pencil or a thumbtack and date the entry. Next, identify the new action the patient must take to get out of the negative emotional state he/she is feeling. Confrontation reduces his or her fears. For example, if he or she is afraid of elevators, have your patient select a "safe person" to ride with him or her at first. When he or she is feeling more secure, have your patient try it alone and reward himself or herself with each success by moving the thumb tack an appropriate distance on the chart away from fear and toward power. Positive reinforcement is a powerful motivator to work through painful emotions.

THE RELATIONSHIP BETWEEN HEART ATTACK AND STRESS

A Short Discussion of Stress and Depression Following a Heart Attack

by Michael Innerfield, MD, Cardiologist

A heart attack, or acute myocardial infarction (MI), is caused by a blood clot that occludes an artery in the heart, blocking oxygen supply to the heart muscle, and leading to muscle death. This blood clot is thought to be pre-disposed by the rupture of an unstable plaque in the wall of the artery (Figure 7). Plaque disruption and thrombosis not uncommonly occur at the site of a previously mild stenosis. In other words, the plaque rupture is an acute phenomenon, akin to an earthquake of the arterial wall. It is difficult to prove exactly what these triggering factors causing plaque rupture are. However, there is mounting evidence that emotional stress can be one of them.

Emotional stress may trigger a heart attack in several ways. It has been well described in the literature how mental stress can cause elevations in blood pressure and heart rate, increase vasomotor tone, and platelet aggregability. It also causes increased oxygen demand, and

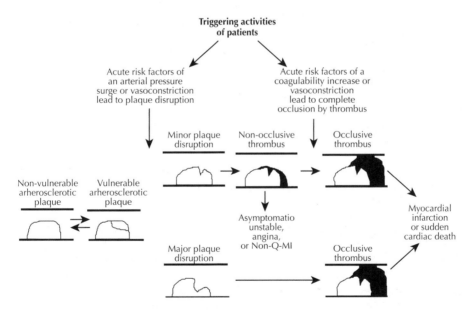

Figure 7: Relationship Between Stress and Coronary Thrombosis

A hypothetical model by which daily activities such as mental stress may trigger coronary thrombosis and precipitate an acute coronary syndrome such as unstable angina or a myocardial infarction. (Redrawn from Muller, J. E., Abela, G. S., Neso, R. W. et al., *J. Am. Coll. Cardiol.*, 1994, 23: 809.)

decreased oxygen supply. Vasoconstriction has been demonstrated during stress in patients with atherosclerosis. In this short treatise, I will briefly review the evidence associating heart attack and stress.

Tofler et al. (1990) reviewed the records of about 900 patients with an acute myocardial infarction, looking for one or more possible triggers. Emotional upset was found in 14%, and was the most common factor given.

Pignalberi et al. (1998) found that in 130 patients hospitalized for MI, about 75% had high levels of emotional stress.

Kawachi followed 34,000 patients for two years. The likelihood of having a fatal cardiovascular event was threefold greater in those patients having the highest level of anxiety, as opposed to those having the lowest level (Kawachi et al., 1994).

Kawachi also studied the effect of anger on the development of heart attack. In about 13,000 patients, those whose personality traits showed frequent volatility and anger were about two times more likely to have a coronary event (Kawachi et al., 1996). It is often asked if an episode of acute anger can precipitate a heart attack. Mittleman tried to answer this question (Mittelman et al., 1995). In the Determinants of Myocardial Infarction Onset Study, 1623 patients were interviewed within one week of an MI, and 2.4% indicated they experienced an episode of anger within two hours of an MI. The most common causes of anger were: family arguments (25%), work (22%), or legal problems (8%). Those with anger were more than twice as likely to have an MI. Interestingly, in this study, those with anger on aspirin or beta blockers were at less risk.

Depression After a Heart Attack

Zeigelstein (2001) demonstrated that about one fifth of patients have a major depressive episode after an MI. It also has been well documented in multiple studies (Ziegelstein, 2001; Frasure-Smith et al., 1995) that depression and other stress factors such as hostility, isolation, anxiety, anger, and marital discord, portend a poorer prognosis in those recovering from an MI. In a sub-study from Italy involving 2500 post-MI patients, those expressing fatigue, anxiety, or depression had a two–three-fold increase in mortality.

Treatment

Supportive treatment of depressed post-MI patients may have a beneficial effect on mortality (see Figure 8) (Frasure-Smith et al., 2000). Spontaneous resolution of depression occurs in about 50% of patients.

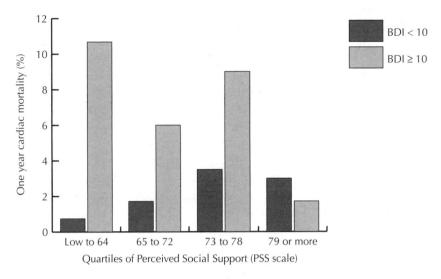

Figure 8: Depression After a Myocardial Infarction Predicts Mortality

In a study of 887 patients, baseline depression was measured by the Beck Depression Inventory (DBI); those with a higher level of depression (DBI ≥ 10) had a higher one-year mortality than those with a lower level of depression. Although the relationship between mortality and depression decreased with increasing levels of perceived social support (PSS), social support was not directly related to survival. (Data from Frasure-Smith, N., Lesperance, F., Gravel, G. et al, *Circulation*, 2000, 101: 1919.)

Thus, a course of anti-depressive treatment would be of benefit in a significant number of patients. Treatment options include pharmacologic and behavioral therapy. Cardiac rehab programs also may be of assistance. The social benefit accrued by sharing experiences with other patients, interacting with staff, and just having a destination and a goal, is significant psychological support in itself.

As for drug therapy, there is a hesitancy among health professionals to prescribe anti-depressant medications because of the propensity for some of the preparations to predispose the heart to potentially fatal arrhythmias. The untoward effect is that on the conduction system of the heart, some of these drugs can prolong the so-called "q-t interval" on the EKG. An extra beat, improperly timed, can develop into ventricular tachycardia or fibrillation, especially if the patient is on tri-cyclics.

The selective serotonin uptake inhibitors (SSRI) appear to be a safer class of drugs. In particular, Sertraline has been shown safe in the post-MI depressed patient. Also, in this same study, Sertraline did not significantly improve depressive scale ratings compared with placebo. However, the subset of patients with a history of depression prior to their MI, did have a significant improvement in symptoms with the drug.

Conclusion

To briefly sum up, there is a body of literature to support the notion that stress and anger can precipitate an acute myocardial infarction by triggering the rupture of a plaque in a coronary artery that is vulnerable to this occurrence. Prophylactic use of aspirin, and perhaps beta blockers, may be of benefit.

Depression and stress are also prevalent after a heart attack. Behavior modification therapy, along with cardiac rehabilitation in a structured environment, are beneficial. Pharmacotherapy may be used in selected individuals. The choice of drug should include that which does not prolong the "q-t interval" of the EKG. Sertraline, though safe, is of limited benefit.

References

Beck, C. A., Joseph, L, Belise, P. and Pilote, L. "Predictors of quality of life 6 months and 1 year after acute myocardial infarction." *American Heart Journal*, 2001, 142:271.

Bush, D. E., Ziegelstein, R. C., Tayback, M., Richter, D., Stevens, S., Zahalsky, H. and Fauerbach, J. A. "Even minimal symptoms of depression increase mortality risk after acute myocardial infarction." *American Journal of Cardiology*, 2001, 88:337.

Frasure-Smith, N., Lesperance, F. and Talajic, M. "Depression following myocardial infarction: impact on 6-month survival." *JAMA*, 1993, 270:1819.

Frasure-Smith, N., Lesperance, F. and Talajic, M. "Depression and 18-month prognosis after myocardial infarction." *Circulation*, 1995, 91:999.

Frasure-Smith, N., Lesperance, F., Gravel, G., Masson, A., Juneau, M., Talajic, M. and Bourassa, M. G. "Social support, depression, and mortality during the first year after myocardial infarction." *Circulation*, 2000, 101:1919.

Kawachi, I., Colditz, G. A., Ascherio, A., Rimm, E. B., Giovannucci, E., Stampfer, M. J. and Willett, W. C. "Prospective study of phobic anxiety and risk of coronary heart disease in men." *Circulation*, 1994, 89:1992.

Kawachi, I., Sparrow, D., Spiro, A., 3rd, Vokonas, P. and Weiss, S. T. "A prospective study of anger and coronary heart disease." The Normative Aging Study. *Circulation*, 1996, 94:2090.

Lesperance, F., Frasure-Smith, N., Talajic, M. and Bourassa, M.G. "Five-year risk of cardiac mortality in relation to initial severity and one-year changes in depression symptoms after myocardial infarction." *Circulation*, 2002, 105:1049.

Mittleman, M. A., Maclure, M., Sherwood, J. B., Mulry, R. P., Tofler, G. H., Jacobs, S. C., Friedman, R., Benson, H. and Muller, J. E. "Triggering of acute myocardial infarction onset by episodes of anger." Determinants of Myocardial Infarction Onset Investigators. *Circulation*, 1995, 92:1720.

Orth-Gomer, K., Wamala, S. P., Horsten, M., Schenck-Gustafsson, K., Schneiderman, N. and Mittelman, M. A. "Marital stress worsens prognosis in women with coronary heart disease." The Stockholm Female Coronary Risk Study. *JAMA,* 2000, 284:3008.

Pignalberi, C., Patti, G., Chimenti, C., Pasceri, V. and Maseri, A. "Role of different determinants of psychological distress in acute coronary syndromes." *Journal of American College of Cardiologists,* 1998, 32:613.

Ruberman, W., Weinblatt, E., Goldberg, J. D. and Chaudhary, B. S. "Psychosocial influences on mortality after myocardial infarction." *New England Journal of Medicine*, 1984, 311:552.

Tofler, G. H., Stone, P. H., Maclure, M., Edelman, E., Davis, V. G., Robertson, T., Antman, E. M. and Muller, J. E. "Analysis of possible triggers of acute myocardial infarction (the MILIS study)." *American Journal of Cardiology*, 1990, 66:22.

Ziegelstein, R. C. "Depression in patients recovering from a myocardial infarction." *JAMA*, 2001, 286:1621.

7
THERAPEUTIC GAMES

Therapeutic games are used to help establish therapeutic alliances with children that enhance the outcome of therapy. They help children cope with trauma, unresolved fears, anxiety, depression, and low self-esteem.

ANGER

Exploring My Anger. Western Psychological Services
Breaking the Chains of Anger. Western Psychological Services
I Can Control My Anger. Childswork/Childsplay
The Anger Control Toolkit. Wellness Reproductions

BEHAVIOR

The Good Behavior Game. Childswork/Childsplay
The Helping, Sharing, and Caring Game. Western Psychological Services
The Odyssey Islands Game. Childswork/Childsplay

COMMUNICATION

Communicate. Western Psychological Services
Life Stories. Western Psychological Services
The Ungame. Western Psychological Services
The Parent Report Card for Teens. Western Psychological Services
Chicken Soup for the Teen's Soul. Childswork/Childsplay
Personality Probe. Childswork/Childsplay
The Positive Thinking Game. Childswork/Childsplay

LOSS

The Goodbye Game. Childswork/Childsplay
The Grief Game. Childswork/Childsplay

FEELINGS

Your Journey Through the Land of Feelings. Blue Heron Games
The Talking, Feeling, Doing Game. Western Psychological Services

MOTIVATION

Never Say Never. Childswork/Childsplay

RESILIENCY

Bounce-Back. Childswork/Childsplay

SELF-CONTROL

Teaching Self Control. Childswork/Childsplay

SELF-CONFIDENCE

The Bridge of Self-Confidence Game. Western Psychological Services

SELF-ESTEEM

Self-Esteem Game. Childswork/Childsplay
Personal Power! POW! Childswork/Childsplay

8
RESOURCES

BOOKS

Anger

Basset, L. (1995). *From Panic to Power*. New York: HarperCollins.

Bilodeau, L. (1992). *The Anger Workbook*. Minneapolis, MN: CompCare Publishers.

Ellis, A. and Tafrate, R. C. (1997). *How to Control Your Anger Before It Controls You*. Secaucus, NJ: Carol Publishing.

Gottlieb, M. M. (1999). *The Angry Self: A Comprehensive Approach to Anger Management*. Phoenix, AZ: Zeig, Tucker & Theisen.

Lee, J. (1993). *Facing the Fire: Experiencing and Expressing Anger Appropriately*. New York: Bantam Books.

Licata, R. (1999). *Everything You Need To Know About Anger*. New York: Rosen Publishing Group.

McKay, M, Rogers, P. D. and McKay, J. (1989). *When Anger Hurts: Quieting the Storm Within*. Oakland, CA: New Harbinger Publications.

Potter-Efron, R. and Potter-Efron, P. (1995). *Letting Go of Anger*. Oakland, CA: New Harbinger Publications.

Weisinger, H. (1985). *Dr. Weisinger's Anger Workout Book*. New York: Quill Publishing.

Anxiety

American Psychiatric Association. (1998). *Practice Guidelines for the Treatment of Patients with Panic Disorders*. Washington DC: American Psychiatric Press.

Balter, L. (1989). *Linda Saves the Day*. New York: Barron's.

Barlow, D. H. (2000). *Anxiety and Its Disorders: The Nature and Treatment of Anxiety and Panic* (Therapist Version). San Antonio, TX: Harcourt Brace.

Barlow, D. H. and Cerny, J. (2000). *Psychiatric Treatment of Panic*. New York: Guilford.

Barlow, D. and Crooke, M. G. (2000). *Mastery of Your Anxiety and Panic*. San Antonio, TX: The Psychological Group.

Basset, L. (1995). *From Panic to Power*. New York: HarperCollins.

Baumgart, K. (1998). *Don't Be Afraid, Tommy*. Waukesha, WI: Little Tiger Publications.

Bodger, C. (1999). *Smart Guide to Relieving Stress*. New York: John Wiley & Sons.

Bourne, E. J. (1997). *The Anxiety and Phobia Workbook*, 2nd ed. Oakland, CA: New Harbinger Publications.

Bourne, E. J. (1998). *Healing Fear*. Oakland, CA: New Harbinger Publications.

Copeland, M. E. (1998). *The Worry Control Workbook*. Oakland, CA: New Harbinger Publications.

Craske, M. G. and Barlow, D. H. (2000). *Mastery of Your Anxiety and Panic*, 3rd ed. (Therapist Version). San Antonio, TX: Harcourt Brace.

Davis, M. (1995). *The Leader's Guide to the Relaxation and Stress Reduction Workbook*. Oakland, CA: New Harbinger Publications.

Ellis, A. (1998). *How to Control Your Anxiety Before It Controls You*. Secaucus, NJ: Carol Publishing.

Fassler, J. (1973). *Don't Worry, Dear*. Nashville, TN: Shawnee Press.

Gerzon, R. (1997). *Finding Serenity in the Age of Anxiety*. New York: Bantam Books.

Goldman, C. and Babior, S. (1996). *Overcoming Panic, Anxiety, and Phobias*. Duluth, MN: Whole Person Associates.

Hipp, E. (1995). *Fighting Invisible Tigers*. Minneapolis, MN: Free Spirit Publishing.

Jacobson, E. (1978). *You Must Relax*. New York: McGraw-Hill Publishing.

Jeffers, S. (1988). *Feel the Fear and Do It Anyway*. New York: Fawcett Columbine.

Kopp, S. (1988). *Raise Your Right Hand Against Fear, Extend the Other One in Compassion*. Minneapolis, MN: CompCare.

Lamb-Shapiro, J. (2000). *The Bear Who Lost His Sleep*. Plainview, NY: Childswork/Childsplay.

Moser, A. and Pilkey, D. (1988). *Don't Pop Your Cork on Mondays!: The Children's Anti-Stress Book*. Kansas City, MO: Landmark.

Moser, A. (1991). *Don't Feed the Monster on Tuesdays!: The Children's Self-Esteem Book*. Kansas City, MO: Landmark.

Nash, M. S. (2000). *The Lion Who Lost His Roar*. Plainview, NY: Childswork/Childsplay.

Selekman, M. (1997). *Solution-Focused Therapy with Children*. New York: Guilford.

Shapiro, L., Shore, H. M. and Williams-Andriani, R. (2001). *Anybody Can Bake a Cake*. Plainview, NY: Childswork/Childsplay.

Shiraldi, G. R. (1996a). *Facts to Relax By*. 2nd ed. Ellicott City, MD: Chevron Publishing.

Shiraldi, G. R. (1996b). *Conquer Anxiety, Worry, and Nervous Fatigue: A Guide to Greater Peace*. Ellicott City, MD: Chevron Publishing.

Werner-Watson, J. (1971). *Sometimes I'm Afraid*. New York: Golden Books.

Wilson, R. R. (1996). *Don't Panic: Taking Control of Anxiety Attacks*. New York: HarperCollins.

Bipolar Disorder

American Psychiatric Association. (1990). *American Psychiatric Association Practice Guidelines for the Treatment of Patients with Bipolar Disorder*. Washington, DC: American Psychiatric Press.

Goldberg, G. F. and Harrow, M. (eds) (1999). *Bipolar Disorders: Clinical Course and Outcomes*. Washington, DC: American Psychiatric Press.

Communications

Faber, A. and Mazlish, E. (1995). *How to Talk So Kids Can Learn*. New York: Rawson Publishing.

Taffel, R. (2000). *Getting Through to Difficult Kids and Parents: Uncommon Sense for Professionals*. New York: Guilford Press.

Coping Skills

Brown, N. (2002). *Whose Life Is It Anyway? When to Stop Taking Care of Their Feelings & Start Taking Care of Your Own*. Oakland, CA: New Harbinger Publications.

Lewis, B. A. (1998). *What Do You Stand For?* Minneapolis, MN: Free Spirit Publishing.

McKay, M., Davis, M. and Fanning, P. (1997). *Thoughts and Feelings: Taking Control of Your Moods and Your Life*. Oakland, CA: New Harbinger Publications.

Napier, N. J. (1993). *Getting Through the Day: Strategies for Adults Hurt as Children*. New York: Norton Professional Books.

O'Toole, D. (2002). *Aarvy Aardvark Finds Hope*. Burnsville, NC: Compassion Books.

Shapiro, L. E. (1996). *The Teens' Solutions Workbook*. Plainview, NY: Childswork/Childsplay.

Stone, V. (1999). *Cops Don't Cry*. Ontario, Canada: Creative Bound.

Taubman, S. (1994). *Ending the Struggle Against Yourself*. New York: Putnam.

Critical Incident Stress Management

Everly, G. S. and Mitchell, J. T. (1999). *Critical Incident Stress Management (CISM): A New Era and Standard of Care in Crisis Intervention*. Ellicott City, MD: Chevron.

FEMA. (1993). *Citizen's Guide to Disaster Assistance*. FEMA Home Study Program. Emmitsburg, MD: Federal Emergency Management Institute (http://www.fema.gov).

Figley, C. (1989). *Helping Traumatized Families*. San Francisco, CA: Jossey-Bass.

Figley, C. (ed.) (1995). *Compassion Fatigue*. New York: Brunner- Mazel.

Figley, C. (2001). *The Green Cross Protocol*. Tallahassee, FL.: Green Cross Foundation.

Figley, C. R., Bride. B. and Mazza, N. (eds) (1997). *Death and Trauma*. London: Taylor & Francis.

Janoff-Bulman, R. (1992). *Shattered Assumptions: Towards a New Psychology of Trauma*. New York: Free Press.

Lamb-Shapiro, J. (2001). *The Hyena Who Lost Her Laugh*. Plainview, NY: Childswork/Childsplay.

Meyers, D. (1996). *Disaster Response and Recovery: A Handbook for Mental Health Professionals*. Collingdale, PA: Diane Publishing.

Death and Bereavement

Caplan, S. and Lang, G. (1995). *Grief's Courageous Journey*. Oakland, CA: New Harbinger Publications.

Fitzgerald, H. (1994). *Grieving Child*. New York: Simon & Schuster.

Fitzgerald, H. (1994). *The Mourning Handbook*. New York: Simon & Schuster.

Frankl, V. (1976). *Man's Search for Meaning: An Introduction to Logotherapy*. New York: Pocket Books.

Goldman, L. (1994). *Breaking the Silence*. Muncie, IN: Accelerated Development.

Goldman, L. (1994). *Life and Loss*. Muncie, IN: Accelerated Development.

Greenlee, S. and Drath, B. (1992). *When Someone Dies*. Atlanta, GA: Peachtree Publishers.

Grollman, E. A. (1993). *Straight Talk About Death for Teenagers: How to Cope With Losing Someone You Love*. Boston, MA: Beacon Press.

Grollman, E. (ed) (1995). *Bereaved Children and Teens*. Boston, MA: Beacon Press.

Grollman, E. and Malikow, M. (1999). *Living When a Young Friend Commits Suicide*. Boston, MA: Beacon Press.

Harris, M. (1995). *The Loss That Is Forever: The Lifelong Impact of the Early Death of a Mother or Father*. New York: Penguin Books.

Heegaard, M. (2002). *When Something Terrible Happens*. Burnsville, NC: Compassion Books.

Jarrat, C. (1994). *Helping Children Cope with Separation and Loss*. Boston, MA: Harvard Commons.

Jozefowski, J. T. (1999). *The Phoenix Phenomenon: Rising From the Ashes of Grief*, 2nd ed. Northvale, NJ: Jason Aronson.

Kubler-Ross, E. (1997). *On Death and Dying*. New York: Simon & Schuster.

Moser, A. and Melton, D. (1996). *Don't Despair on Thursdays!: The Children's Grief-Management Book*. Kansas City, MO: Landmark.

O'Toole, D. B. (1995). *Facing Change: Falling Apart and Coming Together Again in the Teen Years*. South Burnsville, NC: Compassion Books.

Perschey, M. (1997). *Helping Teens Work Through Grief*. Washington, DC: Accelerated Development.

Romain, T. (1999). *What on Earth Do You Do When Someone Dies?* Minneapolis, MN: Free Spirit.

Sanders, C. M. (1998). *Grief: The Mourning After: Dealing With Adult Bereavement*. New York: Wiley.

Viorst, J. (1986). *Necessary Losses*. New York: Simon & Schuster.

Walsh, F. and McGoldrick, M. (eds) (1995). *Living Beyond Loss: Death in the Family*. New York: Norton.

Webb, N. (1993). *Helping Bereaved Children*. New York: Guilford Press.

Wolfelt, A. (1996). *Healing the Bereaved Child*. Fort Collins, CO: Companion.

Worden, J. W. (1996). *Children and Grief*. New York: Guilford Press.

Depression

American Psychiatric Association. (1993). *American Psychiatric Association Practice Guidelines for Depressive Disorders in Adults*. Washington, DC: American Psychiatric Press.
Beck, A. T., Rush, A. J. and Emery, G. (1979). *Cognitive Therapy of Depression*. New York: Guilford Press.
Blackburn, M. and Davidson, K. M. (1995). *Cognitive Therapy for Depression and Anxiety*. Washington, DC: American Psychiatric Press.
Burns, D. (1999). *Feeling Good*. New York: Avon Books.
Butler, B. and Sussman, M. B. (1989). *Museum Visits and Other Activities for Family Life Enrichment*. New York: Haworth.
Cobain, B. (1998). *When Nothing Matters Anymore*. Minneapolis, MN: Free Spirit Publishing.
Copeland, M. E. (1992). *The Depression Workbook: A Guide for Living with Depression and Manic Depression*. Oakland, CA: New Harbinger Publications.
Copeland, M. E. (1998). *The Adolescent Depression Workbook*. Oakland, CA: New Harbinger Publications.
Klosko, J. S. and Sanderson, W. C. (1999). *Cognitive Behavioral Treatment of Depression*. Northvale, NJ: Jason Aronson.
Owen, P. (1995). *I Can See Tomorrow*. Center City, MN: Hazelden.

Dissociative Disorders

Bradshaw, J. (1992). *Homecoming: Reclaiming and Championing Your Inner Child*. New York: Bantam Books.
Braun, B. G. (ed) (1985). *Treatment of Multiple Personality Disorders*. Washington, DC: American Psychiatric Press.
Brenner, J. D. and Marmar, C. R. (1985). *Trauma, Memory, and Dissociation*. Washington, DC: American Psychiatric Press.
Steinberg, M. (1995). *Handbook for the Assessment of Dissociation: A Clinical Guide*. Washington, DC: American Psychiatric Press.
Steinberg, M. (2000). *The Stranger in the Mirror: Dissociation, the Hidden Epidemic*. New York: HarperCollins.

Eating Disorders

Agras, W. S. and Apple, R. F. (1997). *Overcoming Eating Disorders: Cognitive Behavioral Treatment for Bulimia Nervosa and Binge Eating Disorder*. (Therapist Version). San Antonio: TX. Psychological Corp.

American Psychiatric Association. (1993). *American Association Guidelines for Eating Disorders*. Washington DC: American Psychiatric Press.

Danowski, D. and Lazaro, P. (2000). *Why Can't I Stop Eating?* Center City, MN: Hazelden.

Ebbett, J. (1994). *The Eating Illness Workbook*. Center City, MN: Hazelden.

Edell, D. (1999). *Eat, Drink and Be Merry*. New York: HarperCollins.

Levenkron, S. (2000). *Anatomy of Anorexia*. New York: Norton.

LoBue, A. and Marcus, M. (1999). *The Don't Diet, Live It! Workbook: Healing Food, Weight & Body Issues*. Carlsbad, CA: Gurze Books.

Nash, J. D. (1999). *Binge No More*. Oakland, CA: New Harbinger Publications.

Sandbek, T. (1993). *The Deadly Diet*. Oakland, CA: New Harbinger Publications.

Schroder, C. R. (1992). *Fat is Not a Four-Letter Word*. New York: Chronimed Publishing.

Sherman, R. T. and Thompson, R. T. (1996). *Bulimia: A Guide for Family and Friends*. San Francisco, CA: Jossey-Bass.

Wilson, C. P., Hogan, C. and Mintz, I. (eds) (1987). *Fear of Being Fat: The Treatment of Anorexia Nervosa and Bulimia*. Northvale, NJ: Jason Aronson.

Zerbe, K. J. (1993). *The Body Betrayed: Eating Disorders and Their Treatment*. Washington, DC: American Psychiatric Press.

Guilt/Shame

Black, S. and Drozd, L. (1995). *The Missing Piece: Solving the Puzzle of Self*. New York: Ballantine Books.

Breitman, P. and Hatch, C. (2000). *How to Say No Without Feeling Guilty*. New York: Broadway Books.

Elton, R. P. and Elton, F. P. (1989). *Letting Go of Shame: Understanding How Shame Affects Your Life*. Center City, MN: Hazelden.

Hypnosis, Relaxation, Visualization

Allen, J. S. and Klein, R. J. (1996). *Ready… Set… R.E.L.A.X.* Watertown, WI: Inner Coaching.

Araoz, D. L. (1995). *The New Hypnosis: Techniques in Individual and Family Psychotherapy*. Northvale, NJ: Jason Aronson.

Araoz, D. L. (1998). *The New Hypnosis in Sex Therapy: Clinical-Behavioral Methods for Clinicians*. Northvale, NJ: Jason Aronson.

Austin, V. (1998). *Free Yourself From Fear: Self-Hypnosis for Anxiety, Panic Attacks, and Phobias*. London: HarperCollins.

Davis, M. (1985). *Relaxation / Stress, Leaders Guide*. Oakland, CA: New Harbinger Publications.

Davis, M., Eshelman, E. and McKay, M. (1988). *The Relaxation & Stress Reduction Workbook*. Oakland, CA: New Harbinger Publications.

Dowd, E. T. (2000). *Cognitive Hypnotherapy*. Northvale, NJ: Jason Aronson.

Epstein, G. (1989). *Healing Visualizations: Creating Health Through Imagery*. New York: Bantam Books.

Fanning, P. (1988). *Visualization for Change*. Oakland, CA: New Harbinger Publications.

Fisher, S. (1991). *Discovering the Power of Self-Hypnosis: A New Approach for Enabling Change and Promoting Healing*. New York: HarperCollins.

Fuller, G. D. (1984). *Clinical Biofeedback Methods*. San Francisco, CA: Institute of San Francisco.

Gafner, G. and Benson, S. (2000). *Handbook of Hypnotic Inductions*. New York: Norton.

Gawain, S. (1982). *Creative Visualization*. New York: Bantam Books.

Hammond, D.C. (ed) (1990). *Handbook of Hypnotic Suggestion and Metaphors*. New York: Norton.

Lusk, J. T. (ed) (1993). *30 Scripts for Relaxation, Imagery, and Inner Healing*. Duluth, MN: Whole Person Associates.

Rosen, S. (ed) (1982). *My Voice Will Go With You: The Teaching Tales of Milton H. Erickson*. New York: Norton.

Udolf, R. (1992). *Handbook of Hypnosis for Professionals*. Northvale, NJ: Jason Aronson.

Life Management Skills

Korb-Khlasa, K., Azok, S. and Leutenberg, E. A. (1993). *Life Management Skills I: Reproducible Activity Handouts*. Beachwood, OH: Wellness Reproductions.

Korb-Khlasa, K., Azok, S. and Leutenberg, E. A. (1993). *Life Management Skills II: Reproducible Activity Handouts*. Beachwood, OH: Wellness Reproductions.

Korb-Khlasa, K., Azok, S. and Leutenberg, E. A. (1994). *Life Management Skills III: Reproducible Activity Handouts*. Beachwood, OH: Wellness Reproductions.

Korb-Khlasa, K., Azok, S. and Leutenberg, E. A. (1996). *Life Management Skills IV: Reproducible Activity Handouts*. Beachwood, OH: Wellness Reproductions.

Korb-Khlasa, K., Azok, S. and Leutenberg, E. A. (1999). *Life Management Skills V: Reproducible Activity Handouts*. Beachwood, OH: Wellness Reproductions.

Korb-Khlasa, K., Azok, S. and Leutenberg, E. A. (2000). *Life Management Skills VI: Reproducible Activity Handouts*. Beachwood, OH: Wellness Reproductions.

Medical Issues

Canfield, J., Hansen, M.V., Aubry, P. and Mitchell, N. M. (1996). *Chicken Soup for the Surviving Soul*. Deerfield Beach, FL: Health Communications.

Derogatis, L. R. and Wise, T. N. (1989). *Anxiety and Depression in the Medical Patient*. Washington, DC: American Psychiatric Press.

France, R .D. and Krishnan, N. N. (1988). *Chronic Pain*. Washington, DC: American Psychiatric Press.

Hodges, M. and Moorey, S. (1993). *Psychological Treatment in Disease*. Washington, DC: American Psychiatric Press.

Kabat-Zinn, J. (1990). *Full Catastrophe Living: Using the Wisdom of Your Body and Mind to Face Stress, Pain and Illness*. New York: Dell.

Keller, P. (1991). *Psychosomatic Syndromes and Somatic Symptoms*. Washington, DC: American Psychiatric Press.

Maximin, A. and Stevic-Rust, L. (2000). *Treating Depression in the Medically Ill*. Oakland, CA: New Harbinger Publications.

Obsessive-Compulsive Disorder and Phobias

Benson, A. L. (ed) (2000). *I Shop Therefore I am: Compulsive Buying and the Search for Self*. Northvale, NJ: Jason Aronson.

Colas, E. (1988). *Scenes from the Life of an Obsessive-Compulsive*. New York: Pocket Books.

Craske, M. G. and Antony, M. M. (1997). *Mastering Your Specific Phobia*. (Therapist Version). San Antonio, TX: Harcourt Brace.

Foa, E. B. and Kozak, M. J. (1997). *Mastery of Obsessive-Compulsive Disorder: A Cognitive-Behavioral Approach*. San Antonio, TX: Harcourt Brace.

Foa, E. B. and Wilson, R. (1991). *Stop Obsessing: How to Overcome Your Obsessions and Compulsions*. New York: Bantam Books.

Hope, D. A., Heimberg, R. G., Jusher, H. R. and Turk, C. L. (2000). *Managing Social Anxiety: A Cognitive-Behavioral Therapy Approach*. San Antonio, TX: Harcourt Brace.

Hyman, B. M. and Pedrick, C. (1999). *The OCD Workbook: Your Guide to Breaking Free From Obsessive-Compulsive Disorder*. Oakland, CA: New Harbinger Publications.

McGinn, L. K. and Sanderson, W. C. (1999). *Treatment of Obsessive-Compulsive Disorder*. Northvale, NJ: Jason Aronson.

Rapee, R. M. (1999). *Overcoming Shyness: A Step-by-Step Guide*. Northvale, NJ: Jason Aronson.

Rapee, R. M. and Sanderson, W. C. (1998). *Social Phobia: Clinical Application of Evidence-Based Psychotherapy*. Northvale, NJ: Jason Aronson.

Robinson, B.E. (2000). *Don't Let Your Mind Stunt Your Growth*. Oakland, CA: New Harbinger Publications.

Schwartz, J. M. and Bigette, B. (1996). *Brain Lock*. New York: HarperCollins.

Zuercher-White, E. (1997). *Taming Panic Disorder and Agoraphobia*. Oakland, CA: New Harbinger Publications.

Post-traumatic Stress Disorder

Alexander, D. W. (1999). *Children Changed by Trauma: A Healing Guide*. Oakland, CA: New Harbinger Publications.

Allen, G. G. (1999). *Coping With Trauma*. Washington, DC: American Psychiatric Press.

Brenner, J. D. and Marmar, C. R. (1998). *Post-traumatic Stress Disorder: DSM-IV and Beyond*. Washington, DC: American Psychiatric Press.

Brohl, K. (1996). *Working With Traumatized Children*. Washington, DC: CWLA Press.

Davidson, J. R. T. and Foa, E. B. (1992). *Trauma, Memory and Dissociation*. Washington, DC: American Psychiatric Press.

James, B. (1989). *Treating Traumatized Children*. Lexington, MA: Lexington Books.

James, B. (1994). *Handbook for Treatment of Attachment-Trauma Problems in Children*. New York: Maxwell Macmillan International.

Levy, T. and Orlans, M. (1998). *Attachment, Trauma, and Healing*. Washington, DC: CWLA Press.

Matsakis, A. (1994). *Post-traumatic Stress Disorder: A Complete Treatment Guide*. Oakland, CA: New Harbinger Publications.

Matsakis, A. (1998). *Trust After Trauma*. Oakland, CA: New Harbinger Publications.

Matsakis, A. (1999). *I Can't Get Over It*. Oakland, CA: New Harbinger Publications.

Matsakis, A. (1999). *Survivor Guilt*. Oakland, CA: New Harbinger Publications.

O'Hanlon, W. H. and Bertolino, B. (1998). *Even from a Broken Web: Brief, Respectful, Solution-Oriented Therapy for Sexual Abuse and Trauma*. New York: John Wiley & Sons.

Rothblum, B. O. and Foa, E. B. (2000). *Reclaiming Your Life After Rape*. San Antonio, TX: Harcourt Brace.

Williams, M.B. and Poijula, S. (2002). *The PTSD Workbook: Simple, Effective Techniques for Overcoming Traumatic Stress Symptoms*. Oakland, CA: New Harbinger Publications.

Relational Problems (Parent/Child/Partner)

Borcherdt, B. (1996). *Making Families Work and What to Do When They Don't*. New York: Haworth.

Everett, C. A. and Everett, S. V. (1999). *Family Therapy for ADHD: Treating Children, Adults, and Adolescents*. New York: Guilford Press.

Gottman, J. M. (1999). *The Marriage Clinic*. New York: Norton.

Guerin, P. J. (1976). *Family Therapy: Theory and Practice*. New York: Gardner.

McCormack, C. C. (2000). *Treating Borderline States in Marriage: Dealing with Oppositionalism, Ruthless Aggression, and Severe Resistance*. Northvale, NJ: Jason Aronson.

Papp, P. (ed) (2000). *Couples and the Fault Line*. New York: Guilford Press.

Rathus, J. H. and Sanderson, W. C. (1998). *Marital Discord: Clinical Applications of Evidence-Based Psychotherapy*. Northvale, NJ: Jason Aronson.

Rathus, J. H. and Sanderson, W. C. (1999). *Marital Distress: Cognitive-Behavioral Interventions for Couples*. Northvale, NJ: Jason Aronson.

Satir, V. (1977). *Conjoint Family Therapy*. Palo Alto, CA: Science and Behavior.

Satir, V. (1998). *The New Peoplemaking*. Palo Alto, CA: Science and Behavior.

Sharpe, S. A. (2000). *The Ways We Love: A Developmental Approach to Treating Couples*. New York: Guilford Press.

Siskind, D. (1997). *Working with Parents: Establishing the Essential Alliance in Child Psychotherapy and Consultation*. Northvale, NJ: Jason Aronson.

Wexler, D. B. (2000). *Domestic Violence 2000*. New York: Norton.

Self-Esteem

Covey, S. (1998). *The 7 Habits of Highly Effective Teens Book & Journal*. New York: Simon & Schuster.

Donoan, K. (1994). *The Self-Help Directory: A Sourcebook for Self-Help in the US and Canada*. Denville, NJ: American Self-Help Clearinghouse.

Gordon, S. (1981). *The Teenage Survival Book*. New York: Times.

Korb, K. L., Azok, S. D. and Leutenberg, E. A. (2001). *SEALS: Self-Esteem and Life Skills*. Plainview, NY: Wellness Reproductions and Publishing.

Korb, K. L., Azok, S. D. and Leutenberg, E. A. (2001). *SEALS II: Self-Esteem and Life Skills*. Plainview, NY: Wellness Reproductions and Publishing.

Korb, K. L., Azok, S. D. and Leutenberg, E. A. (2001). *SEALS III: Self-Esteem and Life Skills*. Plainview, NY: Wellness Reproductions and Publishing.

McDermott, D. and Snyder, C. R. (1999). *Making Hope Happen; A Workbook for Turning Possibilities into Reality*. Oakland, CA: New Harbinger Publications.

McKay, M., Fanning, P., Honeychurch, C. and Sutker, C. (1999). *The Self-Esteem Companion*. Oakland, CA: New Harbinger Publications.

Mosatche, H. S. and Unger, K. (2000). *Too Old for This, Too Young for That!* Minneapolis, MN: Free Spirit Publishing.

O'Hanlon, W. H. (2000). *Do One Thing Different and Other Uncommonly Sensible Solutions to Life's Problems*. New York: HarperCollins.

Shiraldi, G. R. (1993). *Building Self-Esteem: A 125-Day Program*. Ellicott City, MD: Chevron Publishing.

Zack, L. R. (1995). *Building Self-Esteem Through the Museum of I: 25 Original Projects That Explore and Celebrate the Self*. Minneapolis, MN: Free Spirit Publishing.

Self-Help

Norcross, J. C., Santrock, J. W., Campbell, L. F., Smith, A T. P., Sommer, R. and Zuckerman, E. L. (2000). *Authoritative Guide to Self-Help Resources in Mental Health*. New York: Guilford Press.

White, B. J. (1998). *The Self-Help Sourcebook: Your Guide to Community and Online Support Groups*, 6th ed. Nutley, NJ: Hoffman La Roche.

Sexual Abuse

Bean, B. and Bennett, S. (1997). *The Me Nobody Knows*. San Francisco, CA: Jossey-Bass.

Copeland, M. E. (2000). *Healing the Trauma of Abuse: A Woman's Workbook*. Oakland, CA: New Harbinger Publications.

Katherine, A. (1991). *Boundaries: Where You End and I Begin*. New York: Simon & Schuster.

Loiselle, M. B. and Wright, L. (1997). *Back On Track; Boys Dealing with Sexual Abuse*. Brandon, VT: Safer Society.

Loiselle, M. B. and Wright, L. (1997). *Shining Through: Pulling It Together After Sexual Abuse*. Brandon, VT: Safer Society.

Stark, E. and Holly, M. (1999). *Everything You Need to Know About Sexual Abuse*. New York: Rosen.

Sleep Disorders

Ancoli-Israel, S. (1996). *All I Want is a Good Night's Sleep*. St. Louis, MO: Mosby Year Book.

Ferber, R. (1985). *Solve Your Child's Sleep Problems*. New York: Simon & Schuster.

Morgan, D. (1996). *Sleep Secrets*. Duluth, MN: Whole Person Associates.

Poceta, J. S. and Mitler, M. M. (1998). *Sleep Disorders: Diagnosis and Treatment*. (Current Clinical Practice Series). Washington, DC: American Psychiatric Press.

Reite, M., Ruddy, J. and Nagel, K. (1997). *Concise Guide to Evaluation and Management of Sleep Disorders*. 2nd ed. Washington, DC: American Psychiatric Press.

Waddell, M. and Firth, B. (1994). *Can't You Sleep, Little Bear?* Cambridge, MA: Candlewick.

Stress and Trauma

Ayer, E. H. (1994). *Everything You Need to Know About Stress*. New York: Rosen Publishing Group.

Copeland, M. E. (1998). *The Worry Control Workbook*. Oakland, CA: New Harbinger Publications.

Davis, M., Eshelman, E. R. and McKay, M. (2000). *The Relaxation and Stress Reduction Workbook*, 5th ed. Oakland, CA: New Harbinger Publications.

Everly, G. S. and Mitchell, J. T. (1999). *Critical Incident Stress Management, CISM: A New Era and Standard of Care in Crisis Intervention*, 2nd ed. Ellicott City, MD: Chevron Publishing.

Flannery, R. B. (1993). *Becoming Stress-Resistant: Through the Project SMART Program*. Ellicott City, MD: Chevron Publishing.

Hipp, E. (1995). *Fighting Invisible Tigers: A Stress Management Guide for Teens*. Minneapolis, MN: Free Spirit Publishing.

Levine, P. (1997). *Waking the Tiger: Healing Trauma: The Innate Capacity to Transform Overwhelming Experiences*. Berkeley, CA: North Atlantic Books.

Manning, G., Curtis, K. and McMullen, S. (1999). *Stress: Living and Working in a Changing World*. Duluth, MN: Whole Person Associates.

Matsakis, A. (1998). *Trust After Trauma: A Guide to Relationships for Survivors and Those Who Love Them*. Oakland, CA: New Harbinger Publications.

Rosenbloom, D. and Williams, M. B. (1999). *Life After Trauma: A Workbook for Healing*. New York: Guilford Press.

Toner, P. R. (1993). *Stress Management and Self-Esteem Activities*. West Nyack, NY: Center for Applied Research in Education.

Williams, M. L. and O'Quinne Burke, D. (1996). *Cool Cats, Calm Kids: Relaxation and Stress Management for Young People*. Atascadero, CA: Impact Publishers.

Substance Abuse

101 Ready-to-Use Drug Prevention Activities: http://www.lcps.k12.nm.us/Departments/FedPrograms/Inventory%20list.htm

Alcoholics Anonymous. (1975). *The Big Book*. New York: AA World Services.

Alcoholics Anonymous. (1975). *Living Sober*. New York. AA World Services.

Althauser, D. and Sutker, C. (1998). *You Can Free Yourself From Alcohol and Drugs*. Oakland, CA: New Harbinger Publications.

American Psychiatric Association. (1995). *American Psychiatric Association Practice Guidelines for the Treatment of Patients with Substance Use Disorders: Alcohol, Cocaine, Opioids*. Washington, DC: American Psychiatric Press.

American Psychiatric Association. (1996). *Practice Guidelines for the Treatment of Patients with*

Beattie, M. (1989). *Crack*. Center City, Minnesota: Hazelden. (Pamphlet.)

Bradshaw, J. (1988). *Healing the Shame That Binds You*. Deerfield Beach, FL: Health Communications.

Brown, S. and Lewis, V. (2000). *The Alcoholic Family in Recovery*. New York: Guilford. Press.

Brown, S. and Yalom, I. (1997). *Treating Alcoholism*. San Francisco, CA: Jossey-Bass.

Cook, D. (1998). *Substance Abuse: The Meaning of Addiction*. San Francisco, CA: Jossey Bass.

Cummings, N. A. and Cummings, J. L. (2000). *The First Session with Substance Abuse: A Step-by-Step Guide*. San Francisco, CA: Jossey-Bass.

Daly, D. C. and Marlatt, G. A. (1997). *Managing Your Drug or Alcohol Problem*. (Therapist Guide). San Antonio, TX: Harcourt Brace.

Damond, J. (2000). *Narrative Means to Sober Ends: Treating Addictions and its Aftermath*. New York: Guilford Press.

Dodgen, C. E. (2005). *Nicotine Dependence: Understanding and Applying The Most Effective Treatment Intervention*. Washington, DC: American Psychological Association.

Ellis, A., McInnerney, J. F., DiGillespie, R. and Yaeger, R. J. (1988). *Rational Emotive Therapy with Alcoholics and Substance Abusers*. Boston, MA: Allyn and Bacon.

Fanning, P. and O'Neill, J. (1996). *The Addiction Workbook*. Oakland, CA: New Harbinger Publications.

Fernandez, H. (1998). *Heroin*. Center City, MN: Hazelden.

Johnson Institute. (2000). *How To Get Sober & Stay Sober; Steps 1 Through 5*. Center City, MN: Hazelden.

O'Neill, J. and O'Neill, P. (1992). *Concerned Intervention*. Oakland, CA: New Harbinger Publications.

Scott, T. and Grice, T. (1999). *The Great Brain Robbery*. Center City, MN: Hazelden.

Tanner, L. (1996). *The Mother's Survival Guide to Recovery*. Oakland, CA: New Harbinger Publications.

Tighe, A. A. (1999). *Stop the Chaos: How to Get Control of Your Life by Beating Alcohol and Drugs*. Center City, MN: Hazelden.

Toner, P. R. (1993). *Substance Abuse Prevention Activities*. New York: Prentice Hall.

Suicide

Blumenthal, S. J., and Kuper, D. J. (eds) (1990). *Suicide Over the Life Cycle: Risk Factors, Assessment, and Treatment of Suicidal Patients*. Washington, DC: American Psychiatric Press.

Chiles, J. and Stroshal, K. (1996). *The Suicidal Patient: Principles of Assessment, Treatment and Case Management*. Washington, DC: American Psychiatric Press.

Gordon, S. (1994). *When Living Hurts: For Teenagers and Young Adults*. New York: Union of American Hebrew Congregations.

Ramsey, R. F., Tanney, B. L., Kinzel, T. and Turley, B. (1999). *Suicidal Intervention Handbook*. Calgary, Alberta, Canada: Living Work Education.

Schleifer, J. (1988). *Everything You Need To Know About Teen Suicide*. New York: Rosen Publishing Group.

Therapy

American Psychiatric Association. (1995). *Practice Guidelines for Psychiatric Evaluation of Adults*. Washington, DC: American Psychiatric Press.

American Psychiatric Association. (1996). *Psychiatric Evaluation of Adults: Eating Disorders, Major Depressive Disorders, Bipolar Disorders, Substance Abuse Disorders*. Washington, DC: American Psychiatric Press.

Barlow, D. H. (1993). *Clinical Handbook of Clinical Disorders*. New York: Guilford Press.

Beck, J. (1995). *Cognitive Therapy: Basics and Beyond*. New York: Guilford. Press.

Bisbee, C. C. (1991). *Educating Patients and Families About Mental Illness*. Gaithersburg, MD: Aspen.

Blau, S. and Ellis. A. (eds) (1998). *The Albert Ellis Reader: A Guide to Well-Being Using Rational Emotive Behavioral Techniques*. New York: Carol Publishing.

Cade, B. and O'Hanlon, W. H. (1999). *A Brief Guide to Brief Therapy*. Dunmore, PA: Norton.

Copeland, M. E. (1999). *Winning Against Relapse: A Workbook of Action Plans for Recurring Health and Emotional Problems*. Oakland, CA: New Harbinger Publications.

Figley, C. (1994). *Compassion Fatigue: The Stress of Caring Too Much*. Panama City, FL: Green Cross Foundation, Visionary Productions.

Greenberger, D. and Padesky, C. A. (1955). *Mind Over Mood: A Cognitive Therapy Treatment Manual for Clients*. New York: Guilford Press.

Jongsma, A. E., Peterson, M. and McInnis, W. P. (2000). *Brief Adolescent Therapy Homework Planner*. Beachwood, OH: Wellness Reproductions.

Kendall, P. C. (1991). *Child & Adolescent Therapy Cognitive-Behavioral Procedures*. New York: Guilford Press.

Knell, S. (1993). *Cognitive-Behavioral Play Therapy*. Northvale, NJ: Jason Aronson.

Kreisman, J. J. and Straus, H. (2000). *I Hate You, Don't Leave Me: Understanding the Borderline Personality*. New York: HarperCollins.

Linehan, M. M. (1993). *Skills Training Manual for Treating Borderline Personality Disorder*. New York: Guilford Press.

Linehan, M. M. (2001). *Cognitive-Behavioral Treatment of Borderline Personality Disorder*. Beachwood, OH: Wellness Reproductions.

O'Hanlon, W. H. and Bertolino, B. (1998). *Even from a Broken Web: Brief, Respectful Solution-Oriented Therapy for Sexual Abuse and Trauma*. New York: John Wiley & Sons.

O'Hanlon, W. H. and Rowan, T. (1999). *Solution-Oriented Therapy for Chronic and Severe Mental Illness*. New York: John Wiley & Sons.

Preston, J. (2001). *Shorter Term Treatments for Borderline Personality Disorders*. Beachwood, OH: Wellness Reproductions.

Reinecke, M. A., Dattilio, F. M. and Freeman, A. (eds) (1996). *Cognitive Therapy with Children and Adolescents*. New York: Guilford Press.

Warren, M. P. (2001). *Behavioral Management Guide: Essential Treatment Strategies for Adult Psychotherapy*. Northvale, NJ: Jason Aronson.

Warren, M. P. (2002). *Behavioral Management Guide: Essential Treatment Strategies for The Psychotherapy of Children, Their Parents, and Families*. Northvale, NJ: Jason Aronson.

Warren, M. P. (2005). *Psychotherapy With Adolescents and Their Families: Essential Treatment Strategies*. Carmarthen, UK: Crown House Publishing Ltd.

Vocational Choice

Sussman, M. B. (1992). *A Curious Calling: Unconscious Motivations for Practicing Psychotherapy*. Northvale, NJ: Jason Aronson.

CATALOGS

The expanding list of books and games is in constant flux. Below is a list of several major catalogs to keep you current on new publications and other items as they become available.

Courage to Change
P.O. Box 1268
Newburgh, NY 12551
Tel: 1-800-440-4003
Fax: 1-800-772-6499

Publications Catalog & Resource Guide
NASW Press
750 First Street, NE
Washington, DC 20002-4241
Fax: 202-336-8312

Jossey-Bass
250 Sansome Street
San Francisco, CA 94104-1342
Tel:1-800-956-7739
Fax: 1-800-05-2665
www.josseybass.com

Guilford Publications
72 Spring Street
New York, NY 10012
Tel: 1-800-365-7006
Fax: 212-966-6708
www.guilford.com

Hazelden
15245 Pleasant Valley Road
Center City, MN 55012-0011
Tel: 1-800-257-7810
Fax: 1-651-213-4411
www.hazelden.org

The Haworth Press Inc.
10 Alice Street
Binghamton, NY 13904
Tel: 1-800-429-6784
Fax: 1-800-895-0582
www.haworthpressinc.com

KIDSRIGHTS
8902 Otis Avenue
Indianapolis, IN 46216
Tel: 1-800-648-5478
Fax: 1-800-547-8329
www.jist.com/kidsrights/

Childswork/Childsplay
45 Executive Dr
Suite #201
P.O. Box 9120

Plainview, NY 11803-9020
Tel: 1-800-962-1141
Fax: 1-800-262-1886
www.childswork.com

Self Esteem Shop
32839 Woodward Ave.
Royal Oak, MI 48073
Tel: 1-800-251-8336
Fax: 248-549-0442
www.selfesteemshop.com

The Center for Applied Psychology
P.O. Box 61586
King of Prussia, PA 19406
Tel: 215-277-4020

Wellness Reproductions
P.O. Box 760
Plainview, NY 11803-0760
Tel: 1-800-669-9208
Fax: 1-800-501-8120
www.wellness-resources.com

Western Psychological Services
12031 Wilshire Blvd.
Los Angeles, CA 90025-1251
Tel: 1-800-648-8857
Fax: 310-478-7838
www.wpspublish.com

VIDEOTAPES AND DVDS

Berry, J. (1989). *Human Race Club: Letter on Light Blue Stationary*. Self Esteem Shop, Royal Oak, MI.
Berry, J. (1991). *Human Race Club: Unforgettable Penpal*. Self Esteem Shop, Royal Oak, MI.
Berry, J. (1998). *Casey's Revenge*. Self Esteem Shop, Royal Oak, MI.
Berry, J. (1998). *Human Race Club: Fair Weather Friend*. Self Esteem Shop, Royal Oak, MI.
Berry, J. (1998). *Human Race Club: High Price to Pay*. Self Esteem Shop, Royal Oak, MI.
Berry, J. (1998). *Human Race Club: Lean Mean Machine – Handling Emotion*. Self Esteem Shop, Royal Oak, MI.

Faller, K. (1998). *Interviewing for Child Sexual Abuse*. Self Esteem Shop, Royal Oak, MI.

Hazelden. (2002). *Crack*. Hazelden, Center City, MN.

Hazelden. (2002). *Hemp*. Hazelden, Center City, MN.

Hazelden. (2003). *Cocaine and Crack: A Prevention Video*. Hazelden, Center City, MN.

Meridian Education Association. (1995) *Chill*. Wellness Reproductions, Beachwood, OH.

Simonton, O. C. (1996). *Affirmations for Getting Well Again*. Wellness Reproductions, Beachwood, OH.

Timmerman, E. *A Leap of Faith*. Wellness Reproductions, Beachwood, OH.

REFERENCES

Akhtar, S. (1999). The psychodynamic dimension of terrorism. *Psychiatric Annals, June 29,* 6:350-355.

American Psychiatric Association. (1994). *Desk reference to the diagnostic criteria from DSM-IV*. Washington, DC: American Psychiatric Press.

Araoz, D. L. (1995). *The new hypnosis: Techniques in individual and family psychotherapy*. Northvale, NJ: Jason Aronson.

Araoz, D. L. (1998). *The new hypnosis in sex therapy: Clinical-behavioral methods for clinicians*. Northvale, NJ: Jason Aronson.

Aronson, J. (2000). *The use of the telephone in psychotherapy*. Northvale, NJ: Jason Aronson.

Barber, T. X. (1978). *Hypnosis and psychosomatics*. San Francisco, CA: Proseminar Institute.

Barber, T. X. (1984). Changing "unchangeable" bodily processes by hypnotic suggestions: A new look at hypnosis, cognition, imaginings, and the mind- body problem. In A. Sheikh (ed.) *Imagination and Healing*. Farmingdale, NY: Baywood.

Barlow, D. (2002). *Anxiety and its disorders: The nature and treatment of anxiety and panic*. NY: Guilford.

Bateson, G., Jackson, D. D., Haley, J. and Weakland, J. H. (1956). *Toward a theory of schizophrenia*. NY: Behavioral Science.

Beaton, R., Murphy, S. and Corneil, W. (1996, September). *Prevalence of post-traumatic stress disorder symptomatology in professional urban fire fighters in two countries*. Paper presented at the International Congress of Occupational Health, Stockholm, Sweden.

Becker, E. (1974). *The denial of death*. New York: The Free Press.

Boszormenyi-Nagy, I. and Framo, J. L. (eds) (1965). *Intensive family therapy*. New York: Harper & Row.

Bracken, P. (2002). *Trauma: Culture, meaning & philosophy*. London: Chubb.

Breslau, N., Kessler, R., Chilcoat, H., Schultz, L, Davis, G. and
    Andreski, P. (1998). Trauma and stress disorder in the community.
    Archives of General Psychiatry, 55:626-633.
Caplan, G. (1964). *Principles of preventive psychiatry*. New York: Basic
    Books.
Chessick, R. D. (1978). The sad soul of the psychiatrist. *Bulletin of the
    Menninger Clinic 42*:1-9.
Coffey, R. (1998). *Unspeakable truths and happy endings: New trauma
    therapy*. Baltimore, MD: Sidran Press.
Corr, C. A. (2002, April). Helping adolescents cope with long-term
    illness and death. *The Prevention Researcher*. Vol. 9, No. 2: 9.
Cowley, G. (2003, February 24). Our Bodies, Our Fears. *Newsweek*,
    42–49.
Cunningham, A. (1985). Rollo May: The case for love, beauty, and the
    humanities. *APA Monitor* 16:17.
Einstein, A. (1959). *Philosopher-scientist*. Evanston, IL: The Library of
    Living Philosophers.
Erickson, K. T. (1976). *Everything in its path: Destruction of community
    in the buffalo creek flood*. New York: Simon & Schuster.
Everly, G. S. (1989). *A clinical guide to the treatment of the human
    stress response*. Ellicott City, MD: Chevron.
Everly, G. S. and Mitchell, J. T. (1998). *Assisting individuals in crisis:
    A workbook*. Ellicott City, MD: International Critical Incident
    Stress Foundation.
Everly, G. S. and Mitchell, J. T. (1999). *Critical incident stress
    management (CISM): A new era and standard of care in crisis
    intervention*. Ellicott City, MD: Chevron.
Farberow, N. L. and Frederick, C. J. (1978). *Training manual for
    human service workers in major disasters*. Rockville, MD: National
    Institutes of Mental Health.
Figley, C. (1989). *Helping traumatized families*. San Francisco, CA:
    Jossey-Boss.
Figley, C. (1995). *Compassion fatigue: The stress of caring too much*.
    New York: Brunner- Mazel.
Figley, C. (2001). *The green cross protocol*. Tallahassee, FL.: Green
    Cross Foundation.
Figley, C. R., Bride. B. and Mazza, N. (eds) (1997). *Death and trauma*.
    London: Taylor and Francis.
Flannery, R. B. (1998). *The assaulted staff action program: Coping with
    the psychological aftermath of violence*. Ellicott City, MD: Chevron.
Frank, D. and Mooney, B. (2003). *Hypnosis and counselling in the
    treatment of chronic illness*. New York: Crown House.
Frankl, V. (1976). *Man's search for meaning: An introduction to
    logotherapy*. New York: Pocket Books.

Frankl, V. (1990). Keynote address, Evolution of Psychotherapy Conference. Anaheim, CA.

Friedman, R. A. (2003, December 30). Traversing the mystery of memory. *New York Times*, 5.

Greenson, R. R. (1967). The technique and practice of psychoanalysis. New York: International Universities Press.

Gyatso, T. (Dalai Lama) and Goleman, D. (2003). *Destructive emotions: How can we overcome them?* New York: Bantam Books.

Hammond, D. C. (ed.) (1990). *Handbook of hypnotic suggestions and metaphors*. New York: W. W. Norton.

Harper, J. M. (2002). Children's responses to death. *Trauma Response*, Fall, 2001, Vol. 1, p. 80.

Havens, R. A. and Walters, C. (1989). *Hypnotherapy scripts: A neo-Ericksonian approach to persuasive healing*. New York: Brunner-Mazel.

Herman, J. L. (1997). *Trauma and recovery*. New York: Basic Books.

Hesse, A. R. (2002). Secondary trauma: How working with trauma victims affects therapists. *Clinical Social Work Journal, 30*:3.

Holmes, C. A. V. (1998). *There is no such thing as a therapist: An introduction to the therapeutic process*. London: Karnac Books.

Jozefowski, J. (1999). *The phoenix phenomenon: Rising from the ashes of grief*. Northvale, NJ: Jason Aronson.

Kabat-Zinn, J. (1990). *Full catastrophe living: Using the wisdom of your body and mind to face stress, pain, and illness*. New York: Delta.

Kalb, C. (2003, February 24). Coping with anxiety. *Newsweek*, 51–52.

Laser, E. and Lang, E. (1996). *Methods of non-pharmalocologic analgesia: A sourcebook for practitioners*. The Methods of Non-Pharmacologic Analgesics Workshop, University of Iowa Hospital.

Lerner, M. D. and Shelton, R. D. (2001). How can emergency responders help grieving individuals? *Trauma Response*, Fall/Winter Vol. 8, No. 1: 27.

Levine P. (1997). *Waking the tiger, healing trauma: The innate capacity to transform overwhelming experiences*. Berkeley, CA: North Atlantic Books.

Linehan, M. M. (1993). *Skills training manual for treating borderline personality disorder*. New York: Guilford.

Lusk, J. T. (ed.) (1992). *30 scripts for relaxation, imagery, and inner healing*. Duluth, MN: Whole Person Associates.

Maslow, A. (1968). *Toward a psychology of being*, 2nd ed. New York: Van Nostrand.

Maslow, A. (1987). *Motivation and personality*, 3rd ed. New York: Harper & Row.

Millon, T. (1995). *Disorders of personality: DSM-IV and beyond*, 2nd ed. New York: Wiley.

Mitchell, J. T. (1983a). When disaster strikes: The critical incident stress debriefing process. *Journal of Emergency Medical Services, 8. (1)*:36-39.

Mitchell, J. T. (1983b). Guidelines for psychological debriefings. *Emergency Management Course Manual*. Emmitsburg, MD: Federal Emergency Management Institute.

Mitchell, J. T. (1988a). The history, status, and future of critical incident stress debriefings. *Journal of Emergency Medical Services, 13*, 11: 43-52.

Mitchell, J. T. (1988b). Development and function of a critical incident stress debriefing team. *Journal of Emergency Medical Services*, 132, 12: 43-46.

Mitchell, J. T. and Bray, G. (1990). *Emergency services stress: Guidelines for preserving the health and careers of emergency services personnel*. Ellicott City, MD: Chevron.

Mitchell, J. T. and Everly, G. S. (1993). *Human elements training in emergency services*. Ellicott City, MD: Chevron.

Mitchell, J. T. and Everly, G. S. (1996). *Critical incident stress debriefing: An operations manual for the prevention of traumatic stress among emergency service and disaster workers*. Ellicott City, MD: Chevron.

Mitchell, J. T. and Everly, G. S. (1997). Scientific evidence for critical incident stress management. *Journal of Emergency Medical Services, 22*: 87–93.

Mitchell, J. T. and Everly, G. S. (2001). *Critical incident stress debriefing: An operations manual for CISD, defusing, and other group crisis intervention services*. 3rd ed. Ellicott City, MD: Chevron.

Myss, C. and Shealy, N. (2002). The halographic view of body, mind, emotion, and spirit, Session 4. [CD-ROM]. *The Science of Medical Intuition*. Boulder, CO: Sounds True.

Nagourney, E. (2003, December 30). Scanning a brain for bipolar root. *New York Times*, F6.

National Institute of Mental Health. (2002). *Mental Health and Mass Violence: Evidence-Based Early Psychological Intervention for Victims/Survivors of Mass Violence. A Workshop to Reach Consensus on Best Practices*. NIH Publication No. 02-5138, Washington, DC: U.S. Government Printing Office.

Neil, T., Oney, J., DeFonso, L., Thacker, B. and Reichart, W. (1974). *Emotional first aid*. Louisville, KY: Kemper Behavioral Science Associates.

O'Conner, J. and Seymour, J. (1990). *Introducing NLP: Psychological skills for understanding and influencing people*. San Francisco, CA: Aquarian Press.

Ogden, P. and Minton, K. (2000, October). Sensorimotor psychotherapy: One method for processing traumatic memory. *Traumatology* (6) 3: 12–14.

O'Hanlon, W. H. (2000). *Do One Thing Different and Other Uncommonly Sensible Solutions to Life's Problems*. New York: HarperCollins.

O'Hanlon, B. and Bertolino, B. (1998). *Even from a broken web: Brief, respectful, solution-focused therapy for sexual abuse and trauma*. New York: Wiley.

Ouimette, P. and Brown, P. L. (eds) (2003). *Trauma and substance abuse*. Washington, DC: American Psychiatric Press.

Pert, Candace B. (1997). *Molecules of emotion: The science behind mind-body medicine*. Touchstone, Simon & Schuster, p. 61, pp. 63–72.

Robinson, H., Sigman, M. and Wilson, J. (1997). Duty-related stressors and PTSD

Rosen, S. (ed) (1982). *My voice will go with you: The teaching tales of Milton Erickson*. New York: Norton.

Sapolsky, R. (1993). The vicious cycle of stress. *Scientific American*, pp. 81-91.

Siebert, A. (1996). *The survivor personality*. New York: Berkeley Press.

Simon, R. (2001, November 12). Altered states of America: Coping with life after 9/11. *U. S. News & World Report*, 14.

Slater, L. (2003, February 23). Repress yourself. *New York Times Magazine*, 48-53.

Spiegel, David. (2003, November). Presentation at the 54th annual conference of the Society for Clinical and Experimental Hypnosis, Chicago, IL.

Stolorow, R. D. and Atwood, G. E. (1979). *Faces in a cloud: Subjectivity in personality theory*. Northvale, NJ: Jason Aronson.

Stone, V. (2001). *Cops don't cry*. Ellicott City, MD: Chevron.

Sussman, M. B. (1992). *A curious calling: Unconscious motivations for practicing psychotherapy*. Northvale, NJ: Jason Aronson.

Tuckfelt, S., Fink, J. and Warren, M. P. (1997). *The psychotherapists' guide to managed care in the 21st century*. Northvale, NJ: Jason Aronson.

Van der Kolk, B.A., McFarlane, C. and Weisaeth, L. (eds) (1996). *Traumatic stress: The effects of overwhelming experience on mind, body and society*. New York: Guilford.

Violanti, J. M. (1996). Police suicide: Risks and relationships. *Frontline Counselor*, 4: 6.

Volpe, J. S. (1998). Trauma response profile: Dr. Beverly J. Anderson, PhD, BCETS. *Trauma Response*, IV, 1, 4–6.

Waldholz, M. (2003, October 7). Altered states: Hypnosis goes mainstream. *Wall Street Journal*.

Walker, S. www.netmindbody.com/net_inc_info.html

Warren, M. P. (1991). An Introduction to Death. *Bulletin of the Society for Psychoanalytic Psychotherapy*. Summer, Vol. 6, No. 3: 28.1.

Warren, M. P. (1999). Encoding and decoding: Comparing Milton Erickson's hypnotherapy and Robert Lang's communicative approach. *International Journal of Communicative Psychoanalysis and Psychotherapy*. Vol. 12, Nos. 1–2: 5.

Warren, M. P. (2001). *Behavioral management guide: Essential treatment strategies for adult psychotherapy*. Northvale, NJ: Jason Aronson.

Warren, M. P. (2002). *Behavioral management guide: Essential treatment strategies for the psychotherapy of children, their parents and families*. Northvale, NJ: Aronson.

Warren, M. P. (2004). *Trauma: Treatment and transformation*. New York: IUniverse.

Warren, M. P. (2005). *Psychotherapy with adolescents and their families: Essential treatment strategies*. Carmarthen, UK: Crown House Publishing Ltd.

Williams-Keeler, L. (1998). Psychohistory: The terrible beauty of the confluence of history and psychology. *Trauma Response*, Winter, Vol. 4, No. 1: 32.

RELATED WEBSITES

American Institute of Stress
www.stress.org

American Psychiatric Association
www.psych.org

American Psychological Association
www.apa.org

American Red Cross
www.redcross.org

Center for Post-Trauma Therapy and Education
www.traumaterapiakeskus.com

David Baldwin's Trauma Information
www.trauma-pages.com

Federal Emergency Management Agency (FEMA)
www.fema.gov

International Critical Incident Stress Foundation
www.icisf.org

Mayo Clinic
www.mayoclinic.com

National Center for PTSD
www.ncptsd.org

National Institute of Mental Health
www.nimh.nih.gov

INDEX